Familiar Realities

The Heidelberg Confer

with

Luigi Boscolo, Ivan Boszormenyi-Nagy,
Gianfranco Cecchin, Joseph Duss-von Werdt,
Hermann Haken, Luc Kaufmann,
Theodore Lidz, Norman L. Paul,
Mara Selvini Palazzoli, Eckhard Sperling,
Pekka Tienari, Paul Watzlawick,
Gunthard Weber, Jürg Willi,
Adele R. Wynne, Lyman C. Wynne,
and others

edited by
Helm Stierlin, Fritz B. Simon,
and Gunther Schmidt

BRUNNER/MAZEL, *Publishers* • New York

for the photographs that appear in

Library of Congress Cataloging-in-Publication Data

Familiar realities.

  Based on a meeting held in Heidelberg, Germany from
16–18 May 1985.
  Includes bibliographies and index.
  1. Family psychotherapy—Congresses.   I. Boscolo,
Luigi.   II. Stierlin, Helm.   III. Simon, Fritz. B.
IV. Schmidt, Gunther, 1945–   . [DNLM: 1. Family
Therapy—congresses.   WM 430.5.F2   F1975 1985]
RC488.5.F2756   1987   616.89′156   86-20719
ISBN 0-87630-438-2

Copyright © 1987 by Brunner/Mazel, Inc.

Published by
BRUNNER/MAZEL, INC.
19 Union Square
New York, New York 10003

MANUFACTURED IN THE UNITED STATES OF AMERICA

familiar . . . 1. originally having to do with a family. 2. friendly; intimate; close: as familiar conversation. 3. too friendly; presumptuous; unduly intimate or bold. 4. closely acquainted (with). 5. well known; common; ordinary . . . familiar is applied to that which is known through constant association, and with reference to persons, suggests informality, or even presumption, such as might prevail among members of a family.

(Webster, 1962)

real . . . 1. existing or happening as or in fact; actual; true, objectively so, etc.; not merely seeming, pretended, imagined, fictitious, nominal, or ostensible. 2. a) authentic; genuine b) not pretended; sincere. 3. designating wages or income as measured by purchasing power. 4. Law: of or relating to permanent, immovable things (real property). 5. Math.: designating or of the part of a complex number that is not imaginary. 6. Optics: of or relating to an image made by the actual meeting of light rays at a point. 7. Philos.: existing objectively; actual (not merely possible or ideal), or essential, absolute, ultimate (not relative, derivative, phenomenal, etc.) . . .

(Webster, 1976)

Contents

Contributors

Luigi Boscolo, M.D.
Center for Family Studies, Milan, Italy.

Ivan Boszormenyi-Nagy, M.D.
Professor, Family Therapy Section, Department of Mental Health
Sciences, Hahnemann University, Philadelphia, Pennsylvania.

Gianfranco Cecchin, M.D.
Center for Family Studies, Milan, Italy

Josef Duss-von Werdt, Ph.D., Th.D
Institute for Marriage and the Family, Zürich, Switzerland.

Hermann Haken, Ph.D.
Professor, Institute for Theoretical Physics, University of Stuttgart,
Stuttgart, West Germany.

Luc Kaufmann, M.D.
Professor, Hôpital de Cery, University of Lausanne, Prilly-Lausanne,
Switzerland.

Ilpo Lahti, M.D.
Department of Psychiatry, Oulu University, Oulu, Finland.

Theodore Lidz, M.D.
Sterling Professor Emeritus, School of Medicine, Department of
Psychiatry, Yale University, New Haven, Connecticut.

Juha Moring, M.D.
Department of Psychiatry, Oulu University, Oulu, Finland.

Mikko Naarala, M.D.
Department of Psychiatry, Oulu University, Oulu, Finland.

Norman L. Paul, M.D.
Associate Clinical Professor, Department of Neurology, Boston University School of Medicine, Boston, Massachusetts.

Jukka Pohjola, M.D.
Department of Psychiatry, Oulu University, Oulu, Finland.

Tuula Rönkkö, M.D.
Department of Psychiatry, Oulu University, Oulu, Finland.

Gunther Schmidt, M.D.
Department of Psychoanalytic Basic Research and Family Therapy, University of Heidelberg, Heidelberg, West Germany.

Mara Selvini Palazzoli, M.D.
Professor, New Center for Family Studies, Milan, Italy.

Fritz B. Simon, M.D.
Department of Psychoanalytic Basic Research and Family Therapy, University of Heidelberg, Heidelberg, West Germany.

Anneli Sorri, M.D.
Department of Psychiatry, Oulu University, Oulu, Finland.

Eckhard Sperling, M.D.
Professor, Department for Psychotherapy and Sociotherapy, University of Göttingen, Göttingen, West Germany.

Helm Stierlin, M.D., Ph.D.
Professor, Department of Psychoanalytic Basic Research and Family Therapy, University of Heidelberg, Heidelberg, West Germany.

Pekka Tienari, M.D.
Professor, Department of Psychiatry, Oulu University, Oulu, Finland.

Karl-Erik Wahlberg, Ph.D.
Department of Psychiatry, Oulu University, Oulu, Finland.

Paul Watzlawick, Ph.D.
Professor, Mental Research Institute, Palo Alto, California.

Gunthard Weber, M.D.
Institute for Systemic Therapy, Wiesloch, West Germany.

Jürg Willi, M.D.
Professor, Department of Psychosocial Medicine and Family Therapy, Medical School, University of Zürich, Zürich, Switzerland.

Adele R. Wynne
Marital and Family Therapist, Pittsford, New York.

Lyman C. Wynne, M.D., Ph.D.
Professor of Psychiatry, University of Rochester, Medical Center, Rochester, New York.

Introduction

What use are conferences on family therapy? An unusual question, certainly, possibly even a silly one. Conferences and conventions are obviously here to stay, fixtures in the general landscape of scientific and therapeutic activity. The fact that they keep on happening is an indication that there must be some point to them, quite independent of the actual topics they may be addressing themselves to. The proof of the pudding is in the eating; the proof of the conference is the participation.

Imagine a conference without an audience, without speakers, without the specific atmosphere of the chosen venue. The result is a collection of more or less interesting articles. Then imagine a pop concert, a revue, or some other kind of entertainment involving singing and dancing rather than papers on the theory and practice of therapy. Here we have a parade of artists, comedians, contortionists, ventriloquists—singing, doing splits, showing off their shapely legs, juggling with fragile crockery, and perhaps also indulging in a bit of knife-throwing. The similarity between this kind of show and a conference (particularly one on family therapy) is obviously far greater than that between a conference and the proceedings published later.

Our conclusion then must be that a conference is more than the sum of its papers, more even than the sum of speakers and audience. It is an interactional ritual, where the relational aspects of communication are more important than what is actually being communicated. There is, however, one difference that does distinguish it from most song-and-dance entertainments. In our case, the audience itself is made up of professional singers and dancers, or to put it another way, colleagues and rivals.

Thus answering our initial question—What use are conferences?—is much more difficult than one might have expected. At all events, we cannot be content to look at the official protagonists alone. The spectators are themselves supporting cast, coauthor, and producer, all rolled into one. A conference is in fact a little like a drama where the script is written by the people taking part. In the course of events, relations are formed and coalitions and hierarchies are cemented or dismantled. Form and function, content and contention, the objective and the personal all blend and intermingle when in such a setting new fashions are launched and received or are shot down along with the "stars" who proclaim and embody them.

For the (participating) observer such a conference takes on (ideally) the aspect of a *Gesamtkunstwerk* in which a whole scientific domain is being modeled. The observer is offered the opportunity of finding his bearings in the seemingly endless proliferation of theories and methods. Instead of abstractions on paper he is confronted with tangible personalities. And by defining his own position in terms of the proximity and distance, the affinities and distinctions between himself and those personalities, our participant can finally go some way toward determining where he stands.

A conference, whether successful or not, has effects and repercussions that echo and reecho long after it has run its actual course. It is, in fact, best regarded as an intervention in a self-organizing system.

These were some of the considerations we had in mind when planning the conference marking the tenth anniversary of the Department of Basic Psychoanalytic Research and Family Therapy of Heidelberg University. Our aim was to contribute to the further evolution of concepts and methods in family therapy. To this end, we invited internationally acknowledged pioneers in this field to take the opportunity of describing the theoretical and practical development they had undergone in the past few years. We hoped that the differences between them could become just as apparent as their similarities. In addition, we asked representatives from neighboring disciplines to come and join us to ensure that there would be no danger of the complacency of a closed system gaining the upper hand. But their role was not limited to that of the objective observer on the outside looking in (without family-tinted spectacles!). Their presence was also designed to open up perspectives onto the neighboring disciplines they represented and on the concepts in currency there.

The conference took place in Heidelberg from 16 to 18 May 1985 and was attended by some 2000 participants from 25 countries. One of the results of the conference is this book. In view of what has already been said about conferences, you will hardly expect to find a mere collection of articles. Our aim is rather to spirit you away to a meeting much like the one in Heidelberg. In short, we want to have you take part yourself (again, as if you were actually there).

To engage you in the proceedings, we placed the original papers in a fictional framework. Three (fictitious) participants at the conference are waiting to guide and accompany you through the events. They comment on what they hear and spend much of their time arguing about it. These three people are figments of our imaginations—pure invention. In putting them together we were guided by what we felt we knew about the actual participants. Since it would have been difficult to give all 2000 of them the opportunity to have their say, we decided to construct idealized types representing certain theoretical and practical approaches, currents, or schools of thought. The controversies that divide the family therapy community are meant to be epitomized in the arguments you will be reading. There will be no reticence in expressing personal opinions.

One thing we stress is that these three are not in any way identical with the three editors of this book. They are entirely artificial figures. (After all, what real person can claim that he owes his existence to three parents?) True, they do owe their existence to us and may at times exhibit certain similarities to one or another of us. But we have to admit that at some point we seemed to have lost control over their development. They all follow different theoretical models, subscribe to different epistemologies, profess different ethical values.

We feel that a high proportion of the dissent found among the various schools of family therapy can be traced back to such differences in individual philosophy. And we hope that the disputes acted out by our three fictitious participants may perhaps point up some of the things that family therapists do indeed find it worth their while to argue about.

To ensure that our literary ambitions do not interfere with the standards normally upheld in academic publications, we use two distinct forms of presentation:

1. The Papers. Each paper appears under the name of its authors and is either printed in the form in which it was presented or has since been revised by the authors. The responsibility for the content rests solely with the authors themselves. The text of the papers is printed in Roman type and the bibliographic references are to be found at the end of each paper.

2. Chit-Chat in the Intervals. Here our imaginations were given free rein. Our three (idealized) characters are purely imaginary; any similarity with persons living or dead is entirely coincidental (and of course totally inadvertent). *So as not to confuse the reader even more, these fictional passages are printed in italics.*

Our three characters reflect a blend of fiction and reality. They let off steam, argue, abuse each other, and make up again. At the same time, they selectively utilize comments and questions brought forward by participants from the auditorium during the discussion period following each paper. (Only in rare cases was it possible to identify these participants.)

The length of this preamble betrays a certain amount of insecurity about presenting a book that is unusual in form and does not follow the established conventions of serious academic publications. But we feel that this form may be at least an opportunity to do justice to the substance of the conference. And of course we hope that reading the book will be as entertaining as most people found the conference.

Helm Stierlin
Fritz B. Simon
Gunther Schmidt

Familiar Realities

The First Day

Breakfast Chit-Chat

The scene is a small, typically German, typically romantic hotel, with a no less typically German name, "Student Prince." Three people are breakfasting together. They had met the evening before, when they found themselves standing side by side in the queue outside the Congress Hall where the Heidelberg conference is taking place. Waiting there patiently, they somehow got to talking (which shows that none of them suffers from major contact difficulties). As soon as each was safely in possession of a name badge, earphones, and advertising package, they decided to use the foldout guide to Heidelberg to find a place to have a meal together. It turned out that they not only took an immediate liking to each other but were all staying in the same hotel (chance does play these funny tricks sometimes). And so it was something of a foregone conclusion that from then on they would be inseparable companions for the duration of the three-day conference.

It proved to be a very enjoyable evening, with plenty to drink and a great deal to talk about. We only intend going into those details that may be required by the conversational gambits put forward by our three friends. Let it be said straightaway that these were not always entirely germane to the issue. At times, indeed, it was difficult to avoid the impression that these verbal skirmishes were of a more provocative than argumentative nature, more flirtatious than strictly scientific. Tact and discretion forbid us from dwelling on this aspect. Our sole interest in these three is, after all, their status as people who are in some way concerned with the psychosocial problems of others and, in two cases at least, even make a living out of them.

Who are these three? The most striking of them is certainly Maria Callous. She is in her thirties and a psychologist by profession. She has just finished an advanced course in Italian and her favorite dish is pasta asciutta (although you'd never guess by looking at her). At the moment she is very pleased with the way things are going professionally as she has just been entrusted with the directorship of a child-care advisory center. She is strictly "systemic" in her approach, meaning in concrete terms that she is an adherent of the so-called Milan Model. Her more intimate friends sometimes inadvertently leave the "i" out of her name, which she invariably finds a little embarrassing.

Theo Riedhammer is an entirely different kettle of fish. He is a trained psychoanalyst. Experience (he is in his mid-forties and has had a psychotherapeutic practice of his own for some years) has taught him that the couch is not the answer to everybody's problems and for that reason he has taken up family therapy. He does not see this as in any way a danger to his identity as a psychoanalyst. Up to now he has always been able to find analytic justification for his family therapy decisions. His feelings toward system theory are very mixed. He concedes that, intellectually speaking, this kind of approach does have a certain fascination. Where he draws the line is when he hears what the "systems people" (this is what he normally calls them; when he gets worked up he usually switches to "systems hardliners") get up to with their clients. That "rubs him the wrong way," it is "profoundly incompatible with the moral requirements that are simply indissociable from therapy per se whatever its nature." After all, as he emphasizes again and again, he sees his work as "emancipatory." "Monadic" approaches to psychology are anathema to him. An active member of the student movement when young, he considers himself politically aware. His children, however, invariably react aggressively when he uses adjectives that start with "socio-." They tend to conclude such discussions with remarks like "the same old late-sixties bullshit again." Despite all this, Theo considers himself deep-down to be left-wing. He, too, adores Italian food.

From Theo's remarks in their first exploratory exchanges the evening before, Maria very quickly formed the conviction that his way of conducting family therapy could only be called "antediluvian," a "throwback to the Neanderthal era, a relic of the primeval dawn." For his part, despite the personal liking he had taken to Maria, Theo could not close his eyes to the fact that "she manipulates her patients in the most shameful and unconscionable way." He interpreted this as the expression of inadequately worked out omnipotence fantasies. The way these two aired their differences of opinion that evening caused the third member of the group ("Doc") to reflect that what Theo would like best would be to get Maria on the couch without further delay. His own conjectures with regard to other people's omnipotence fantasies, however, pointed in an entirely different direction. But then he didn't really know much about that. After all, he wasn't one of them.

At least that was how he saw it. His interest in the conference was accordingly pretty limited. The names of the speakers meant nothing to him; he had never even heard of most of them. He had come to visit

Heidelberg rather than attend the conference. His daughter, a psychology student about to take her final exams, had originally put her name down as a participant. The day before the conference was due to start she had rung her father on her way back from holidays in Spain. Her car had broken down and she wouldn't be back in time for the start of the conference in Heidelberg. She had asked him to try to get a refund for the conference fee, a cripplingly large sum in her present straitened circumstances. To cut a long story short, his long-distance negotiations with the conference secretariat got him nowhere. The only "concession" that was offered him was that someone else could take his daughter's place. Half defiant at this attitude and half intrigued by the idea, he decided to step in for her himself. What did he stand to lose! Heidelberg is a beautiful city, the weather forecast looked promising, and there was no need to go and listen to the papers if he didn't want to. All in all, it could turn out to be a welcome break, and tax deductible in the bargain.

Not that this version of himself as an "outsider," "not one of them," was accepted by the others without demur. Theo interpreted his "tall story" as an attempt to keep the whole subject of "family" at arm's length, "a defense mechanism pure and simple." Of course it wasn't at all his way to come up with such snap judgments in a private context, particularly over drinks and without being asked. All the same, the scepticism he felt at the authenticity of Doc's "weekend idyll" became obvious when he insisted on knowing what it was that had made this psychologist daughter of his want to come to the conference in the first place. Hadn't she perhaps at some stage expressed the desire to take her whole family to a therapist? (Answer: "Yes.") Well, there you are!

Maria was not much interested in the internal dynamics of Doc's family and whether this was the conscious or unconscious reason for his participation. She was out to convince him that in his profession he was predestined to think along "systemic" lines. A country doctor, down-to-earth and full of practical intelligence, he really did have a great deal in common with the doctors in Westerns: mid-fifties, weatherbeaten features, unflappable. The name "Doc"—and here Theo and Maria were unanimous for once—was the only one that fitted; however, when Doc attempted to explain his motives for coming to the conference, his nickname was temporarily modified to "Doc Holiday." As a country doctor, Maria insisted, Doc was always confronted with the whole system, not only the individual person (Maria: "I don't believe there is any such thing as individuals"),—but the whole family, pets, and farmyard animals were included.

Anyway, the evening passes in a very relaxed atmosphere, with these three "individuals" (let us stick to the term for the moment at least, whatever objections there may be to it) soon developing a high degree of familiarity, intimacy even, despite the differences in character. From the bantering tone they employed, we can see their certainty that none of them was likely to take umbrage, the touch of self-irony that they all felt they could allow themselves.

So here they are, slightly hung over, in the "Student Prince," digging into a spread far more sumptuous than the normal German hotel breakfast. . . .

Theo: Well, Doc, been dreaming of your daughter again?

Doc: Why should I dream about her? I'm glad to have one night's peace from her at last.

Maria: Put two men together and what do you get? One male chauvinist trying to score points off another. You've no idea how boring you are!

Doc: Nothing to get steamed up about, Maria. After all, you are young enough to be my daughter.

Maria: Precisely. I was just thinking how awful it would be.

Theo: No time for that now. We've got to be going if we don't want to be late. I've heard it's likely to be crowded.

Doc: Hard to say. The usual mutual congratulation ritual first off, of course—I'm all right, you're all right, how much poorer the world would be without our major and significant contributions to science, the dazzling lucidity of Professor Such-and Such's remarks, etc., etc.

Maria: I wouldn't try going in for the sales promotion profession if I were you. Look, this morning we have Stierlin's welcoming remarks, Duss-von Werdt, and Haken. Josef Duss-von Werdt is the Director of the Institute for Marriage and Family in Zürich. Very much the practical therapist, but by all accounts able to inquire critically into the methods and foundations of such therapy. Hermann Haken teaches theoretical physics in Stuttgart.

Theo: I can't see for the life of me what a physicist is doing here, least of all a "theoretical" one.

Maria: That just shows your complete lack of systemic imagination. Haken has spent a lot of time on self-organization processes. Ultimately it is possible to define all living creatures, social systems, and so on, in terms of self-organization. The question remains, of course, to what extent the abstract principles worked out mathematically by a physicist can be applied to human beings and the way they organize their life together.

Theo: Can't see it leading anywhere myself.

The discussion continued for a while longer, without any agreement being reached. Maria argued that "from a systemic angle" there was a good deal to be said for looking into the organizational processes underlying human knowledge acquisition (she saw herself, after all, first and foremost as an "epistemologist"). Theo objected that history had shown time and again how dangerous it was, socially and politically, to start drawing conclusions on human behavior from mechanistic studies.

At all events, Doc decided to postpone his shopping to a later date and to join the others in attending the morning session.

Opening

Helm Stierlin

Ladies and Gentlemen, on behalf of the members of our department, I should like to extend a very warm welcome to you all, both to those of you who have undertaken long journeys to be with us here in Heidelberg today and to those of you from not quite so far afield. The fact that this congress—the first major international family therapy congress on German soil—should be taking place in Heidelberg gives rise to a number of historical reflections. Planned to coincide with the tenth anniversary of our institute, it also falls within a period in which two other anniversaries are occupying us, the six-hundredth anniversary of the foundation of the University of Heidelberg, Germany's oldest, and the fortieth anniversary of the occupation of Heidelberg by American troops at the end of World War II. (Some of the posters you will see around the town refer to this event as the "liberation" of the city, others to its "fall.")

Looking specifically at the history of our university, we might, for example, ask to what extent this congress will be looking at topics and issues that other thinkers and researchers working at this university have also been concerned with. Hegel is one who springs to mind: appointed Professor of Philosophy some 170 years ago, in the year 1816, shortly after the appearance of his *Phenomenology of Mind*. I would also mention Erich von Holst and Viktor von Weizsäcker, both of whom I was privileged to have as teachers. Erich von Holst may legitimately be regarded as the founder of a cybernetic approach to biology, while Viktor von Weizsäcker was the first to pursue such an approach in the field of psychosomatic medicine. Both were thus operative in laying the foundations of a systemic approach as typified most recently by Gregory Bateson.

Turning our attention to the "fall" or "liberation" of Heidelberg, we come across difficult and considerably more ominous aspects of Heidelberg's history which we—as inquirer into the nature of social systems and relations—would be extremely ill-advised to ignore. Heidelberg became a "brown" university very early on. Goebbels studied here and more than

10

60 professors, most of them Jewish scholars, were dismissed and prose-cuted in the early stages of the Nazi era, among them the holder of the chair of psychiatry at the time, Professor Willmanns, the father of Ruth Lidz, who is with us here today, together with Theodore Lidz. Incidental-ly, Ruth's grandfather, Viktor Meyer, must also be counted among Heidel-berg's great scholars. His grave, in the Bergfriedhof Cemetery, is situated not far from the grave of Max Weber, another scholar from Heidelberg University who attained worldwide renown.

I myself started my studies in Heidelberg in 1946 and have many vivid memories of the period immediately after its liberation. The Old Bridge, which crosses the Neckar only a few hundred yards away from this con-gress center, was still in ruins, blown up by fanatical Nazi diehards. And the inscription over the main entrance of the New University, where the majority of our workshops will be taking place, had just been changed. In its original form, as suggested by the Germanist Friedrich Gundolf, it had read "Dem lebendigen Geist" ("To the lively mind"). The Nazis changed it to "Dem deutschen Geist" ("To the German mind") but now it had been changed back to "To the lively mind" and that seems to be an equally good motto for this symposium.

Finally, we may perhaps be permitted to mention the tenth anniversary of our department. It seemed to us that there now exists something akin to an international family of family therapists and we felt that, however modest it may appear alongside those other anniversaries I have men-tioned, our entry into double figures might be a suitable moment to invite the members of that family to a family reunion—albeit in full awareness of the fact that a congress like the present one is bound to be something more than just an informal get-together. We could not of course invite all the members of the family of family therapists. We decided rather to concentrate on those whose work has been most fruitful for us in the course of the years, those who have come to see us repeatedly, those we owe most to, those we feel united with in growing friendship. We are very glad that a not inconsiderable number of the internationally acknowledged initiators and investigators of family therapy may be numbered among them, pioneering figures who have contributed to the emergence of the new—or perhaps no longer so new—familiar realities that will be con-cerning us in the course of this congress. But we are no less glad that so many of the younger generation have come to join us, in search of a dialogue with the senior figures among us. The fact that our family reunion has attracted so many guests is intensely gratifying. It is a source of par-ticular pleasure that there are among them visitors from such faraway countries as Japan, New Zealand, and Australia, not to mention Canada and the United States. And we are also overjoyed that a number of colleagues from Eastern European countries, notably Poland and Hungary, are able to be with us, always bearing in mind that for them (although for different reasons) the journey here is fraught with as many difficulties as it is for our colleagues from Australia and the United States. (I may perhaps add, as another interesting historical fact, that none of our colleagues from East Germany—so near and yet so far—have been able to join us.) And we are, in conclusion, glad that you have come to this congress with the expectations that one may legitimately have of a meeting of this size. You may rightfully assume, we feel, that the quality of the papers, discussions, and workshops, the romantic atmosphere of Heidelberg, and the autopoietic resources that you, the participants, can call upon, will contribute to the success of the congress. So, once again: Welcome to Heidelberg!

Ten Years Are (No) Reason to Celebrate

Joseph Duss-von Werdt

Dear grandmothers with sons-in-law!
Silent majority of normal parents!
Dear part-time children and rare full-time fathers!
All-too-maligned nonworking mothers!
Old foster-fathers and new surrogate mothers!
Wifeless fathers and only children in your multitudes!
Expelled and bound delegates from near and far!
Last generation before the test tube babies and other spare parts from
    the bio laboratory!
Symptom-carriers, index patients, and homeostatics!
Autopoiets and morphogeneticists!
Children from good homes, including those who have gone off the
    rails!

In short:
Dear family realities, in all your over 1000 forms (so they tell me).

For ten years now, family therapy here in Heidelberg has figured as the
universally well-known branch of a founding enterprise which it is rather
hard to localize. It is thus a birthday that has brought us together, though
not for a party with ice cream and party games, as when a child reaches
double figures, but for a family reunion encompassing several generations
that have supported the cause of family therapy through the years and
still continue to do so. My position in this clan is that of grandson, uncle,
brother, and adoptive father, all in one. As a grandson, I belong to the
third generation. I am an uncle because I instruct nephews and nieces in
family therapy. My relationship to Helm Stierlin is that of a brother. And
I see myself as an adoptive father because I lay no claim to having begotten
any family therapy concept of my own. I have brought roses with me as

a birthday present. Why roses and not some more seasonal offering, like daffodils or lilies of the valley? Because roses smell nicer—and because they also have thorns. So they are the most fitting flowers to strew along the path that I should like to tread in your company today as we look together at some of the reflections that this anniversary may inspire in us.

I

In terms of a human life span, family therapy is entering the notoriously crisis-ridden middle years. As a product of the postwar years, it grew up in unstable family surroundings. After 40 years and more, its relations to its parents and siblings are anything but well defined. Any one of the family theories developed in that time could probably be used to substantiate a diagnosis pointing to pathological elements in those relations. If one assumes that two things are of the essence for the establishment of a resilient identity—definite knowledge about one's origins and a nice, comfortable feeling of "belonging"—then the child we are interested in is obviously at a disadvantage from the start. Nobody knows exactly who the parents were. Hardly surprising, therefore, that there should be bitter disagreement about who is actually responsible for the really rather gratifying progress made by this unlikely infant. Genetically, the child is a mystery; itself a product of a multiple birth, it has managed to reproduce itself multiracially.

Families with more respectable pedigrees started falling out over the child. Some of their members, well-established local squires and undisputed lords of the manor, laid claim to the *jus primae noctis*. Others turned the child from their door, proclaiming it a bastard. Whereas the former group saw their own traditions mirrored and guaranteed a further lease on life, the latter spoke of a betrayal of their heritage, with the High Church representatives hinting darkly at the possibility of inquisition. In all their published exegeses and apologias, the phrase "as the founder of our branch of science so rightly said" recurred time and again, leaving no doubt that all future development had been anticipated way back and that there would never be anything new under the sun of human intellectual endeavor, just the "mixture as before" for the duration, meaning of course that this must be accepted as "eternal truth."

This internecine strife within the house of origin had all kinds of consequences. At fairly regular intervals, a couple of family members left the fold in which they had grown up and went and teamed up with the rejected foundling. But this separation process was by no means entirely free of internal and external conflicts. After all, we remain the children of our parents all our lives, and with our spiritual and intellectual mentors who later take over *in loco parentis* the same thing happens. Others married into this new line, as was the case here in Heidelberg. Such paradigmatic pairings are no easy matter. However great the infatuation, each of the partners wanted to ensure its—albeit related—individuation and not just merge imperceptibly into the other. The initiator of this marriage will himself be describing later how successful the partners have been in this endeavor and what they have been through in the process. In their immediate vicinity, that is, in the extradyadic context, the new couple was not always given a very friendly reception. However happy a marriage may be, it isn't necessarily going to make everybody happy as well. But the two now have ten years of wedded bliss to look back on. At critical points in those ten years, the family was enlarged by new arrivals. The children's names are unusual. One is called "malign clinch" (between the parents, spiteful tongues have been heard to say). The second-born rejoices in the name of "coevolution," obviously conceived to celebrate a newfound harmony. Whether it will stay that way remains to be seen; it is after all still at a very tender age. But there can be no doubt—the first rose is for the ten-year-old family.

II

In contrast to the unanimity with which the detractors of family therapy either looked down on it as a persona non grata—and hence completely ineligible in terms of the marriage market—or else dismissed it out of hand as a nonperson, its own representatives were anything but like minded. Although some embarked on mixed marriages, others held family therapy to be not just an immaculate but an entirely spontaneous conception, self-generated without any kind of parental agency, something completely and entirely novel. This new paradigm relegated everything else to oblivion, just as all revolutions do, at least in the eyes of their own perpetrators. This was zero hour!

But either this proclamation was premature or the opportunity has gone for good. For as far as I can see, the revolution hasn't taken place. In fact, it's even been shorn of its first letter. "Evolution" is now the "in" word, with a "co" tacked on for good measure. It would be nice if one could take this as a sign that the age of revolutions is over and a more constructive era has dawned.

At the same time, other developments were brewing outside the confines of family therapy. Opponents came along to challenge it, asserting that man was a tribal animal and not a family creature. In his beginning was the tribe and that was where he was destined to return. More substantial objections were put forward by sociologists and social critics. The most extreme among them felt not only that the end of the family was in sight but that everything possible should be done to accelerate that end, systematically. So what point was there to family therapy? It was *bound* to be reactionary!

These critics were inaccurate in at least one respect. They equate the family with its western middle-class (or "bourgeois") form. It is of course true that no amount of restorative effort will prevent this form itself from becoming obsolete in the course of history. At one point, it was a new alternative to other existing forms. But if it should turn out to be the last family type in human history, then—probably not for the reasons adduced by its critics—it would be the end of history altogether. But as long as social critics believe that there is no other family form in existence today apart from the middle-class "bourgeois" family that they have more or less astutely stylized as such, they are contributing just as much to the preservation of a "bourgeois" order of things—to which, in their view, this kind of family belongs—as the therapy they rail at for attempting to help the "bourgeois" families manifestly still in existence. This is to greatly overrate the sociopolitical influence of family therapy. All the same, we who practice it would, I feel, do well to take the pronouncements of critically minded social therapists seriously. Nor should we ignore the uncritically minded of the species, who, with their idyllicized ideologies about a family form that has never existed, are just as far off the mark as regards family reality. Sharpening our perception of this point would do us all a world of good. I shall return to this question later.

III

For the moment, I should like to remain with the further development of family therapy. In the course of its lifetime, it has become something of a globetrotter, has experienced deportation and colonialism. Often and in the most unlikely venues it has been put through its paces, like a performing bear, for a huge variety of audiences. But now the novelty, the sensational element, is beginning to wear off. And this is certainly to its advantage; sensationalism is incompatible with coming of age. Things have quieted down, here in Heidelberg as elsewhere. The experimenting goes on, as does the research, the encouragement, the training. And a new terminology, a new language is being fashioned. *The Language of Family Therapy* is the title of Heidelberg's latest publication (3). This is an ambitious claim, for family therapy has never acquired a mother tongue. It grew up on a hybrid diet of scraps from other people's dialects, had to learn to speak Cybernetics, Systemics, Analytics, Astrophysics, Biophysics, Chemistry, and much else besides. And when I see all this lumped together, all I can say is that the theoreticians of this form of therapy must be true linguistic enthusiasts, fervid collectors of exotic words. Linguistically they are living, as it were, on borrowed terms. But this is precisely the point where I want to proffer them another rose. With linguistic confusions taking on Babel-like proportions all around, we find here in Heidelberg a heroic attempt being made to invoke a long-forgotten academic tradition of *esprit de corps* and present the language of family therapy in dictionary form. The idea behind this is not to create a kind of Esperanto but rather to provide an aid to understanding, a translation manual. And this is something that is typical of the kind of work that has been done here ever since the Department of Basic Psychoanalytic Research and Family Therapy came into existence. In therapy its aim has always been to differentiate *and* connect, to stress individuality *and* relatedness. And the same applies to its conceptual efforts. Indeed, this congress itself, with its broad variety of topics, is an eloquent testimony to this attitude.

For our guild of professional individualists, this conference is a challenge. There may be the temptation to make use of it to emulate the trend toward one-upmanship that is beginning to surface again in the economic field, to play one side off against the other, gain personal kudos, form monopolies; or to see it as a species of hit parade, ranging from familiar evergreens to the very latest new-wave avant-gardism. But neither would be a true reflection of the *genius loci* and its striving for communication, fairness, impartiality, and loyalty; however discerning and critical in spirit the discussion and inquiry may be, I do not think that I have strayed from my topic. I was talking about language. And I often ask myself whether families would understand what we are talking about if they could hear us talking about them in our professional jargon. What kind of reality is it that is being put into words? Is it family reality at all? Or is it experienced reality as it affects the people concerned?

Language creates reality, or at least a construction of reality, as epistemology teaches us—another of those subjects we had to learn and ought to know more about! Reality is therefore dependent on language. And language itself? If reality is to be talked about using language, then that language must be perception-dependent. Reality is always perceived reality. And vice-versa: I can perceive something by virtue of its being; through my perception of it, it becomes reality (for me).

The Greeks called perception "aisthesis," the root of our word "aesthetics." And this is another word that has found its devotees in our profession. In its original sense it does not mean something that would be the preserve of art museums, fashion designers, and cosmeticians. Taken literally, it can indeed have to do with beauty; above all, however, it refers to "rightness," correct proportions, measure. Aisthesis does indeed create reality, but it is at the same time mimetic. It takes the measure of reality, measures it up, rather than measuring itself presumptuously *against* reality. It seeks to correspond to what it perceives, to be as truly receptive to it as possible, not to alienate or to distort it but rather to have a part in it.

Is the way we talk about the family mimetic? Can it be? Is it not rather the case that the language of therapy must have something "thetic," something normative about it, express in language the way things *should* be? But how can we know the way things should be? What is the yardstick? Is it not presumptuous to speak of "the" family in the singular as if we had some infallible measure of what that is? Must aesthetic language not be rather more circumspect here?

Our language tends to lose its sense of just measure in another respect as well, when it seeks to express not just perception but—no more, no less—Truth. It is then that the necessarily subjective element of perception is negated, then that seeing becomes identical with what is seen. If, for example, I say "the family *is* a system" and mean that ontologically, in the sense of an entity, and not epistemologically, in the sense of a category, then I have lost the measure of it, I am using the wrong system of measurement. It is tantamount to equating a perceptual category with a reality independent of perception. This way lies dogmatism, lies clericalism, inquisition, excommunication.

I am greatly impressed by the modesty with which Gregory Bateson in 1969 undertook a critical review of the double-bind theory he had developed 13 years earlier (1). He warns against a reification of our concepts. Double bind belongs to a different reality, a different logical type from the one inhabited by these roses. It is not "out there," but "in here," a "mental reality." It is not a visible thing. After all, who has ever come across Oedipus in person, to have his complex demonstrated "in the flesh"?

Once we start reifying concepts, communication becomes difficult if not impossible. Concepts are ways of seeing things and as such can always change. For this reason, they must never become irrevocable.

Family reality does not present itself in the singular but in an endless plurality. Its measure can be taken only by employing a multiplicity of languages, by description and redescription over and over again, because it can be experienced and perceived in a multiplicity of ways. (Families in crisis themselves have a tendency, incidentally, to reify their concept of themselves and we then do our best to offer them a different view of themselves, to thaw out their self-images.)

Whoever speaks of families is invariably also speaking personally. We cannot speak neutrally *about* them, as though we were outside looking in. Both cognitively *and* existentially we all participate in families because we ourselves are sons, daughters, grandchildren, relatives. It would be fascinating to examine fully elaborated theoretical concepts of family to find out what bearing the origins and present family life of their creators have on the aspects they concentrate on and the language used in them. And much the same kind of inquiry could be undertaken for the declared critics and/or fans of the institution "family" in the ranks, say, of our politicians. Whereas some obviously think in terms of Happy Families, others will tend more toward "My Family and Other Animals." This would certainly be borne out in their language.

To my ears, the language used by the Heidelberg concept is an appropriate one, deserving of a rose. It is appropriate because it is inexact. Its central terms "binding," "expelling," "delegation," "related individuation" are fuzzy, soft-edged, intuitive, and for that reason hard if not impossible to verify scientifically. They are rather aesthetic categories in the sense I used the word in earlier. This may be annoying for those for whom reality is only that which has been scientifically proven. But let's be honest. How many of you would like to live in a scientifically screened reality? I wouldn't, for one. For me it would be the worst kind of deprivation.

The point about the language under discussion here is its therapeutic appropriateness. The words I mentioned refer to relational qualities, not to objectively measurable transactions accessible to direct observation. Who, after all, has actually witnessed as a recordable datable event how someone in a family has been "delegated" the role, say, of bringing a little excitement into the boring routine of things? And yet this term is an appropriate intuitive reflection of something which may not be a discrete event but rather a process extending over a period of time. If we could live with a family and have a part in its existence, then we should probably find all kinds of indicators pointing to such a process. And the research approach appropriate to it would be process research.

But there are ways of gaining access to realities besides the scientific method; for instance, art and therapy. These are not characterized by any fundamental mistrust of personal experience, of subjectivity, that necessary pendant to objectivity. Science is not an absolute. Those who still confuse "scientific" with "precise," "definite," "exact," or reification with "objectivity" have simply not yet awakened to the fact that soft-edged categories such as "probability" and "uncertainty" have been in use in the so-called exact sciences for decades. Their world has become more alive. Should the human sciences, they of all things, try to be more exact than the mathematical sciences? What is the price that humanity then has to pay in order to enjoy the questionable benefits of scientifically exact therapy?

IV

The Heidelberg Family Concept was developed further and is still being developed. It seems to be moving in the direction of what recently was termed the "evolutionary paradigm." The family album with illustrations of homeostasis is obviously a thing of the past.

Concepts are thought systems and as such are subject to the laws governing all human systems. They can be open or closed. If one attempts to keep them consistent and preserve their inner "logic," they close up and become rigid. All they provide then are redundant answers but no more questions—and certainly none with respect to themselves. They breed an insatiable hunger for self-confirmation, become encrusted with intellectual and conceptual stucco like a parody of rococo.

By contrast, concepts that have not been sterilized into immunity against new experience transcend themselves by virtue of their very nature. Experience keeps us moving. As Heraclitus says: "We never step into the same river twice."

Cabinetmakers do not have only *one* plane. Their experience with different kinds of wood and their expression of their ideas in wood have led to the invention of an impressive array of instruments. The same is true, mutatis mutandis, of therapy concepts. They too have an instrumental character for the practice and training of—and some aspects of the research into—therapy. However, it is not research but experience that tests them for their suitability. And they remain suitable as long as they maintain an appropriate give-and-take relationship with family realities. These, in their turn, are caught up in a constant process of change. To the extent that concepts of family perceive and reflect this change, they will remain open and changeable themselves.

V

I should like here to work in a critical comment that seems to me to apply to all the family concepts I am familiar with. And it is to them that I should like to dedicate most of the thorns on my roses.

Family theories largely agree that a family should be open toward the outside, should possess a certain autonomy, and should be able to organize itself as far as possible, if it is to be considered functional. But do these theories take sufficient account of the fact that that which is on the other side of that open boundary is going to influence the autonomy and the development of the family, either positively or negatively? They may indeed refer to this fact. And yet as far as I can see they still concentrate on the "inner space" of the family as if it were something independent, something clearly separable from its environment. Concentrating on the individual is an approach that must be rejected, they agree. But aren't they doing the same at one remove by concentrating on the individual family? The interest taken in internal processes is merely transposed from the individual to the family.

I cannot exist as an individual without a multidimensional environment. I need air, light, food, clothing, information, attention, relationships, somewhere to live. If emancipation takes the form of freeing one's self from these environments, then its first stage is isolation, its last perhaps suicide. If therapy sees its goal only in the emancipation or protection against what is then by definition a hostile environment, it is putting a stranglehold on that individual and cutting him off entirely from sources of invigoration that may have been meager enough already.

To put it another way, what we think of as so obviously being an individual is not a living unit sufficient unto itself. To declare something absolutely individual is to betray in the use of one's terms something akin to a murderous intention. Ab–sol–ute means i–sol–ation, being cut off, unrelated, an abstract entity. In my paranoid infatuation with myself, I may regard everyone else as a negation of that self, as a denizen of Sartre's hell. But even then it remains posited by myself. Nothing can survive for very long on the Either–Or principle.

What happens if we transpose this to the family level? A family is just as unable to exist without a multidimensional environment as an individual is. Its surroundings may set it at risk or help it thrive. The art of family survival is to keep this dialectic in equipoise. And if this is beyond it, family therapy should help it become more skilled in that art.

Internal and external factors together form family reality. A family in its demarcation from the outside world can organize itself only if it can integrate constant organizational influences from outside. Self-organization and organization from outside—or if you prefer it in English autopoiesis and allopoiesis—are both constantly present and often in conflict with one another. In its internal allocation of roles, for example, the family is organized more from the outside than self-organized. It is not the man of the house who allocates or prescribes himself the role of being mainly responsible for the material welfare of the family by going out to work. It is not by choice that it is the mother who is marked down by fate and nature to be largely if not exclusively responsible for the children, the cooking, the housework, and the like. Not all children want to be literate; some would rather stay illiterate and not be forced to go to school and learn to forget everything that doesn't fit in between A and Z.

Thus talking of pathological families can quite simply be discrimination, nothing less. Psychosomatic, depressive, neurotic, and other phenomena are interactive processes that combine with unemployment, cramped living conditions, financial worries, multiple burdens on all the family members. They have nothing to do with deprivation in early childhood, authoritarian upbringing, intrafamilial exploitation, and all the rest of it. They have quite simply to do with unemployment, cramped living conditions, financial worries, etc., etc. Psychologizing is not going to explain that away; the very attempt is cynical from the outset.

If family environments with their burdens and resources are not part of a therapy concept, then that concept is blind in one eye. It privatizes the family. The impairment of the family situation by social, political, housing, and traffic conditions, by wrong-headed schooling and polluted air is spirited away. Who does this exonerate, who does it put the blame on? It is surely only an oblique way of saying that everything is the family's fault after all, even the television programs—after all, the family switches them on! Responsibility is made synonymous with blame. And putting the blame on the family has the inestimable advantage of taking away the blame from us.

If we as therapists restrict our perspective to the inner space of the family, we are not only going to miss out on essential elements of family reality. We are declaring ourselves to be agreeable to the notion that the family is its own worst enemy. And when it realizes that, as it undoubtedly will, then it is going to turn in on itself and keep us on the outside. The immediate feedback it will get, of course, is that it is its own worst enemy.

The monocle was still in fashion when present-day psychotherapy essayed its first steps. Since then spectacles with two eyeglasses have become the norm. So we should seriously ponder Gregory Bateson's conviction that one's vision needs to be at least binocular if it is to have even an inkling of what is going on between two things in relation to one another, for example, a family and its environment.

Of course, none of this is new to you. I hope. For I prefer to carry coals to Newcastle rather than pride myself on having something so esoteric to say that nobody is interested in hearing it. But saying such things and having them listened to is not enough. I suspect myself—and not only myself—of not drawing the necessary conclusions from what I have said and you have heard. Does extending our field of vision mean that we in doing so are ipso facto enriching our therapeutic practice? Therapeutic concepts are not picture books; they hope and seek to be a blueprint for action. Can this action for families be reduced to psychotherapy or to the family alone, if I really do keep both eyes open?

The word most often used by therapists probably is "change." This is taken for granted to such an extent that there is little reflection about why, how, and to what end something should change. And if it so happens on some occasion that all our therapeutic hocus-pocus fails to change anything, then the family is obviously just rigid, obstinate, a "hopeless case." But it might well be that for that family a new home, employment, or better working conditions, a school for children rather than children for school, a little more so-called quality of life as exemplified by better sound-proofing, aids to integration into the community, and so forth, would be just what the doctor ordered. I can of course turn up my nose and say that such "marginal factors" are the preserve of the social workers, the education and social welfare authorities and have nothing to do with the "essentials" of therapy, which is something only understood by a tiny minority, an elite. And indeed snobbery is definitely one way of matching one's inefficiency with an imposing exterior.

Probably many of those present are engaged in social work. I do not presume that it is their intention to attain by stealth the status of therapists. Nor do I want to spark a discussion about where the line should be drawn between social work and psychology. But I would like to present a rose to the ladies and gentlemen active in social work, with the following dedication: To all those who, when family therapy has failed, have been the last resort but the only really effective source of assistance.

The conclusion I draw from the critical comments that have made me deny us therapists a rose, leaving us only with the thorns, is the following: It is a one-sided attitude that reduces family therapy to a matter concerning medicine and psychotherapy alone. Family therapy should be more alive to the fact that it *is* by its very nature situated in the middle ground between family privacy and the public, social domain. And that is not a comfortable place to be. This is where things are bound to turn political. This is where the decision is taken whether family therapy should be used to fudge problems that need to be tackled on the social plane or whether it should rather at least point them up for what they are. This is where, in actual cases, I am called upon to ask myself whether I wish to regard active support for changes in family environments as unethical activism or as a logical consequence of my view of the nature of therapy. Discussions with social workers and socialists could be useful here. And they wouldn't all have to take place under such headings as "the socially underprivileged," "lower-class families," or "employment for down-and-outs." There are other social problems that beset us members of the middle and upper classes, for example, "the decline of the family among the wealthy."

VI

Concepts of family are becoming more and more "ecological." That situates them squarely back on their own terrain, as "ecological" comes from "oikos," which was to the Greeks what the family is to us. Another succulent bit of terminology is the word "holistic." This is fairly easy to say but pretty difficult to live up to. We are told to grasp the whole, as if the very injunction to do so were sufficient to make it possible. I cannot grasp the whole unless I am able to get outside that of which I am necessarily myself a part. That point outside of the world from which the whole planet could be moved is something that neither Archimedes nor anyone since has succeeded in finding. Hoping to find it now is in my view presumptuous, for man has reached a point where, in his overweening folly, he can shake the world off its axis in an entirely different sense. This is a late consequence of that old hybris that encouraged men in thinking that they were not part of the whole but could rather do with it as they wished. Doesn't this global arrogance have its localized likenesses in concepts, institutions, *and* their personal representatives—in me, myself?

VII

Ladies and gentlemen, I was ironical where I felt things to be particularly serious. My criticism is part of a resolve to improve myself. If I have seemed overly reflective, please do not take it amiss. As has been the case before, I no longer feel so sure of myself.

There remain the roses that I have brought with me. I chose roses as a metaphor to express the idea of "both . . . and." Their scent is balm; their thorns are barbs. They have a healing power but can also injure. Their leaves feel like warm velvet but can be as cool as wet pebbles. The wood of the rosebush is sturdy and hard; flutes can be made out of it. An either–or will never produce a rose, nor would it let one blossom. For scent and thorns are both sentences out of its dialogue with the soil, the animal world, and the air.

Rose, Oh pure gainsaying, bliss of being nobody's sleep under so many eyelids.

I do not want to close with this inscription on the poet Rilke's gravestone but rather offer you another text to go with the roses as a birthday tribute to the Department of Basic Psychoanalytic Research and Family Therapy on the threshold of its second decade. The text is taken from Erhart Kästner's book *Kreta* (2).

Who can claim that he knows himself well enough to say why he finds this or that affecting him? Things felt elsewhere and at other times continue to resonate softly, high or low, of their own accord, like the wires of a piano when a violin is played in the same room. We do not see images but images behind images, as in a hall of mirrors. Often what is at first glance reality can become translucent and then it is not something complete unto itself but many things in one and is wedded and blended, brings forth other things out of itself and is hardly namable anymore. A person one sees reminds me in his movements of others. The sound of one voice recalls that of another, beloved or hated. An autumn day recalls hopes, a scent fulfillments. Yesterday is today. Always the one builds into the other. The longer one fashions the tapestry that is called life and its strange patterns, the richer the weave becomes, the fuller the harmonies. The experience of advancing years is the experience of growing abundance.

REFERENCES

1. Bateson, G. (1972). Double bind, 1969. In G. Bateson, *Steps to an ecology of mind* (pp. 271–278). New York: Ballantine.
2. Kästner, E. (1975). *Kreta*. Frankfurt: Insel. (Originally published 1943)
3. Simon, F. B., Stierlin, H., & Wynne, L. C. (1985). *The language of family therapy. A systemic vocabulary and sourcebook*. New York: Family Process Press.

Synergetics and Its Application to Psychosocial Problems

Hermann Haken

WHAT IS SYNERGETICS ABOUT?

The main topic of this congress is family therapy. As was shown in this discipline, in particular by the work by Stierlin (7), the family is a strongly formative force which may act in a positive but also in a negative way on the growing child. Thus we have to deal with a problem in which we have to elucidate the relation between an individual and the group he or she belongs to.

Such a problem is treated in a seemingly different discipline of science, synergetics. Synergetics, which came to prominence in the natural sciences or, more precisely speaking, in physics, has matured to an interdisciplinary field of research (1, 3). In this paper I attempt to outline basic concepts of synergetics and its possible applications to psychosocial problems.

The word synergetics is taken from the Greek and means "science of cooperation." Generally, synergetics is the study of how the individual parts of a system cooperate and self-organize their behavior in ways by which the whole acquires special states of order or structure. Thus we shall consider how such self-organized collective ordered states arise and then how they can be influenced from the outside. An essential aspect of synergetics is the search for general principles independent of the nature of the individual parts of the systems, parts which may be atoms, molecules, cells, or even humans. Because all matter, including man, consists of atoms, one might get the impression that I am propagating here a pronounced materialism, but, as we shall see, this is not the case at all. Rather, we shall study in an abstract manner typical relations between a system and its parts. As it will transpire, we shall not propagate any reductionism that attempts to understand the properties of the total system by

26

means of the properties of its parts alone. To the contrary, it will turn out that at the level of the total system entirely new concepts are needed.

The general principles unearthed by synergetics, which are discussed later, allow us to transfer results obtained in one discipline to another so that surprising new insights can be obtained into facts which have long been known in that other discipline.

Our procedure is illustrated in Table 1. Starting from well-known processes in physics, chemistry, and biology one may derive a mathematical description. This description turns out to be part of a general mathematical principle that can be represented by abstract relations which, interestingly enough, in turn can be represented by relations expressible in common language. In this way we may find applications, in particular in the framework of this meeting, to psychology, group dynamics, and psychiatry.

In the scope of this paper it is not possible to represent the individual steps of the mathematical description. Therefore, I shall present only a

Table 1

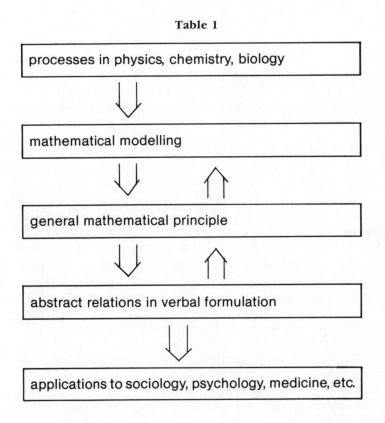

few examples from the natural sciences in order to elucidate the starting point of synergetics. The formulation chosen allows an immediate application to the fields just mentioned. From the very beginning I should stress that synergetics introduces concepts that are value free. An evaluation can be done only in the context of the individual disciplines. For instance, "left" and "right" are value-free concepts which, however, acquire immediately a value in politics where the value then depends on the person who does the evaluation.

SOME EXAMPLES FROM THE NATURAL SCIENCES

At a first glance these examples may seem to be primitive to someone who deals with psychosocial problems. Nevertheless, these examples allow us to elucidate basic principles of synergetics. Examples of material structures which are studied by synergetics are provided by cloud streets in the sky, that is, regularly arranged stripes of clouds. A related example stems from fluid dynamics where a fluid, when heated from below, can spontaneously form honeycomb cells. A further example is provided by chemical reactions where spirals are formed which turn around, spread, and eventually hit each other. Similar spiral waves can be found in certain states of development of slime mold. Here the individual cells live on a substrate but when food becomes scarce they start to produce a specific kind of molecule, cAMP (cyclic adenosine-3',5'-monophosphate), and release it into the substrate where it diffuses. When cAMP hits other cells they are induced to increase production of that molecule. By the interplay of diffusion and increased release spiral waves are formed. The individual cells can sense the gradient of concentration of cAMP and are thus enabled to migrate toward the middle of the spiral by means of their pseudopodes.

A further example is provided by the new light source called laser. Whereas the atoms of a gas discharge lamp emit light in the form of individual wave tracks, like the wave formed when pebbles are thrown into water, in the laser a beautiful coherent light wave is generated. This can be achieved only if the atoms emit their light in a well-correlated fashion, as if an internal consensus of the atoms had been achieved. Here again a new structure, in the form of the coherent light wave, has arisen.

All these examples have in common that at the level of the total system spatially or temporally a well-ordered structure is formed.

In the following discussion a misunderstanding should be avoided. In particular, when we think of applications of these concepts to the psychosocial disciplines the word "structure" should be preferred to the word "order." When speaking of order we think of something very regular, maybe even on the order of a cemetery. The word "structure" on the other hand allows for many more applications. Instead of the word "structure" we also use the word "pattern," for instance, in the sense of behavioral patterns.

FUNDAMENTAL CONCEPTS AND PRINCIPLES OF SYNERGETICS

Undoubtedly we shall bore the reader who is not familiar with the natural sciences if we try to derive from the just mentioned examples the general concepts of synergetics. Readers interested in that derivation are referred to my popularization, *The Science of Structure—Synergetics* (3), or to my books written in the terminology of mathematics, *Synergetics. An Introduction* (1) and *Advanced Synergetics* (2).

Let us therefore try to formulate an important new principle, the "slaving principle." *Long-living, slowly varying quantities enslave short-living, quickly varying quantities.* Later I shall explain this principle by means of some concrete examples. The long-living or slowly varying quantities are called "order parameters." In the context of humans they may be represented by individuals but in synergetics we are mainly concerned with the idea that order parameters are collective states, as we shall see. The short-living, quickly varying quantities are also called "enslaved variables." The ordered state of the total system is brought about by the mutual conditioning of order parameters and enslaved variables. In the technical jargon of synergetics enslaved variables are called "slaved." It already is clear that this mutual conditioning may become a vicious circle.

Because synergetics originated from the natural sciences the word enslavement or slaving could there be used in a value-free manner. I have retained it in the field of psychology and sociology as a terminus technicus in order to stress the particular relation between order parameters and slaved quantities. I am fully aware of the fact that in spite of all my claims that this word is a terminus technicus it irritates sociologists. Nevertheless, I think it is important to draw one's attention to this specific relationship in order to make people conscious. While Karl Marx was speaking of religion as being an opiate for the masses I have occasionally the impression that in some schools of sociology important relations in connection with the slaving principle are intentionally ignored.

Let us now discuss some concrete examples which are represented in Table 2. From the natural sciences we mention the example of the light field and atoms. In the laser the light field is a slowly varying quantity which remains in the laser for a relatively long time and thus is able to force the atoms to oscillate in the same rhythm and at the same time to enhance the light wave by light emission.

The next example is taken from the psychosocial area but is still rela-

Table 2

Order Parameter	Slaved Individuals
Light field	Atoms
Language	Baby
Habits	Child
Customs	Child
Culture	Child
School	Child
Family (adults, but collective climate too)	Child

tively harmless. The language of a people is, compared with the life of individuals, a slowly varying quantity. When a baby is born he or she will be dragged into the language. According to the jargon of synergetics he or she is enslaved by the language. This example elucidates the fact that the terminus technicus "enslavement" or "slaving" is value free. On the one hand the growing child will be enabled by the language to live in its social surrounding—yes, even to survive—at the same time the child will be enabled for a specific social surrounding only. It could not use its language within any other people. In this way a child is shaped in a specific way so that the terminus "enslavement" seems to be adequate even in the sense of everyday language. When a child has grown up he or she carries the language of his or her people further, which illustrates the effect mentioned earlier that order parameters and enslaved individuals condition each other. Without individuals the language of the people (the order parameter) cannot exist, but in turn the language enslaves the individuals.

What was just said applies practically without any change to habits and customs conceived as order parameters and to the youngsters as enslaved individuals. Culture also acts as an order parameter in the sense used here.

The closest interaction between order parameter and enslaved individuals takes place at school and in particular in the family. Indeed in the context of family therapy Stierlin (7) also speaks of enslavement. Incidentally, here it becomes quite clear how general concepts of synergetics need a specific interpretation in each individual science, for instance, in which way the enslavement is brought about within a family and which shapes it acquires. Stierlin speaks of transactional modes where he distinguishes between three types: the binding mode, where a child becomes too strongly bound up with the family; the expelling mode, where a child is prematurely expelled from the family; and the delegating mode, where the child is under pressure to comply with exorbitant parental expectations and is thereby subjected to massive stress. These transactional modes can entail specific behavioral patterns and psychological problems in the child.

Lidz rejects the word enslavement in the psychosocial context, as he observed in a discussion remark, because he prefers the word enablement. However, his written remarks demonstrate how strong the slaving principle (enslavement as now used in common language) is. For instance, Ruth and Theodore Lidz admit that at least 45 out of 50 schizophrenic patients come from massively disturbed or highly eccentric marriages or from those which were a total failure.

Lidz and Fleck (6) underline the importance of the transmission of culture where they not only speak of enablement but where they illustrate its very dramatic results as this is elucidated by the following section of their book.

> The two paths of maturation, the unfolding of his genetic endowment and the assimilation of the culture, are inextricably intertwined. Man's biological nature establishes certain imperatives—such as the complete dependency of the infant and the late occurrence of pubescence—and each culture must take these into account. The value systems and meanings inherent in each culture set imperatives also, to insure that each new member will be able to live in and to transmit the culture—imperatives which profoundly affect physiological functioning. Simply illustrated, a Christian's appetite and gastric juices may be stimulated by pork, but a Mohammedan will be repelled by it.

I definitely do not support the interpretation of the slaving principle as being exclusively negative; I just want to stress that this principle appears Janus-faced. Indeed, as we have seen by means of the example of language, the ordered state need not necessarily be negative but it can also be quite essential for a living together. In this way also Stierlin (7) differentiates between the ways in which a child is subjected to the order (or ordered state) that is represented by his mother and that of an adult who submits to an arbitrary or dictatorial authority.

Finally, the chosen formulation of the enslavement principle wants to sharpen our conciousness. We can escape the enslavement by our own language if we learn other languages, for instance, those from the Far East. We may get acquainted with other cultures, maybe not in order to throw away our own but to accept it in a conscious and positive manner. Maybe this should be done also by parents with respect to their children and vice-versa!

THE FORMATION OF STRUCTURE
STABILITY AND INSTABILITY

The transition from the disordered light of a lamp to the ordered light of a laser can be visualized in an impressive way which can be transferred to a series of processes in psychology and sociology, provided we adopt a sufficiently high level of abstraction. To this end we symbolize the amplitude of the light field by the position of a ball in a vase or by a ball between two slopes (Fig. 1a). The irregular emission processes in the lamp can be visualized by a soccer team that kicks the ball in an entirely random fashion (which is not so seldom in actual games). The field amplitude E will then undergo an entirely chaotic motion but essentially around the zero point (Fig. 1b).

In order to understand the behavior of a laser we imagine that the bottom of the vase or of the valley is deformed (Fig. 2a). Now a new stable position originates which remains practically unaffected under little pushes. Thus a new stable amplitude of the laser light field connected with this new stable position (Fig. 2b) is formed. By means of these simple pictures we may illustrate basic concepts of synergetics which I believe are also relevant for psychosocial problems.

Evidently the equilibrium position on the right-hand side is symmetrical to an equilibrium position on the left-hand side, that is, the system (in our concrete example the laser) can adopt two positions in principle but it can realize only one of them at any time (Fig. 3a, b). The originally given potentiality of selection, which is symmetric, is "broken," to use a word

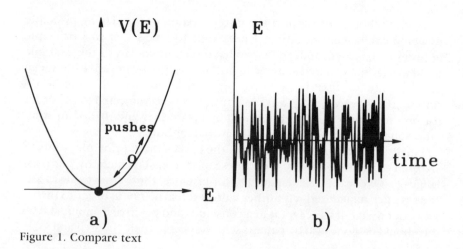

Figure 1. Compare text

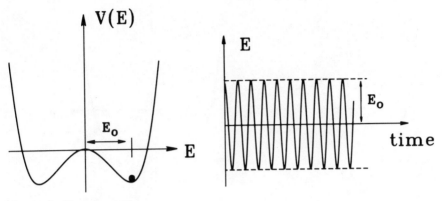

Figure 2. Compare text

in the jargon of synergetics. The right position can mean that the light wave is running to the right, whereas the left position means that the light wave is running to the left (Fig. 3c, d). To generate such a wave, respectively, the atoms must oscillate in a specific way. In the corresponding cases the two states are not compatible with each other. The laser can oscillate only in one state or the other. Now one might think that we do not like the oscillation of an individual atom in one of these two specific states. We then may extract the atom and put it into the other mode of oscillation. But at the moment we reinsert the atom it will be dragged into the old state of oscillation. The atom is enslaved by it. A different situation will occur if we bring it into a laser with the adequate state of oscillation or if we put all atoms simultaneously into the other state of oscillation. A further possibility is the following. We first bring the system into the state of a lamp, that is, into a noncollective state, and then we generate again a laser state for which the wanted mode of oscillation is initiated from the outside. When we imagine that the behavior of the atom is only an example illustrating the validity of the slaving principle, important consequences for the behavior of a person with disturbed behavior in a family and of his treatment come to mind and the application of this physical example to problems of family therapy may be left to the reader.

The phenomenon of "symmetry breaking" can be found in an impressive manner also in the human brain. Figure 4 is ambivalent and at first no specific picture can be perceived. But if the observer is given the additional information "consider the white as foreground" he will recognize a vase. If he or she is told "consider both sides as foreground," he or she will immediately recognize two faces. Only with such additional informa-

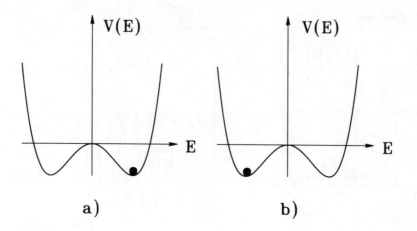

a) b)

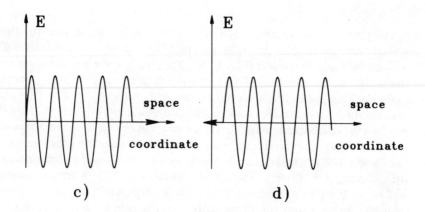

c) d)

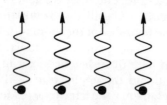

atomic oscillation

(symbolic)

atomic oscillation

(symbolic)

Figure 3. Compare text

Figure 4. Vase or faces

tion is the observer able to recognize the corresponding object where an incidental selection is made by the information given.

The phenomenon of symmetry breaking has been used for a long time in psychology where the symmetry is broken by the internal bias of the test person. Thus in the apperception test a picture showing two female faces is presented to a test person. The two faces are more or less without any expression. Because of his or her bias the test person will give a special interpretation to the faces and thus will reveal to the doctor his or her internal state.

THE ROLE OF ORDER PARAMETERS

Numerous examples adduced by synergetics have revealed at least in the areas of physics, chemistry, and biological models that the collective states even of complex systems may be described by few order parameters. If the condition of a system's surroundings are changed even in a rather unspecific way the order parameters can undergo dramatic changes.

An illustrative example is again provided by the laser as shown in Fig. 5. The laser may have a disordered phase (a) or a phase with a coherent wave (b). Then with further increased energy input light flashes (pulses) (c) or, if the losses by the mirrors are increased, macroscopic chaotic oscillations may occur (d). Finally, the phenomenon of intermittency is observed where quiet phases alternate with unpredictable chaotic outbursts (e).

Dramatic changes of macroscopic behavior are also found in biology. We may recall the different gaits of horses, in particular the walk, trot, and gallop. Detailed experiments of Kelso (5), who studied human hand movement, also show abrupt transitions between different kinds of motion. His results can be well modeled mathematically by the methods and concepts of synergetics (4). In this context I should like also to remind the reader of the papers by Erich von Holst, who was a professor at Heidelberg.

Generally, order parameters determine and guide behavioral patterns. A great repertoire of order parameters guarantees a great adaptability of the system. In this sense certain classes of mental illness can be interpreted as a decrease of the number of order parameters, or to put it differently, by a small dimensionality of the attractors. Here again abrupt transitions between different behavioral patterns typically occur. I suppose that this was what Stierlin (7) spoke of as "de-differentiation."

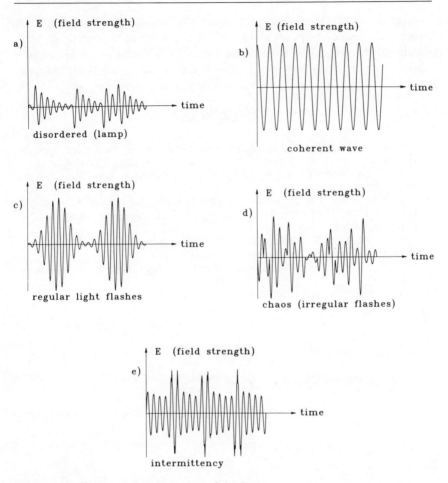

Figure 5. Different emission modes of the laser

CONCLUDING REMARKS

In this paper I have tried to elaborate on some basic concepts of synergetics and to indicate some possible applications to psychosocial problems. Of course, I could present only a few aspects of the field of synergetics which over the past years has grown immensely. It seems to me that in synergetics we may unearth important and far-reaching analogies between different fields of scientific study. As a consequence we may not only describe phenomena well known in one field by new words or concepts, but, far more important, we may formulate concrete models; moreover, processes in areas which did not seem to be mathematizable can be mathematized. At least in this way synergetics offers an operational approach which may be applied successfully in quite a number of concrete cases, as in psychology, group dynamics, and psychiatry.

REFERENCES

1. Haken, H. (1983). *Synergetics. An introduction.* 3rd. ed., New York: Springer.
2. Haken, H. (1983). *Advanced synergetics.* Berlin: Springer-Verlag.
3. Haken, H. (1984). *The Science of structure. Synergetics.* New York: Van Nostrand Reinhold.
4. Haken, H., Kelso, J. A. S., & Bunz, H. (1985). *Biol. Cybernetics, 51,* 347–356.
5. Kelso, J. A. S. (1981). On the oscillatory basis of movement. *Bulletin of the Psychonometric Society, 18,* 63.
6. Lidz, T., Fleck, S., & Cornelison, A. R. (1965). *Schizophrenia and the family.* New York: International Universities Press.
7. Stierlin, H. (1977). *Psychoanalysis and family therapy.* New York: Jason Aronson.

Lunch Chit-Chat

"I need a good stiff drink! That really does take the cake! What were the organizers thinking of, inviting a speaker who has the gall to try to convert us to his reductionist way of looking at things!

"What have clouds, spiral waves, and slime mold got to do with human beings?" Theo was having difficulty in controlling his anger. If the waiter had not arrived at that moment to take our three friends' orders for lunch, he might very well have started getting personal.

Doc, the country medic, had been greatly impressed by Duss-von Werdt's remarks. He ordered chopped veal à la Zurichoise with globs of cream sauce, while Theo plumped for a substantial hotpot (no doubt an expression of his continued striving for integration) and Maria (once she had downed a double grappa) called for the usual spaghetti, then offered her two pfennigs:

"My dear Theo, you've obviously got hold of the wrong end of the stick again. Haken was talking about abstract mathematical relations describing organizational principles in various material areas. His remarks were free of any kind of value judgment."

"But listen," Doc intervened, "Haken doesn't seem to me to be free of value judgments at all. With his enslavement principle he seems to be trying to give power structures of tyrannic dimensions the status of a law of nature. At least those are the associations I was getting."

"Wrong again," Maria retorted, "although I do admit that the term enslavement is a very unfortunate choice. He's not saying that one element of the system enslaves the other, but that all elements together create a rule, an ordering parameter, which all are then subject to. Language is such a parameter. All those who speak it both confirm and change its structure. At the same time those speakers are bound to observe its rules."

Maria was once again interrupted by the waiter, this time asking whether anyone wanted dessert. "The normal order of courses: entree, main course, dessert, coffee—is that an ordering parameter? The menu that enslaves us all?" Theo asked rather simply.

"Only if we let ourselves be enslaved! I want more soup instead of

coffee! If that were to become the fashion I wouldn't be the one enslaving the soup-lovers. However much enslavement there is, there's still room for individual responsibility!"

"Who's on this afternoon then?" asked Doc, to put an end to this verbal skirmishing.

"Three stars—Ivan Boszormenyi-Nagy, Paul Watzlawick, and Lyman Wynne."

"Never heard of them!" said Doc. "Should I have?"

"Well yes," was Theo's rejoinder. "But if you want to find out more about them, you can always look them up in this book."

The Context of Consequences and the Limits of Therapeutic Responsibility

Ivan Boszormenyi-Nagy

The thesis of this paper is that an ethical-existential dimension is the crucial fiber of relationships and of therapy, that the ethical-existential dimension is anchored in the transgenerational chain of living and thus transcends both individual psychology and systems of relational feedback, and that the knowledge and monitoring of lasting relational consequences is the greatest therapeutic resource, whereas the stubbornness of some of these consequences constitutes a major limitation of therapeutic prospects. I propose not to let curiosity about the epistemology of behavior prevent the ontological investigation of the sources and forms of relational consequences for being.

Certain relational consequences lead to reciprocal freedom for the use of life's options, others to one person's unilateral use of the other's stagnation. One principal cause of such unilateral use of others is an actual justification to be vindictive: the dilemma of destructive entitlement. Many of therapy's limitations are anchored in therapeutic ignorance about actual justifications, based on people's factual victimization.

It appears to me that, inadvertently, most therapeutic publications understate the value and mandate of therapy. Authors on therapy seem to be inclined to ignore the fact that successful therapy has lasting, transpersonal, and even transgenerational consequences. By focusing on here-and-now behavioral change, theoreticians implicitly deny that therapy's consequences are inseparable from prevention. This is all the more striking since we live in an era in which the validity of therapy is increasingly being questioned by the representatives of government, the deans of medical schools, and others.

Family therapy experience has revealed a new connection between

41

therapy and prevention. In close relationship self-serving behavior and altruism are often hard to separate. Having acted with due integrity toward a vulnerable partner serves the interest of the doer as well as the recipient. The adage about sound sleep resulting from clear conscience contains an important psychosomatic hypothesis of insomnia. Bad conscience was assumed to be the consequence of unaccountable action and insomnia a consequence of bad conscience. The context of consequences thus bridges the realms of accountability for actions with the territories of physiology and relational ethics. In this scenario the circumstance of bad conscience is more a psychological consequence than a cause.

Contextual therapy, instead of discarding the knowledge of individual psychology, subsumes its terms into the terms of the dimension of the ethics of relational responsibility. Far from being a derivative of any religious or even value ethic, the ethics of relational responsibility is the ontic substrate of active concern without which higher animal life of any sort is inconceivable. All higher animals take good care of their offspring, who in turn take care of their young. If they fail in this task the consequence is that rather than turning out to be neurotic, the offspring will not survive.

In terms of individual psychodynamic psychology, a person's reliance on neurotic defense mechanisms signals a certain weakness of ego. From the vantage point of relational ethics, his behavior represents an unaccountable, selfish use of his partner, who perhaps is more maturely, that is, more considerately, related to him. The Freudian notion of "reality testing" is a unilateral concept. Who is reality? In a relational sense what from a patient's side represents his "external reality," that is, his human environment, is at the same time the live "psychic reality" of his partner. Conversely, the patient's psychic reality represents each of his partner's external realities. A multilateral, relational outlook has to consider both persons as simultaneously coexisting, interlocking psychic *and* external realities.

Consequence is an important concept: Life is a context of consequences. If consequence is defined as "something necessarily following from a set of conditions" (5), the entire evolution of all species and the development of every individual living being is necessarily part of a chain of enduring consequences, with each link following from preceding sets of conditions. Conversely, the life of each of us as individuals leads to consequences for the lives of others. Furthermore, the survival of each species is the consequence of the conservatism of genes throughout the chain of individuals. The emergence of a new species hinges on consequences of genetic mutation. The survival of every human civilization depends on the consequences of their cultural arrangements.

I propose that consequence is an important form of relatedness. The fact that I will have lasting consequences for my son's life and perhaps even for my grandchildren's lives is a more lastingly decisive impact than the circumstance of how long I will have a chance to communicate, transact, or exchange with them. Consequence flowing from person to person from generation to generation is a crucial component of relational reality.

In part the distinction between social interaction and therapy is that therapy is purposely aimed at helpful consequences. A friendly discussion during a cocktail hour with my friend about his son may have, as a by-product, a beneficial effect on his parenting behavior. In therapy, however, the beneficial consequence is the purpose.

The goal of therapy is not a scientific one. Its medium is the subject of ontology, not epistemology. The therapist has to be biased toward the health of the client whom he offers to help, benefit, and cure. In this sense the therapist is in a conspiracy with the client. The benefit should come to the client on his or her own terms. Whether it is open or covert, ever since Hippocrates this conspiracy has been regarded as essential to the ethics of the therapeutic contract. Even if in order to get his weatlth, the patient's relatives want to kill him, at least his physician is expected to be partial to his health interests.

In family therapy all relatives become the therapist's charges. Their conflicting interests become a challenge to the therapist: how to find a way to be partial to everybody's welfare. The prospect of catalyzing multilaterally beneficial consequences is both the main limitation and the main resource of therapy.

However, as further experience accumulates, it becomes increasingly clear to the family therapist that the heaviest, lasting, and most irreversible consequences tend to accrue for the developmentally vulnerable young offspring. For instance, take the outcome of a painful marital conflict. As the wife gets liberated from her neurotic marital bond and her husband finds a new spouse, in turn, their young children become passively subjected to the loss of the security of the world of their family of origin. The offspring's helpless exposure to these consequences then makes the therapist inherently accountable to become an expert advocate for the obvious underdog: the young child who can neither divorce the family nor hire a lawyer.

By extending the logic of the flow of consequences, it becomes clear that the greatest impact of events of the present is likely to hit posterity. The more the family therapist has learned, for example, about what victimizes the children of mistrustfully feuding parents, the more it becomes his task to help minimize the damaging consequences for posterity. Therapy expands thus from the individual through the nuclear family to transgenerational solidarity. However, the therapist's relevant partiality to the target of the heaviest prospective injury makes him at the same time automatically partial also to the parents. In the long run the parents' emotional help is best served by their having done their best in the interest of their children's and grandchildren's well-being.

SPONTANEITY AND CONSEQUENCES

Although therapy contains elements of effective influence, not all manipulation of people is therapeutic. The difference between manipulation of people and therapy is that therapy helps people in a direction that is compatible with both their interests and their spontaneous strivings and life goals. A mere manipulative prescription or suggestive influence can easily be wiped out of the client's repertory of behaviors as soon as it conflicts with his spontaneous tendencies. Whether individual or relationally based, sophisticated therapy approaches try to build on the understanding of people's own spontaneity or motivation, rather than on imposing a therapeutic doctrine.

The spontaneity of a person's moves is codetermined by the nature of predictable consequences of his actions. Perhaps Freud's reality principle could be understood as the patient's capacity for anticipating and coping with the consequences of his actions as they might affect his life. This somewhat teleological guideline for monitoring one's motives is indispensable for the understanding of animal survival. A bird's building a nest in the spring anticipates the consequence that soon there will be eggs which will need protection and warm incubation. In a way the bird's spontaneous moves for constructing a nest are consequences of what will be future consequences of sexual behavior.

Through friendship or sexual needs the individual is invested in relating to others. Furthermore, the act of reproduction creates an indispensable relationship between mother and offspring. Moreover, through reproduction consequences of current acts point beyond just parent and child. If as a parent I care about my child, inherently I care about his child too.

By the same logic, the grandparent cares about the grandchild's child and even his grandchild. The chain is virtually endless. It melts into transgenerational species solidarity. The concept of legacy in contextual therapy addresses those expectations that benefit the transgenerational quality of life and survival. A capacity for understanding the guidelines of such legacies is an important resource for the therapist.

The more the therapist knows about the context of transgenerational consequences, the more will he be able to help his clients with their essential life issues, rather than just with here-and-now symptomatic criteria of their behavior. Yet there is a paradox in the fact that, because of a lack of truly relational goal definitions, family therapy, which started out to transcend the limitations not only of the symptom but even of the individual patient role, has often slipped back into limited, symptom-based goal criteria. Many times its otherwise sophisticated systems-based conceptualizations are incapable of providing the tools for addressing relational mechanisms beyond the scope of here-and-now observable behavior. I hypothesize here that essential help is tied to affecting those forces that determine long-term, decisive relational consequences. What then are life's long-term consequences? Examples include the following:

Lack of reproduction versus becoming a parent;
Psychosomatic inclinations versus health;
Lack of trust and suicidal inclination;
Inability to form commitments to close relationships;
Adjusting to life as a dependent, parasitic "borderline" personality rather than a creative partner.

If helping means the promotion of beneficial consequences, then knowledge of consequences becomes a chief therapeutic tool. Even though as scientists we have not developed a strict causal knowledge of behavioral or psychic pathology, as therapists we cannot help but notice sets of conditions that probably, if not necessarily, lead to beneficial or detrimental consequences from the vantage point of some relating party. For example, even if a father and his five-year-old daughter consensually and recursively validate each other's needs for affection and excitement, the therapist knows that the consequences of incest will eventually be emotionally costly to at least the offspring. As a minimum, the daughter will lose the kind of innocence that would enable her as a teenager to invest peer relationships with primary sexual intimacy. Yet most likely, sooner or later the daughter might run into conflict with society's mores. Moreover, as a destructively entitled adult, she will be inclined to inadvertently victimize someone else, possibly her children. Contextual therapy proposes to raise the father's trustworthiness by addressing that level of his spontaneity which considers long-range consequences from his daughter's vantage point.

NEGENTROPY AND RESOURCES OF PARENTING

Therapy fits into Schroedinger's original use of the concept "negentropy"[1] as a characteristic of life's sustaining mechanisms. By the term negentropy he refers to the capability of living systems to reverse the universal entropic tendency of all higher structures of energy and matter toward disintegration. Instead, Schroedinger (4) states, living systems are capable of building molecules of a higher order of complexity. Bateson (1) implied that this feature of life points to the central mystery of evolution.

The term negentropy addresses a potential of all living beings as a whole. In our current use the concept pertains to the creatively self-maintaining tendency of the human species. On the other hand, from the vantage point of the Earth's biology as a whole, survival of human posterity is clearly a limited goal. Yet it is outside the human ontological realm to be concerned about the survival of an ecosystem dominated entirely, for instance, by cockroaches and worms, even if it is epistemologically feasible to imagine such a postradioactive world. From a human vantage point, protection of the environment means concern about an environment that enables human survival.

The quality of human relationship is a consequence of a multilateral input. In human relationships the quality of parenting influences can determine the development of the offspring's personality and relational attitudes. In analogy to entropy in the inorganic world, careless neglect, exploitation, or hostile scapegoating can produce an even less parental further offspring. Conversely, in analogy to negentropy, the human relationship process has pockets of trust resources for the production of a more parental, responsibly giving offspring than were the offspring's parents.

Neglectful parenting, however, is not the only source of threat to the quality of human survival and relational integrity. In society at large human intelligence seems to be the creator of an increasing order: Reason has helped build and maintain civilizations. Conversely, unbridled greed and hatred are presumed to lead human groups to destructive behavior and, ultimately, to wars. Yet it is human intelligence and reason channeled

---

[1]The terms entropy and negentropy are used here in a framework different from their communicational implications.

into technical development that enable the greatest violation of social responsibility, ultimately endangering the health and survival of all life on Earth. Unless there is a comparable growth in the ethics of accountability for consequences to posterity among humans, there is little hope for maintaining a healthy environment or safety of survival. In the social sense accountable concern rather than intelligence alone represents negentropy.

Although there seems to be no direct connection between the prevention of environmental damage and therapeutic-preventive concern about relational deterioration, both are connected through a common underlying ethical issue: Is it true that today's self-serving expediency has to be diametrically opposite to a noble, altruistic regard for the welfare of posterity? Or, conversely, can the caring person benefit through being validated by his integrity of due caring? Accountability for relationship thus can meet self-serving effectiveness.

SELF-VALIDATION AND FREEDOM THROUGH THE EARNING OF ENTITLEMENT

In relationships among partners of equal power, for example, two adult peers, it is in both partners' self-serving interest to try to sustain fair reciprocity to keep the relationship. Peers can thus maintain an approximately equal amount of investment in the prospect of a continued relating. By contrast, relational unequals, for instance, an adult offspring and her aging parent or her small or unborn child, cannot be expected to invest an equitable degree of reciprocal concern in the relationship. The more powerful partner's caring cannot be expected to be returned on equal terms by the weaker one. Part of the actor's investment is rewarded by his earning of freedom through establishing his ethical worth. Whether he gains an awareness of worth is a question irrelevant to that of an actual ethical self-validation and therefore earned existential freedom.

It is the therapist's task to elicit each client's moves toward self-validation. As people begin to experience the liberating effect of receiving through giving and become self-motivated to earn the rewards of self-validating concern about the well-being of others, the therapist's role starts to shift from elicitor to supporter of a self-reinforcing spontaneous process. The forms of concern are manifold; for example:

Due acknowledgment of a child's caring offsprings;
Exoneration of seemingly monsterlike parents;
Help rather than condemnation of a mother-in-law.

The therapist's assistance to family members in discovering pockets of residual trust, that is, options for receiving through giving, represents an input into relational negentropy. Every positive present input into the generational chain is bound to improve the lot of posterity. The sum total of families with their formula of surviving trust adds up to transgenerational solidarity and paves the way toward a trustable human environment. As a minimum, through helping family members reconnect self-gain with due consideration, the therapist can contribute to the high preventive goal.

The effort spent in self-validation, the establishment of the self's ethical worth, is the price we pay for personal freedom and satisfaction. Close relationships can be sustained only if they are trustable. *A*'s relationship with *B* is trustworthy if *A* tries both to claim his own terms and wishes and, at least from time to time, to consider *B*'s interest as well. Yet the fully genuine dialogue of relating requires that *B* exhibit the same type of multilateral concern. An attempt at the fair equitability of consideration characterizes building trustworthy relating as opposed to a mere effective manipulating of the partner's need for a "sense" of trusting. The ethic of reciprocal due consideration is the deepest fiber of viable relating. This dimension of relational bonds is more crucial than the dimension of the psychology of liking, empathizing, and so on. Consequently, therapeutic concern about the fairness and integrity of parent–child relationships is likely to bring out a far more intensive emotional response than addressing of emotion does.

Freedom earned through due consideration is an ethical-ontological rather than epistemological or psychological proposition. The freedom is, however, an important condition of psychological and even psychosomatic well-being. As constructive liberation it enables its owner to live with a wider choice of options and a lessened inclination for self-destructive behavior or psychosomatic symptom choice. Earned freedom or entitlement enables one to enjoy his life's options for intimacy or beauty on the one hand and for creativity on the other. Entitlement enables one to risk offering trust that is necessary for relational commitment and for claiming one's own side and giving generous consideration. For example, the incestuous father who through his sincerity decides to help his daughter regain trust not only does earn self-validation for himself but also makes a beneficial input into posterity.

On its negative side, earned freedom can take the form of destructive entitlement, earned at the cost of having been exploited or mistreated despite one's best effort and good faith. Moreover, through helplessness the very young child is inherently entitled to caretaking. His balanced physical and emotional development depends on the quality of care he has received. If he gets seriously shortchanged by his destiny, he not only develops a mistrustful character type, but he also *becomes*, not just feels, entitled to compensation or vindication.

ENTITLEMENT TO BE DESTRUCTIVE

In human relations the greatest disintegrative force is not a mere absence of "good enough" parenting, to use Winnicott's words. It is not simply a lack of having learned good parenting patterns from one's formative environment. A far more sinister disintegrative form is the accumulation of destructive entitlement as the new offspring is placed into a world of injured justice. The "injured justice of the human order," in Martin Buber's (3) words, creates in my view justification for vindictiveness. This is a far tougher consequence than even ignorance or a hurt sense of deprivation is. Disregard for the existence of destructive entitlement therefore constitutes a major limitation of therapeutic effectiveness.

In order to restore trust in the family of the incestuous father, for example, the contextual therapist is likely to utilize the three-generational leverage of searching for ways in which to acknowledge the father's own past childhood victimization as a giving parent. His destructive entitlement has to be discovered and credited, but in return he has to offer the sincerity his hurt child is entitled to.

The incestuous father of a grown-up daughter first reacted with this statement: "I don't remember anything but if I did things like that, I am sorry." This attitude, of course, did not satisfy the daughter since it left her version in doubt. After several months in therapy the father was able to say: "It did happen but I remember no details." This statement gave an immense relief to the daughter and all family members seemed to progress rapidly afterward.

The father's sagging ego strength was enhanced by a therapeutic offer of self-validation through considering posterity's interests. Addressing him as a prospectively responsible parent offers him more support than merely empathizing with him, making him accountable or restructuring his action patterns with others. The therapist contracts with and addresses the father's options for responsible integrity in action rather than with the psychology of his ego–superego relationship. This is not teaching of insight but inducement of the use of relational self-delineation and self-validation resources, so that the parents learn to experience liberation from the earning of entitlement.

Almost three decades of multigenerational work with families has convinced me that one of the great sources of an "entropic" increase of relational mistrust is the consequence of the progressive fragmentation of Western family life. Much has been written about the faults of rigid, tradition-bound family structures. They sure are confining and at times even boring. However, at the opposite extreme, fragmented nuclear families and fragmented parenting units can have escalatingly detrimental consequences for the offspring.

The increasing anxiety of the progressively more bereft, alienated parents often finds no one else to lean on for security than their small child. The child easily gets destructively parentified and often sexually or violently abused. In other, less overt cases of exploitation the child is placed in the role of a referee between mistrustfully feuding parents or between mother and grandmother. In many other cases the symptomatic role itself parentifies the child, for example, in the case of school phobia in which having the child stay home symbolizes to the parent a safe possession of a parent surrogate and thus a compensation for the parent's early loss of his or her parent.

It has to be added that, as a consequence, destructive entitlement does accumulate on the side of anybody victimized by mere "distributive injustice." A person having been dealt a rotten hand by destiny, for example, through being a carrier of a hereditary or cogenital disease, or through early loss of parents, is less fortunate than his average contemporary. Without knowing any actual person to blame, whom can the damaged one ask: "Why me?" Thus not every injustice originates from personal malice. Since unfair, inequitable victimization or burdening of people leads to real handicaps and therefore destructive actual justifications, the extent of fairness of the victim's life situation becomes an important determinant of his relational attitudes. Whether he recognizes this circumstance or blocks his awareness of it, it is the therapist's task to liberate his client's relationship from the shadow of conflicting, currently victimizing prior justifications.

This is more than a pious idealistic dream. Behind this concise goal lies the complexity of coping with the context of relational consequences, which is easier said than done. Contextual therapy (2) bases its methodological principles on how to cope with the consequences of relationships both for the self and for others. Its transgenerational scope places this therapy next to other efforts explicitly aimed at the prevention of irreversible damages to human survival.

The therapist cannot create a just or fair world, of course, but he or she can go a long way toward restoring the trustworthiness of the world in which at least someone cares about the innocent underdog of crippling victimization. Mere sympathy, however, is not therapy. The therapist has to place the expectations of responsible decision making on his client.

As the therapist cares to raise the question of each side's fairness and justifiability, he gives evidence of his courage by risking the strongest of emotional reactions. When he expects each client to take a spontaneous position and make a decision about his next moves, he challenges the client's entire system of defensive operations. A seemingly simple, rational question—What can you do about your side of the relationship?—covers more emotional ground than interventions aimed at expressing emotion or at thinking about the sources of emotion. The client may sleep better or "open up sexually" for the first time in years. The client's responsible caring about posterity is not sacrificial then. It is bound to benefit the self too.

In sum, in clinical and historical perspective, therapy will not fulfill its mandate until it can address transgenerational solidarity. A major step in this direction hinges on a rejoining of people's attitudes split into self-serving versus self-denyingly altruistic categories. As each partner learns to integrate due consideration for the other's interests with an active claiming of the self's rights and needs, not only does their relationship benefit, but, automatically, they will invest in posterity's trust reserves and well-being as well.

REFERENCES

1. Bateson, G. (1979). *Mind and nature.* New York: Dutton.
2. Boszormenyi-Nagy, I. (1979). *Contextual therapy: Therapeutic leverages in mobilizing trust* (American Family, Report 2). Reprinted also in R. J. Green & J. L. Framo (Eds.) (1981). *Family therapy: Major contributions.* New York: International Universities Press.
3. Buber, M. (1966). *The knowledge of man: A philosophy of the interhuman.* New York: Harper and Row.
4. Schroedinger, E. (1962). *What is life? The physical aspects of the living cell.* New York: The University Press.
5. *Webster's Third New International Dictionary of the English Language* (1971). Springfield, MA: G. L. Merriam Co.

Hypnotherapeutic Principles in Family Therapy

Paul Watzlawick

The title of this paper might give the impression that it deals with the hypnotherapy of entire families. What I want to present, instead, are thoughts on *language* and *reality* in family therapy, with particular attention to the behavioral effects of certain uses of language that have been part and parcel of hypnotic techniques for a long time. It may be unnecessary to point to the fact that what follows can at best amount to an overview.

Hypnosis is the *enfant terrible* of psychotherapeutic orthodoxy. On the one hand, the often surprising results of hypnotic interventions are undeniable; on the other hand, it is difficult, if at all possible, to reconcile them with the postulates of the classical theories of therapeutic change. In the psychodynamic model, hypnosis at worst represents the anathema of purely symptom-oriented treatment; at best it has some usefulness as a tool for lifting repressed material into consciousness, for instance by means of time regression in the service of facilitating insight.

Different and even incompatible as the respective tenets and techniques of the classical schools of psychotherapy may be, they have one thing in common: the use of language as a means of description, explanation, and, above all, interpretation. This language is called *indicative* or—in terms of the lateralization theory of the brain—*left-hemispheric*. For a long time, in fact until the middle of our century, it was considered the language of science *par excellence*. But even at best, this language can only provide an intellectual, rational understanding of meaning or of cause–effect relations that have so far remained outside somebody's comprehension. This alone accounts for the well-known fact that indicative language is ill-suited for the communication of those experiences whose nature cannot be expressed rationally. The brain researcher Galin (3) once pointed to this difference by contrasting the experience of listening to a piano concerto (which cannot be "described") with the appreciation of the sentence "Democracy requires informed participation" (which can be communicated only in the indicative mood).

It is obvious that therapy is concerned far more with conveying experiences than with intellectual appreciations. A good joke can achieve much more than an exhaustive (and exhausting) explanation although—or maybe because—the point or the punch line of a joke violates the rules of indicative language and its underlying logic. The famous hypnotherapist Milton H. Erickson was known for his ability to resort to suggestions that violated the rules of grammar, syntax, or semantics, to juggle with puns or other plays on words (which in the traditional perspective would have been attributed to slips of the tongue or even primary-process thinking), and to take full therapeutic advantage of the confusion he thereby managed to create. And long before him—in fact, for millennia—the powerful effects of specific uses of language for the purpose of providing immediate emotional experiences were already known and utilized in rhetoric, drama, poetry, and ritual. Consider the second half of Hölderlin's poem "The Middle of Life" (in Michael Hamburger's translation):

> But oh, where shall I find
> When winter comes, the flowers and where
> The sunshine
> and the shade of the earth?
> The walls loom
> speechless and cold, in the wind
> weathercocks clatter.

Or permit the opening lines of Leopardi's poem "La sera del dì di festa" (The Evening after the Fair," translated by John Heath-Stubb) to influence your mood:

> The night is soft and clear, and no wind blows;
> The quiet moon stands above roofs and orchards
> Revealing from afar each distant hill.

The clinical usefulness of this language, its potential for conveying completely different experiences, for achieving very different emotional effects, rather than the dry, objective language of explanation and interpretation, has for a long time been confined to hypnosis. What I would like to suggest is that more than any other particular therapeutic skill, a familiarity with this language may provide new, effective approaches to the solution of human problems, the handling of resistance, and the modification of behavior. Therefore, these approaches can be helpful in family therapy. Let us examine at least some of them.

What is a suggestion? Although many divergent definitions have been proposed, it is safe to say that it is a communication that changes—even if at times only temporarily—somebody's view of his reality. Basically, any suggestion amounts to the request: Behave *as if* such and such were the case. Thus it is a behavior prescription, often, but not necessarily given in covert form. For instance, the suggestion "Imagine that you are biting into a thick, juicy slice of lemon" will provoke immediate salivation in most of us; in other words, it will elicit a physiological reaction that we cannot produce for ourselves voluntarily in any other way. The decisive difference lies in the as-if character of the situation. In other words, the recipient of the suggestion is invited to create in his mind a different reality (after all, he does not "really" bite into a lemon) and this imagination leads into a concrete effect. At first sight this outcome may seem hardly re-markable, but on closer examination it reveals its practical usefulness for bringing about therapeutic change. Admittedly, this perspective is not at all new. As early as 1911 the German philosopher Hans Vaihinger pre-sented his *Philosophy of As If* (12), a work of over 800 pages that greatly influenced Alfred Adler and to a lesser degree Sigmund Freud. Vaihinger presents countless examples in support of his contention that not only in our individual lives, but also in the natural sciences as well as in the humanities and in the wider social contexts, we always act on the basis of unproven and unprovable "as-if" assumptions. And even though these assumptions can make no claim to being "true" or reflecting "reality," they are more or less useful fictions that produce desirable or undesirable *concrete* results, whereupon the fiction need no longer be part of the situation and "falls out," to use Vaihinger's expression. An example of such a useful fiction is the imaginary number i, the square root of minus one. It not only defies imagination but violates the basic laws of arith-metic, since no number multiplied by itself can give a negative value. This has not prevented physicists and engineers (especially in the field of electronics) from nonchalantly including i in their computations and arriving at concrete, useful results.

What practical conclusions can be drawn from this for therapy? First, it enables us to dispense with the naive notion that to have any effect at all, an interpretation must be in some sense "true," since the theory on which the interpretation is based is itself considered to be true. That this delusion of "truth" then makes it possible to declare all other theories and hypotheses to be "untrue" and provides the basis for endless and useless "scientific" debates is mentioned here only in passing. Not truth, but only effectiveness toward a given purpose can be the goal of science. Although the number *i*—or for that matter any other number concept— is "only" a fiction, its effectiveness and usefulness are beyond doubt. What matters, here and elsewhere, are not interpretations or explanations as such, but the realization that imaginary assumptions provide fictitious bridges to practical results.

What are the optimal preconditions for this technique of change? Let us recall the essence of every suggestion: the demand to imagine and/or to behave *as if* something were the case that "is not" the case in the world image of that person. But since this world image is itself but a composite of as-if fictions, a new "reality" is thereby constructed (13)—provided, of course, that the new fiction is acceptable to the recipient of the suggestion. This means that it must not be too alien or contradictory to the way this person has so far constructed his or her "reality." Out of this necessity grows one of the basic rules of the Ericksonian approach: *Learn and use the client's language.* This is a significant departure from the techniques of the classic therapies whose first phase is largely taken up by the task of teaching the *patients* a new "language"; that is, the constructs and con- ceptualizations of that particular school of therapy, with a view to getting the patients to see themselves, their problems, and their causes as well as their present situations in this new conceptual framework. The very opposite takes place in hypnotherapy. There it is the *therapist* who tries to learn, as quickly as possible, the subject's "language," that is, the subject's way of conceptualizing the world. The only language spoken and understood by an overprotective mother is the language of maternal responsibility and sacrifice; with the engineer or computer expert one must try to speak the crystal-clear language of binary logic (rather than attempting to bring him into touch with personal feelings—something his spouse has already tried in vain for 20 years); with the starry-eyed, esoteric youth we may have to speak the language of Eastern thought. Of course, any one of these languages is only the form, the "package" used to in- troduce the particular as-if fiction.

Another characteristic of hypnosis is the avoidance of so-called *n*- words, that is, of negations (no, not, nobody, nowhere, never, etc.). Ac- cording to a plausible paleolinguistic hypothesis, negation is a relatively late acquisition of human (digital) language. This would account for the undeniable fact that in a state of hypnotic regression negations are often not "received" and that a suggestion, containing an *n*-word, can easily have the opposite effect. Similarly, a child is more likely to forget the admonition "Don't forget to . . . " than the equivalent positive formulation "Remember to . . . ." Applied to psychotherapy in general, this means that negations (and in a wider sense therefore also negative remarks and judgments) by the therapist may produce unintended and contrary results, causing resistance and an unwillingness to go along with the as-if fiction of the therapeutic intervention. Thus rather than criticize an attempted solution as pointless or counterproductive, it may be considerably more effective to remark: "You seem to have tried just about everything possible to get rid of your problem—maybe together we can come up with something *additional* that might be done."

Closely related to this is the *use of resistance* in hypnotherapy. Instead of following the classic procedure of interpreting it in terms of its supposed origin in the past and thereby at best reinforcing it, it is considerably more effective to *prescribe* it. Prescribed resistance ceases to be resistance, for it leaves the clients only two possibilities: either to continue that particular form of resistance which now, however, owing to its having been prescribed, amounts to compliance rather than resistance or to stop that behavior in order to resist the request to engage in it. In terms of the pragmatics of human communication, a therapeutic double bind is thereby created.

A still more complex pattern of communication is the *creation of resistance* in the service of therapeutic change. Essentially this consists of explaining to the family what kind of problem solution might be most effective under the circumstances, but immediately defining it as something that the family members will most probably be unable to carry out. The more condescending, authoritarian, and pessimistic the therapist manages to sound when expressing this opinion, the greater the likelihood that the family members will feel challenged by this pessimism and will be motivated to prove to him how wrong he is.

A separate paper would be necessary to present yet another form of intervention taken directly from hypnotherapy, *reframing*. It is the most immediate practical application of an as-if fiction. The family presents the problem in their view; the therapist puts it into another perspective, another frame, which may be equally applicable or even more plausible. The much-quoted example is that passage from Mark Twain's *Tom Sawyer* where Tom succeeds in reframing his punishment (to paint a fence) as an unusual privilege, so that his friends—who at first tease him for having to work on a Saturday afternoon—eventually are eager to pay him for permission to paint the fence themselves.

The references to poetry at the beginning of this paper may give the unintended impression that the therapist should use poetic language. This would be asking a bit too much. But the *telling of stories* is an age-old technique of opening new perspectives and facilitating change. Tales, especially witty or wise ones, may not only appeal in and by themselves, but also facilitate identification. And since they are always about other times and circumstances and deal with fictitious people, it is entirely up to the listener to decide how much of the story appears to be similar to his own life situation. He can identify himself with a story *à distance*, as it were, that is, apparently without commitment and therefore with a minimum of resistance. Milton H. Erickson was known for his frequent use of stories—either from his personal life (8) or others that he freely invented at the spur of the moment to fit a given situation—in order to conceal in this "wrapping" a suggestion that would probably have been rejected or disqualified if given in a more direct and overt form. For those interested in the use of such archetypically therapeutic stories, books like Peseschkian's *The Merchant and the Parrot* (7) or the writings by Idries Shah (9), too numerous to be listed here by title, can be recommended.

The common denominator of all the interventions mentioned so far is the fact that the therapist plays an *active* role. He deliberately influences, even though at times—as in story telling—this influence may be covert. This active stance becomes particularly obvious in the so-called *direct behavior prescriptions*. While a suggestion attempts to communicate to its recipient an as-if fiction that is different from the way he has so far *seen* his situation, the behavior prescription attempts to get him to *act* as if he lived in a reality that is quite different from the one he has so far constructed for himself—as if, for instance, his problem were already solved. In this connection it cannot be stated too strongly that those as-if behaviors should be very simple. Their often trivial simplicity accounts for their surprising, almost "magical" effects. And yet they are behaviors that were possible at all times but were not resorted to, because in the frame of the family's reality construction there was no room for, or sense in, resorting to them. This, incidentally, may also be the reason why such unorthodox ways of dealing with somebody's "reality adaptation" are rejected by many therapists. Yet it is known that such surprisingly abrupt and unplanned problem solutions may emerge spontaneously in the course of treatment. The famous somersault by one of Michael Balint's patients is a classical example (2). He was working with a patient, "an attractive, vivacious, rather flirtatious girl in her late 20's, whose main complaint was an inability to achieve anything." This was due, in part, to her "crippling fear of uncertainty whenever she had to take any risks." After two years of psychoanalytic treatment

> she was given the interpretation that apparently the most important thing for her was to keep her head safely up, with both feet firmly planted on the ground. In response, she mentioned that ever since

her earliest childhood she could never do a somersault; although at various periods she tried desparately to do one. I then said: "What about it now?"—whereupon she got up from the couch and, to her great amazement, did a perfect somersault without any difficulty.

This proved to be a real breakthrough. Many changes followed, in her emotional, social and professional life, all towards greater freedom and elasticity. Moreover, she managed to get permission to sit for, and passed, a most difficult post-graduate professional examination, became engaged, and was married. (2, pp. 128–129)

(And now Balint uses almost two pages to explain that this breakthrough does not contradict object relation theory, and that such an unexpected and unplanned remission does not "replace interpretation, it was in addition to it" [p. 134].)

A further characteristic of the language of behavior prescriptions is its *injunctive* and *performative* nature, occasionally also referred to as *deontic*. To define these terms very briefly: *Injunctive* comes from the Latin *injunctio* (order, admonition) and is defined in this sense for instance by George Spencer-Brown (11) as that class of communications which requires the recipient to engage in a certain action which, in turn, may lead to a totally new experience. The second term, *performative*, was coined by the British philosopher of language John L. Austin (1), who introduced the important distinction between utterances that state or explain something (called *constative*) and other "speech acts" through which something is actually achieved or accomplished and thus, in a very real sense, *performed*. If the president of an assembly utters the words "The meeting will come to order," he has not made a remark about (i.e., described) something but has thereby created a specific, concrete interpersonal situation. *Deontic*, finally, is a term introduced by the philosopher Ernst Mally in his *Logic of Will* (6), a logical system dealing with the structure and the interpersonal effects of command sentences.

The three logical domains just mentioned intersect and overlap, even though on closer examination they seem to be going into different directions. But their common denominator remains their pragmatic, reality-creating effect, which has always been an important part of hypnotic technique but is equally applicable to human relationship systems, such as couples, families, and even larger contexts.

The brief therapy model developed at the Mental Research Institute in Palo Alto relies on interventions of this kind. They entail a reversal of the classical principle of insight as a *precondition* of behavioral change. In the MRI model, what matters and produces change are actions carried out by the family in compliance with specific behavior prescriptions. The most elegant and complex applications of this technique are *family rituals*, as described by Selvini (10) and van der Hart (5), whose performance leads to the experience of a new "reality." Here, then, insight is the *consequence*, the *effect* of a behavior change, very much in accordance with Heinz von Foerster's (4) Aesthetical Imperative: "If you desire to see, learn how to act."

REFERENCES

1. Austin, J. L. (1962). *How to do things with words*. Oxford: University Press.
2. Balint, M. (1969). *The basic fault*. London: Tavistock.
3. Galin, D. (1947). Implications for psychiatry of left and right cerebral specialization: A neurophysiological context for unconscious processes. *Archives of General Psychiatry, 31:* 576.
4. Foerster, H. von (1973). On constructing a reality. In E. Preiser (Ed.), *Environmental design*. Stroudsberg: Dowden, Hutchinson & Ross. Reprinted in P. Watzlawick (Ed.) (1984). *The invented reality*. New York: Norton.
5. Hart, O. van der (1983). *Rituals in psychotherapy*. New York: Irvington.
6. Mally, E. (1926). *Grundgesetze des Sollens*. Graz: Leuscher & Lubensky.
7. Peseschkian, N. (1982). *The merchant and the parrot*. New York: Vantage.
8. Rosen, S. (1982). *My voice will go with you*. New York: Norton.
9. Shah, I. 22 Books (dates vary). Los Altos, CA: Institute for the Study of Human Knowledge.
10. Selvini Palazzoli, M., Boscolo, L., Cecchin, G., & Prata, G. (1977). Family rituals: A powerful tool in family therapy. *Family Process, 16:* 445–454.
11. Spencer-Brown, G. (1973). *Laws of form*. New York: Bantam.
12. Vaihinger, H. (1924). *The philosophy of "as if."* New York: Harcourt Brace.
13. Watzlawick, P. (Ed.) (1984). *The invented reality*. New York: Norton.

The Quest for Intimacy

Lyman C. Wynne and Adele R. Wynne

The marital couple that most recently consulted with us complained of a problem we have heard again and again in our practice of marital and family therapy. The husband and wife agreed, in despair, exasperation, and seeming self-contradiction, "We no longer have anything in common. We can't agree on anything. We think we still love each other, but we have lost all intimacy." Edward, 47, and Helen, 43, have had their lawyers draw up divorce papers. Pausing before the papers are legally filed, they were now seeking last-minute help to see if their marriage could be salvaged. Edward went on to describe what he meant by "no intimacy": "I am living in a house of strangers. We never sit down for dinner together. We all do our own thing. I need to communicate—I want to know what she is *feeling*." Helen's version differed considerably: "I'd like him to accept me for what I am. It's true, I don't like to cook or clean. I do like to sit and relax in the same room with him, just read, watch television. He talks constantly. He's always wanting to know what I'm thinking."

Despite eight years of marital dissension, this couple is quite capable, we were surprised to learn, of having experiences that they do regard as "intimate"—but only when they are on a holiday together. Indeed, just the preceding week, after leaving the offices of their divorce lawyers, they had taken off for a "wonderful" four days at a mountain resort: "No arguing, played tennis, ate and drank, walked and talked, played bingo, rested, and made love—that's *never* been a problem" (this last activity reported with exuberance).

Indeed, one could say that the relationship of Edward and Helen would have been a success as an affair but had been a failure as a marriage. Although they succeeded earlier in working together as a business team,

Revision published in the *Journal of Marital and Family Therapy,* Volume 12, October 1986. Copyright 1986 American Association for Marriage and Family Therapy. Reprinted by permission.

their negotiating competencies evaporate when they confront the most mundane household problem solving. Their failure, after months of angry dispute, to work out a plan of having meals together is but one example. Each had been married previously and each has two teenage offspring who are experts in igniting parental quarrels. For example, parental disagreement escalates into open warfare over what to do when a teenager leaves a wet towel on the hallway carpet.

Helen has had enough serious psychiatric symptomatology in the past to qualify amply for wearing the badge of a DSM-III (or ICD-9) psychiatric diagnosis. Her symptoms were successfully treated with prior individual psychotherapy and medication, but she and Edward have continued to be intensely dissatisfied with their marriage. They restlessly demand an elusive quality of relatedness that they variously and vaguely label as better "intimacy," "closeness," "love," "communication," and "acceptance." When we ask this couple, and others like them, why *this* kind of relationship is so important, they respond with puzzled exasperation: "It's obvious. What is a marriage without intimacy?" When we turn to our colleagues in marital and family therapy, we find that they often describe this field as therapy of "intimate relationships," a term that seems to have been regarded as self-explanatory.

When we consider historical, ethnic, and social class variations in marital relationships, the current public and professional consensus about the importance of intimacy stands in sharp contrast to the rarity with which intimacy has been regarded as important or has even been identified in other settings and times. Yet as we review the vicissitudes of relatedness for ourselves and others, we remain impressed by both the power of intimacy and by its ephemeral inconstancy. All too often, intimacy transiently is experienced as meaningful but fails to build into enduring relatedness. How can these puzzling discrepancies be understood and integrated with the theory and practice of marital and family therapy?

DEFINITION OF INTIMACY

In an extensive review of the research literature on intimacy, Schaefer and Olson (38) conclude that our field has "barely paused" to define, clearly conceptualize, or validate the nature of intimacy. Perhaps the topic has been regarded as too popular or too amorphous for "serious" study. We have concluded that it would not be useful to broaden and loosely equate intimacy with such terms as closeness, warmth, love, and sexuality. Among those besides Schaefer and Olson who have struggled with the concept of intimacy are Clinebell and Clinebell (7), Dahms (8), Doherty and Colangelo (9), Gilbert (14), Jourard (22), Levinger and Raush (26), and Waring and Reddon (40). Drawing on their suggestions and our own observations, we propose the following working definition of intimacy: Intimacy is a subjective relational experience in which the core components are *trusting self-disclosure* to which the response is *communicated empathy.*

Intimacy may be asymmetrically complementary, with one person disclosing more than the other. It is important to recognize that self-disclosure in itself does not necessarily generate intimacy, for example, when divorcing couples use self-disclosure to "prove" how little they care for one another. Rather, a key component is the willingness to disclose, verbally or nonverbally, or to allow to be revealed, personal feelings, fantasies, and emotionally meaningful experiences and actions, positive or negative, with the expectation and *trust that the other person* will emotionally comprehend and accept what is being shared and *will not betray or exploit this trust.* As an indication that this trust is justified, an intimate experience has not taken place, in our definition, until there is empathic feedback, that is, until acceptance and acknowledgment are communicated, verbally or nonverbally.

Several implications of this definition are relevant to our discussion. Intimate experience is necessarily intermittent, partly because these distinctive interchanges are incompatible with much of daily life, the going-and-coming of what Buber called the world of I–It (5). Buber's world of I–Thou, which has much overlap with what we are calling intimacy, may be cyclically renewed through relatedness in the world of I–It, but I–Thou experiences cannot be forcibly induced or prolonged. (Buber's profound influence on our formulation is discussed at greater length by Wynne [43, 45.]

Although intimate experience subjectively feels all-encompassing at the time, the actual context and content may be limited to one of several realms, such as sexual, intellectual, esthetic, spiritual, or recreational (38). Also, under special circumstances, intimacy may occur in a brief encounter, even with a relative stranger, because there is little likelihood of a further relationship with opportunities for possible betrayal. Over time intimacy occurs with wide variations in frequency and depth of involvement of the "total selves" of the participants. However, within the context of more enduring relatedness, intimacy may recur and become more reliable. Understandably, intimacy can most readily be achieved in dyadic relatedness, but it may emerge in triads and larger groups when, in a protective setting, trust and openness are explicitly valued.

In an effort to clarify further our concept of intimacy, we shall consider the topic within three contexts: (1) a developmental or epigenetic model for relational systems; (2) an evolutionary and historical perspective; and (3) the closely related topic of the problematic contribution of gender differences.

AN EPIGENETIC MODEL OF RELATIONAL SYSTEMS

First, let us consider how intimacy fits into a recently published model that organizes enduring relational processes within a developmental perspective (44). In enduring systems of which the family is the prototype, four major relational processes unfold in sequence:

1. *Attachment/caregiving*, complementary affectional bonding, prototypically manifest in parent–infant relatedness;
2. *Communicating*, beginning with the sharing of foci of attention and continuing in the exchange of meanings and messages;
3. *Joint problem solving* and renewable sharing of tasks, interests, and activities; and
4. *Mutuality*, the flexible, selective integrations of the preceding processes into an enduring, superordinate pattern of relatedness.

Our special use of the term "mutuality," introduced by Wynne, Ryckoff, Day, and Hirsch (46), should be clarified further. In coping with divergence and conflict, growth and aging, and discontinuities in the life cycles of individuals and family–relational systems, mutuality involves both distancing and reengagement. In mutuality, relatedness is reshaped, sometimes drastically reorganized, but with continuity of the participants.

A pivotal criterion for recognizing mutuality, perhaps applicable in research, is that reengagement with change takes place after a crisis or a disruption of relatedness. The relational patterns change in ways that are appropriate for new circumstances, while retaining other patterns that continue to be valued and that "work." The kinds of change may be either first order (changes of content but not in the structure of the relational system) or second order (changes in the rules or organization of the system) (41).

Returning to the principle of relational epigenesis, this formulation means that the four basic relational processes characteristically build upon one another in becoming focally significant and ascendant during development. In each phase, new biologic, behavioral, and relational patterns

emerge that help shape the normative or dysfunctional patterns of the next
phase. Figure 1 outlines this schema, including examples of dysfunctions
of each process.

Edward and Helen exemplify a couple with relational difficulties in
each of these four primary processes. We found it interesting that their
contributions to this problem do not follow traditional sex role patterns.
Helen has largely turned her back on household chores as a form of
caretaking and is more concerned with establishing her personal identity
in a career. Edward feels that her lack of interest in housekeeping means
that she does not really care for him and this, in his view, destroys the
basis for intimacy that he explicitly craves. Although they agree that they
have a communication failure, they do not share the same idea of what
constitutes "communication." Helen berates Edward when he repetitious-
ly demands that she "talk to him about what is going on in her head."
She insists that just "being together" is a better way of relating. Joint
problem solving in household tasks are neglected. And they fail to recover
from their quarrels in a restorative mutuality.

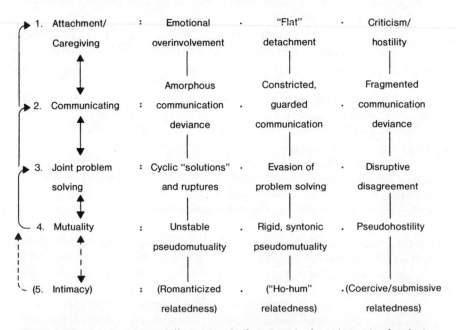

Figure 1. Major processes and illustrative dysfunctions in the epigenesis of enduring
relational systems. The sequence may stop progressing at any stage. Intimacy is
not essential for enduring relatedness, but if and when it becomes *reliably* available, intimacy is a subjective corollary of mutuality.

Note that despite the centrality given by this and other couples to "being intimate," we have *not* included intimacy as a primary relational process in our epigenetic model. Earlier, we regarded intimacy as a fifth stage emerging after mutuality, but we realized that such a formulation, however well it may fit popular ideals, was flawed on several grounds. First, intimacy is not so much a *process* as it is the subjective corollary of more basic relational processes; intimacy is evoked *in association* with these processes under conditions of trust and communicated acknowledgment. Second, although mutuality maximizes the opportunity for intimacy, intimacy can occur in association with *any* of the other basic processes, for example, with the nonverbal exchanges of mother–infant caregiving and attachment, as well as with communication and problem solving "in depth." Third, the elusive and episodic nature of intimacy disqualifies it for inclusion as a primary process in a generalized formulation of relational development.

Another important feature of this model should be noted: Over the life cycle, *these relational processes become linked to one another in a circular or spiral, not lineal, manner.* Out of marital mutuality may arise new cycles of triadic parental caregiving and attachment of the infant. Caregiving and attachment between spouses and long-time friends may reemerge as ascendant during illness and aging. Changes in the structure of the family, or the community, require fresh problem solving. In short, even after sustained mutuality is achieved, relatedness may usefully return to earlier processes for a period of time.

Olson's Circumplex Model

The concepts that we have used have similarities with as well as differences from those of others. Without comprehensively reviewing this literature, our formulation may be clarified by comparison with at least one other model for the study of family relationships, the well-known Circumplex Model of Olson and colleagues. Olson, Russell, and Sprenkle (34) define cohesion as "the emotional bonding which family members have toward one another" (p. 70). Their term "bonding" is similar to attachment/caregiving, though Olson does not mention attachment/caregiving among the 40 concepts he surveyed in his study on "cohesion." In agreement with Bowlby (3), Ainsworth (1), Hinde (19), and many others, we regard bonding as having a basic biological component, with evolutionary origins. Schaefer and Olson (38) speak of cohesion quite globally as "a *resultant condition* of the dynamic processes within the group. Intimacy is actually part of the myriad of processes. A sharing of intimate experiences is a precondition for cohesion'' (p. 50). We believe that intimate experience flows out of and recursively strengthens *all* of the basic relational processes, but is not necessarily a *precondition* for any of them.

Olson and McCubbin (33) describe communication as a ''facilitatory'' dimension in his model, but it is not clear just how communication relates to the primary dimensions of cohesion and adaptability. We suggest that a developmental framework helps ''locate'' communication processes. Joint problem solving is omitted from Olson's schema, but perhaps is encompassed within ''adaptability.''

The reciprocal coping processes of mutuality, as sketched out here, resemble most closely what Olson and McCubbin call adaptability, in which there is a balance between change and stability, between morphogenesis and morphostasis (42). However, adaptability has been widely used as a concept that applies to *individual* psychological systems—how a person relates to the environment—and does not imply so clearly the *reciprocal* adaptability that we regard as crucial in theories of systems. Also, we prefer to view the integrative functions of mutuality in a developmental context, not cross-sectionally in time, as rated in the measures of the Circumplex Model.

Family Structure and the Family Life Cycle

Our model for understanding the unfolding of relational *processes* differs from and, in a sense, is orthogonal to concepts of *structural* change in family systems. The most widely used structural model depicts the *hierarchical* organization of families in genograms that depict age, sex, and generation of the family members in their hierarchical organization, which changes during the family life cycle. These changes in family composition are most readily noted at the time of exits and entries of family members (6, 10, 17, 18). Normatively, the family life cycle has been divided in varying detail, from 4 to 24 stages (36). Such marker points include the birth of a baby, the departure of a child to school, the adolescent leaving home, and the reentry to the home of the retiring breadwinner(s).

Superimposed on this normative pattern, premature deaths, divorce, remarriage, illness, and dislocations take place unexpectedly and often inexorably, regardless of how far relational development has proceeded. Therefore, structural changes over the family life cycle and the *qualitative* changes in relational processes identified in our epigenetic model may take place in reasonable synchrony or, more often, with timing that seems developmentally unfortunate. For example, divorce that is precipitated by failures in communication or joint problem solving is often followed by persistent, vindictive custody and alimony conflicts—evidence of a "stuck" relational process that continues despite the legally recognized dissolution of the relationship. With divorce or remarriage, if attachment/caregiving is to become established not only between the new spouses but also between stepparents and stepchildren, a starting-over in relational processes is necessary, however confusing that may be. Past relational experiences, with the skills and "invisible loyalties" (3) that are carried into, and help shape, each new relationship, mean that the intricate skein of relational processes recursively unfold and must ceaselessly be reintegrated. Thus in this formulation attention must be given to the interplay between the changes of the family life cycle and the epigenesis of relational processes.

AN EVOLUTIONARY VIEW OF RELATEDNESS

While the diversity of family patterns across cultures and over time is enormously fascinating, this very diversity makes it difficult to identify those processes that are truly fundamental. Here we wish to make what is no doubt a rash leap, to consider what may be called the evolutionary basis of enduring relatedness. It is our assumption that certain basic qualities of relational systems developed during the course of evolution in order for the human species to survive—so far. Our sources are not so much those of the speculative sociobiologists such as Lumsden and Wilson (27, 28), who speak very generally of gene–culture coevolution. We find more congenial and interesting the work of researchers such as Paul D. MacLean, who has studied specific components of relatedness from an evolutionary standpoint, components that correspond in surprising detail to the relational processes we have described. In discussing the coevolution of the brain and the family, MacLean (31) wryly commented: "It helps to allay pessimism about the future of the family if it is recalled that the family, as a biological institution, has survived 180 million years, having originated with the earliest mammals living in Late Triassic times. This is a length of time that would allow the election of more than 40 million United States presidents" (p. 405).

MacLean (29) noted that one can recognize in lizards more than 25 special forms of basic behavior patterns that are also seen in human beings. In the evolutionary transition from reptile to mammal, MacLean (30, 31) identified three additional developments that appear crucial for family-related behavior: (1) nursing, in conjunction with maternal care; (2) the separation call, necessary for maintaining maternal–offspring contact; and (3) play, which inhibits destructive fighting within the nest and promotes later affiliation and joint exploratory behavior. Nursing behavior can be linked to what we have called attachment/caregiving; the separation call can be regarded as the starting point of audiovocal communication; and play can be reasonably viewed as the developmental starting point for joint problem solving. However, these findings raise certain questions and suggest limitations for our model. For example, is there a "functional" sex difference, biologically rooted, for a different kind of participation by females in relatedness compared to males? How do the concepts of play and affiliation outside the family fit into our relational scheme? And what possible place could intimacy needs have in this evolutionary picture?

First, it seems important to recognize that language is the most distinctive evolutionary acquisition of the human species. Although important experiences of intimacy undoubtedly take place in attachment/caregiving and in preverbal communication, it seems to us that the full richness of intimacy cannot occur without the human capacity for language. This conclusion is implicit in our definition of intimacy, in which we emphasize trusting self-disclosure, which may be nonverbal but becomes far more complex with words. Also, we emphasize communicational feedback, acknowledgment, and acceptance that can either confirm the experience of intimacy or mask and muddle it. It seems plausible to regard intimate experience as a valuable reinforcement, supplementary but not essential, for strengthening relational systems that have been crucial for human evolution but have had many opportunities for going astray.

GENDER DIFFERENCES IN INTIMACY

In the much shorter time frame of recorded history, the consuming quest for intimacy appears to be a recent and special phenomenon. The historian Howard Gadlin (13), in a particularly perceptive critique of the history of intimate relations in the United States, argues that intimate relations, as we understand them today, did not emerge until the early decades of the nineteenth century. In earlier times, clearly exemplified in colonial America, people's lives were completely intertwined in close physical proximity. Men were dominant over women in an extremely clear hierarchical organization, but the small, extrafamilial community maintained pervasive surveillance over the "well-ordered family" and intruded into the details of family life. In that context, "intimacy" between family members was prescribed and shaped by the mold of social status. Formality in relatedness then became a means of "preserving some distance in face of an overbearing intimacy" between persons who were intertwined in every waking and sleeping moment (13, p. 36). Under such circumstances, self-disclosure and societal feedback did not take place in isolated rare moments but as part of a continuous stream of life experience. Confirmation and acknowledgment of what the other person behaviorally and verbally revealed was an essential ingredient of the cultural norm. Intimacy in the contemporary Western sense was not *sought* but was a problem to be limited and contained by formal rules. The informality and spontaneity that we often associate with intimacy today would have made relatedness far too intense and continuous to be bearable in such traditional contexts.

With rapid urbanization and industrial development in the nineteenth century in Europe and America, the world of work became severed from the world of the home. Changes in social structure brought disconnectedness both between persons and between the parts of an individual's life. One result was the painful loss of what had previously often been onerous: intimacy became recognized as a "need" when it became erratically difficult to achieve. Here we can only touch upon the complex contradictions of the Victorian era. While the family became idealized as the "haven in a heartless world" (23), intimacy to a considerable extent became more regularly achieved in same-sex relationships of both men and women (2). Mother–child relationships and sexuality within marriage provided opportunities for discrete areas of socially approved intimacy. There is considerable historical and literary evidence to support the view that affiliative relational systems, not the family, became more dominant. Men tended to bond with other men in the pub and club. However, competition in the workplace often left men wary of revealing their hidden vulnerabilities and not open to intimacy in their male relationships. Women with women, in sewing or child-raising circles around and in the home, quietly gained same-sex intimacy, while paying the price of being oppressed by men who now existed in a world more apart.

Social and economic changes from the Victorian era to the contemporary scene have opened up greatly the need and the opportunity for broader-based intimacy between the sexes. However, gender differences continue to generate relational difficulties, including problems in achieving intimacy. At the level of **attachment/caregiving** there is an extensive pediatric literature on "bonding" of mothers to infants, which is said to take place, if conditions are optimal, abruptly after the birth of an infant (e.g., 20, 24). Yet there is also evidence that fathers may become affectively bonded to their infants (e.g., 35). An interesting study of a different kind was conducted by Sawin and Parke (37), who show that in feeding newborns, fathers are as active participants in dyadic interaction with infants as are mothers. This study also showed that the father's involvement in triadic interactions with the mother and infant together appeared to enhance the mother's interest and affect directed toward the infant. Finally, these authors studied parental responsiveness to infant signaling by calculating the conditional probabilities of parental behaviors occurring within ten seconds following specified infant behaviors. In this measure of sensitivity to infant behavior, the fathers were no less sensitive or responsive to infant behaviors and signals in the neonatal feeding context than were mothers.

As in the animal data, the finding on sex differences in the early attachment/caregiving seem to suggest that the differences are pivotally related to the timing and quality of early contact with the infant. Despite this seeming evidence that the biologic *potentiality* for involvement in attachment/caregiving is similar for males and females, the ordinary reality is that fathers have less practice in realizing their potentialities for contributing to family relatedness and of having the subjective experiences of satisfaction and frustration that are associated with parental caregiving. If the subjective experience in parenting is positive, intimacy thereafter may be more highly valued and widely sought.

At the level of **communication**, there is no reason to believe that there are gender differences in the potential for communicational skills. Perhaps females more readily integrate nonverbal modes of communication by building, epigenetically, upon their more intense and prolonged involvement in attachment/caregiving. Additionally, because women generally have been less able than men to satisfy their needs and demands by the use of force, they may have developed greater use of verbal persuasion and responsiveness to subtle emotional connotations of language. Men have traditionally delivered the thundering, pompous orations at meetings, including those on family therapy. This is not the stuff of intimacy.

The relational systems that emerge epigenetically from attachment/caregiving broadly diverge, one stream flowing into familial relatedness, the other into affiliative systems, which more often separate the sexes than join them into the same social units. Jessie Bernard (2) described very well how family theorists have neglected the importance, cross-culturally, of same-sex relatedness, which is more *homophilic* than *homosexual*. Such woman-to-woman and man-to-man relatedness grows through communicational sharing, as well as through joint problem solving. Homophilic intimacy begins with the play between childhood chums and continues in gratifying adult friendships, but in our modern, mobile society, it is increasingly harder to sustain. Insofar as injustices of unequal rights for the sexes are being corrected, role complementarity between the sexes has become less and less clear-cut in the workplace. Secondarily, the increased sharing of domestic roles, while desirable for both sexes in many respects, requires greater skill and experience in problem solving and communication.

Carol Gilligan (15) eloquently described the "different voice" of males and females as they deal with the issues of attachment and separation. In accord with the biologic and evolutionary evidence, she does not see these sex differences as absolute, but rather as differences in goals and priorities and as different constructions of truth. Comparatively, males of Western cultures are not primarily concerned with establishing and sustaining relatedness, but are more involved with the issue of achieving separation, with defining and empowering the self through autonomy and individuation. Females have more fully valued and sought to create and sustain community and intimacy through the elaboration of attachment and caregiving, much as has been described in our model of relational epigenesis. Gilligan points out that for males, attachment often appears to be a paralyzing entrapment, and caring an inevitable prelude to compromise. Women more often view autonomy, rather than attachment, as illusory and dangerous. Not only Freud but also other male developmental theorists, such as Jean Piaget, Erik Erikson, Daniel Levinson, and Lawrence Kohlberg, have formulated theories, as Gilligan points out, in which attachment/caregiving and its relational derivatives are conceptualized at best as way stations for those who have not achieved the "mature" goals of separateness and independence. These theorists, and their followers, will protest that the goal is not to achieve independence in isolation, but within the context of relatedness. However, a careful and, in our view, balanced reading of these theorists leaves no doubt that they believe the primary human struggle and challenge is to resist and overcome the suction of symbiotic relatedness, to go beyond, for example, Erickson's "basic trust" to stages of autonomy, initiative, and identity *before* intimacy becomes regarded as a focal issue (11, 12). From the feminine vantage point of giving equal or first priority to relational development rather than individual growth, an alternative construction of truth would consider how intimacy may be a valued by-product at *each* stage of development, beginning with attachment/caregiving.

In psychoanalytic theories, emphasis has been given to the idea that before reaching about 18 months, children of both sexes make a primary identification with their mothers (39). However, even earlier, this identification takes a different course according to gender. Ricki Levenson (25) examined these differences in a way that is pertinent to our present discussion:

> For a boy the process of separating and individuating from his mother is aided by her perception (and eventually his own) that he is "other" by dint of his maleness. She brings all her personal and cultural history with males into her half of the "dual unity." From the moment she lays eyes on the genitals of her child, her ways of handling, looking at, reacting to him or her differ. In addition, the boy is helped in cognitively clarifying exactly what his differences from his mother are by "disidentifying from his mother" (16), identifying with his father, older brother or, as Kohlberg (21) points out, with this society's myths and images of maleness. As his individuality evolves and he pleasurably and painfully realizes his separateness from his mother, he enters the rapprochement phase, in which he attempts to reunite with her and must, with her help, accept the fact that they are two separate individuals. As he woos, cajoles, and tries to coerce her into being there only for him, his identification as a male helps keep him defended, secure from the temptation to regress and become re-engulfed by the comforting and, at the same time, frightening symbiotic union (32). If he regressed defensively, out of fear of losing her love, he would lose not only his autonomous functioning, but, because it is now attached to his maleness, he would be in jeopardy of losing that maleness itself.
>
> For a female, on the other hand, her first love relationship with mother is not only symbiotic but colored by her mother's and eventually her own perception of their sameness.

Returning to evolutionary considerations, let us take it as a given that it has been necessary for men to be physically active, aggressive, perhaps hostile (although this is more questionable) in order to hunt, to defend against predators, and to obtain food supplies. Audiovocal communication to maintain contact with others was highly functional for survival, and play in the nest was preparatory for affiliation in the field. MacLean (31) and others have observed that even nest play differs for male and female mammals. Males are more rough and tumble, with fighting that parents may have to interrupt, while the nest play of female infant animals is quieter, less competitive, and a more likely precurser of social intimacy.

Going on to the level of what we have called **joint problem solving**, the most dramatic change has occurred in contemporary marriages and families compared to the Victorian era. When the traditional spheres of the sexes were sharply separated, *joint* problem solving between husband and wife was minimally necessary. Cultural norms, in which the spheres, activity, and authority of males and females were clearly delineated, limited the areas of controversy between the sexes and granted ultimate power to the husband. If a wife was a nag, it was from a position of powerlessness, not because change was going to be jointly negotiated.

In the contemporary scene, several major societal changes that are underway have substantially increased the need for *joint* problem solving by husbands and wives. In many countries and communities, dual-career marriages are now the norm rather than the exception. *Both* women and men are in the workplace and return to domestic tasks together but have no models from the immediately preceding generation for regulating how the division of tasks and authority can be resolved. Today, men commonly expect and may even demand that they be allowed to share in childrearing, but residual ambivalence and inconsistency in such matters is everywhere. However, with success in this joint problem solving, intimate sharing, arising out of this sphere of marital relatedness, is increasingly being discovered.

On the other hand, countless disputes continue as couples *demand* intimacy but fail to establish the conditions under which it may spontaneously flow, especially in joint problem solving about childrearing and daily household tasks. Divorcing couples tend to view lack of intimacy as their root difficulty, rather than to acknowledge their lack of attention to the underlying foundation from which intimacy could arise. In therapy, work on problem solving is certainly not very glamorous, but like the issues of attachment/caregiving and communications skills, it is a conceptually sound base for effective enrichment and intervention with troubled relationships.

CONCLUDING NOTE

Schaefer and Olson (38) propose a distinction between intimacy that is an "experience," limited in time and content, and intimacy that is a "relationship," which is said to exist when "an individual shares intimate experiences in several areas and there is the expectation that such experiences will recur and that the relationship will persist over time. . . . While intimate experiences are elusive and unpredictable phenomena that may occur spontaneously, an intimate relationship may take time, work, and effort to maintain" (p. 50). Although we partially agree, our misgivings about this distinction are threefold: (1) We do not agree with the goal of *maintaining* intimacy. If couples give primary or continual attention to maintaining intimacy, their expectations will be illusory and their efforts often misdirected. (2) The use of the word *intimacy* to apply both to the experience and to the relationship blurs what we regard as a crucial distinction; we believe that it would be less confusing to use the term intimacy to refer only to intimate experience. (3) We view the "time, work, and effort to maintain" relatedness as a complex and primary task; researchers, clinicians, and the public alike are likely to gloss over and be diverted from this larger task by the seductive appeal and immediacy of intimate experience. In efficacious family therapy, the focus will shift depending upon where leverage for change can be most effectively applied—relatedness that accepts and copes with divergence, separation, and conflict, and that welcomes but does not demand intimacy.

It should be obvious that we are not enthusiastic about what Schaefer and Olson call the "highly marketable enrichment programs" that "teach the 'how to's' of being intimate" (38, p. 47). We see many professionals—not including Schaefer and Olson—"buying into" a muddled, culture-wide mystique about intimacy. In our view, professionals in the marital and family field should take leadership in challenging the enshrinement of "intimacy." Somewhat paradoxically, professionals may be able to enhance the contribution of intimate experience to the quality of life by *not* accepting "the overriding predominance of intimacy as a cultural value" (38, p. 47).

The couple described at the beginning of this paper perhaps speaks, in part, for many, if not all of us. We, like they, need reminding that intimacy can be intensely pleasurable, but it is necessarily short lived. It is illusory to believe that trusting self-disclosure and an empathic response can be achieved through demand or willfulness. Paradoxically, intimacy emerges not when it has been sought directly but when it is embraced serendipitously. It is to the more basic relational processes that we, as family therapists, must direct our primary concern and attention. If the elusive phoenix of intimacy is to return again and again, the relational nest must be in good repair.

REFERENCES

1. Ainsworth, M. D. S. (1982). Attachment: Retrospect and prospect. In M. C. Parkes & J. Stevenson-Hinde (Eds.), *The place of attachment in human behavior*. New York: Basic Books.
2. Bernard, J. (1985). The marital bond vis-à-vis the male bond and the female bond. *Newsletter of the American Family Therapy Association, 19*: 15–22.
3. Boszormenyi-Nagy, I., & Spark, G. M. (1973). *Invisible loyalties: Reciprocity in intergenerational family therapy*. New York: Harper and Row.

4. Bowlby, J. (1969). *Attachment and loss* (Vol. 1). New York: Basic Books.
5. Buber, M. (1937). *I and thou*. Edinburgh: T. & T. Clark.
6. Carter, E. A., & McGoldrick, M. (Eds.). (1980). *The family life cycle: A framework for family therapy*. New York: Gardner.
7. Clinebell, H. J., & Clinebell, C. H. (1970). *The intimate marriage*. New York: Harper and Row.
8. Dahms, A. (1972). *Emotional intimacy*. Denver: Pruett.
9. Doherty, W. J., & Colangelo, N. (1984). The family FIRO model: A modest proposal for organizing family treatment. *Journal of Marital and Family Therapy, 10*: 19–29.
10. Duvall, E. M. (1962). *Family development* (rev. ed.). Chicago: Lippincott.
11. Erickson, E. H. (1950). *Childhood and society*. New York: Norton.
12. Erickson, E. H. (1956). The problem of ego identity. *Journal of the American Psychoanalytic Association, 4*: 56–121.
13. Gadlin, H. (1977). Private lives and public order: A critical view of the history of intimate relationships in the United States. In G. Levinger & H. L. Raush (Eds.), *Close relationships: Perspectives on the meaning of intimacy*. Amherst: University of Massachusetts Press.
14. Gilbert, S. J. (1976). Self-disclosure, intimacy and communication in family. *Family Coordinator, 25*: 221–231.
15. Gilligan, C. (1982). *In a different voice: Psychological theory and women's development*. Cambridge, MA: Harvard University Press.
16. Greenson, R. (1963). Dis-identification. *International Journal of Psychoanalysis, 49*: 370–374.
17. Haley, J. (1973). *Uncommon therapy: The psychiatric techniques of Milton H. Erickson*. New York: Norton.
18. Hill, R. (1964). Methodological issues in family development research. *Family Process, 3*: 186–206.
19. Hinde, R. A. (1982). Attachment: Some conceptual and biological issues. In C. M. Parkes & J. Stevenson-Hinde (Eds.), *The place of attachment in human behavior*. New York: Basic Books.
20. Klaus, M. H., & Kennell, J. H. (1976). *Maternal–infant bonding*. St. Louis: Mosby.
21. Kohlberg, L. (1966). A cognitive-developmental analysis of children's sex role concepts and attitudes. In E. Maccoby (Ed.), *The development of sex differences*. Stanford, CA: Stanford University Press.
22. Jourard, S. M. (1964). *The transparent self*. Princeton, NJ: Van Nostrand Reinhold.
23. Lasch, C. (1977). *Haven in a heartless world: The family besieged*. New York: Basic Books.
24. Leiderman, P. H., & Seashore, M. J. (1975). Mother–infant separation: Some delayed consequences. In *Parental–infant interaction*. Ciba Foundation Symposium 33 (new series). Amsterdam: Elsevier.
25. Levenson, R. (1984). Intimacy, autonomy and gender: Developmental differences and their reflection in adult relationships. *Journal of the American Academy of Psychoanalysis, 12*: 529–544.
26. Levinger, G., & Raush, H. L. (1977). *Close relationships: Perspectives on the meaning of intimacy*. Amherst: University of Massachusetts Press.
27. Lumsden, C. J., & Wilson, E. O. (1981). *Genes, mind, and culture*. Cambridge, MA: Harvard University Press.

28. Lumsden, C. J., & Wilson, E. O. (1983). *Promethean fire: Reflections on the origin of mind*. Cambridge, MA: Harvard University Press.
29. MacLean, P. D. (1978). Why brain research on lizards? In N. Greenberg & P. D. MacLean (Eds.), *Behavior and neurology of lizards*. Bethesda: NIMH.
30. MacLean, P. D. (1982). A triangular brief on the evolution of brain and law. *Journal of Social Biol. Struc., 5*: 369–379.
31. MacLean, P. D. (1985). Brain evolution relating to family, play, and the separation call. *Archives of General Psychiatry, 42*: 405–417.
32. Mahler, M. S., Pine, F., & Bergman, A. (1975). *The psychological birth of the human infant*. New York: Basic Books.
33. Olson, D. H., McCubbin, H. C., Barnes, H., Larsen, A., Muxan, M., & Wilson, M. (1983). *Families: What makes them work*. Beverly Hills: Sage.
34. Olson, D. H., Russell, D. S., & Sprenkle, D. H. (1983). Circumplex model of marital and family systems: VI. Theoretical update. *Family Process, 22*: 69–83.
35. Peterson, G. H., Mehl, L. E., & Leiderman, P. H. (1979). The role of some birth related variables in father attachment. *American Journal of Orthopsychiatry, 49*: 330–338.
36. Rogers, R. (1960). Proposed modification of Duvall's family life cycle stages. Paper presented at the American Sociological Association Meeting, New York, August 1960.
37. Sawin, D. B., & Parke, R. D. (1979). Fathers' affectionate stimulation and caregiving behaviors with newborn infants. *Family Coordinator, 28*: 509–513.
38. Schaefer, M. T., Olson, D. H. (1981). Assessing intimacy: The PAIR inventory. *Journal of Marital and Family Therapy, 7*: 47–60.
39. Stoller, R. J. (1968). *Sex and gender* (Vol. 1). New York: Science House.
40. Waring, E. M., & Reddon, J. R. (1983). The measurement of intimacy in marriage. The Waring Intimacy Questionnaire. *Clinical Psychology, 39*: 53–57.
41. Watzlawick, P., Weakland, J. H., & Fisch, R. (1974). *Principles of problem formation and problem resolution*. New York: Norton.
42. Wertheim, E. S. (1973). Family unit therapy and the science and typology of family systems. *Family Process, 12*: 361–376.
43. Wynne, L. C. (1970). Communication disorders and the quest for relatedness in families of schizophrenics. *American Journal of Psychoanalysis, 30*: 100–114.
44. Wynne, L. C. (1984). The epigenesis of relational systems: A model for understanding family development. *Family Process, 23*: 297–318.
45. Wynne, L. C. (1986). Mutuality and pseudomutuality reconsidered: Implications for therapy and a theory of development of relational systems. In D. Schwartz, J. Sacksteder, & Y. Akabane (Eds.), *Attachment and the therapeutic process*. New York: International Universities Press.
46. Wynne, L. C., Ryckoff, I., Day, D. & Hirsch, S. (1958). Pseudomutuality in the family relations of schizophrenics. *Psychiatry, 21*: 205–220.

Dinner Chit-Chat

Theo: No, but that was just too much, actually hearing Ivan Boszormenyi-Nagy in the flesh. . . .

Maria: Too much? You can say that again! I couldn't have taken much more of it!

Theo: You hear, I just don't understand you systems people at all. Here was finally someone with the guts to tackle the problems that everyone else gives a wide berth to. After all, that's what human relations are *really* about, questions of justice, responsibility, fairness, loyalty, and mutual acceptance.

Maria: Oh, come on, give me a break. . . .

Theo: He's the only one of all the major family therapists to address himself earnestly to the ethical dimension in family interaction processes. And that includes the relationship between therapist and family, a relationship of true humanity. . . .

Maria: What I can't stomach is the context of the consequences of his missionary pronouncements. Although I share many of the values he represents I find his claim to have found the sole true path more than problematic: He appeals to Martin Buber and other higher beings so that he can proclaim his own personal values as the true ones. And as he is in possession of the truth, he can of course decide what is good and what is bad. And it's only a short step from there to papal encyclicals and excommunication. For me, moralizing of that kind is always bound up with intolerance and a well-developed lust for power.

Theo: You're mixing up taking a well-defined ethical stance with moralizing. For him (and for me) there really is such a thing as a just order of things which we all have to do our bit to create and maintain. If we don't, there's always the danger that what he calls the "destructive entitlement" will take on catastrophic proportions and people will exploit each other more and more. Pretty awful prospects for the future of our children!

Maria: It's not his values I'm criticizing; it's his claim to having found the truth.

77

Theo: But you are criticizing him from a position which looks at all truth as relative and the product of some kind of do-it-yourself construction. And all that can lead to is Watzlawick and his own special brand of nihilism. That's just sleight-of-hand with which you can jusitify any kind of psychotherapeutic techniques, manipulations, and tricks. All that's required is a little cosmetic treatment on the surface. But the basis of trust, which is the foundation of all genuine human relations, is ignored, or rather destroyed.

Maria: If there's one thing Watzlawick's position isn't it's nihilistic! On the contrary. When he says we construct our own reality, what he means is that our values, morals, and ethics are of our own making. That is to say we cannot hide behind some higher authority but have to accept the responsibility ourselves for the values we opt for. And the upshot of that is that we cannot consider our values as the true ones in any absolute sense but have to tolerate other people's values, even if they're different.

Theo: Whatever they look like? The values of people who batter their children, beat hell out of their wives? . . . to stick to the harmless examples!

Maria: Of course situations can arise where conflicting values have to be weighed against each other. But even if I decide that protection for battered wives and children is more important than tolerance for the batterer, it still remains a value option of my own which determines my actions and which I alone am accountable for.

Doc: Would somebody pass the pepper, please? If this soup had as much pep to it as your argument, I'd be more than content. But there was one thing I wanted to ask you. What significance do your differences of attitude have for practical therapy work?

Theo: The therapist's attitude on such questions is of absolutely essential significance. If a therapist does not feel ethically obliged to create trust, be sincere, eschew cheap tricks and manipulation, how can he expect trust and positive reciprocity to develop in families?

Maria: The question is what does one consider to be manipulation? There's no way that you can avoid manipulation fully. As soon as we start arguing, I'm manipulating you and you're manipulating me and Doc is probably doing it to both of us. Didn't he just get you to pass the pepper? As soon as there is any kind of interaction between people, there's bound to be manipulation. And if someone approaches me for therapy, he is in fact asking for manipulation. I am being asked to do something with my patients that they haven't done themselves. They are manipulating me into manipulating them.

Theo: What you're doing is watering down the term "manipulation" until there's nothing left of it. I take it that's what you people mean by reframing. And magicking the ethical problem away like that is certainly one way of solving the problem! But the central issue still remains whether we are going to be guided by strategic considerations in our dealings with one another or by honesty and sincerity.

Maria: You're implying that people can do without strategies in their dealings with one another. But every human being, every animal—if we're going to appeal to nature in this—behaves strategically in every conceivable context. And part of a strategy is to protest that one is not pursuing any particular strategy. What, I ask myself, are those people out to achieve whose strategy is to keep stressing their own honesty and sincerity. Every check forger, con man, and PR agent knows what a good strategy that is.

Theo: You can't really mean that! You can't be sincere in arguing that way!

Doc: I must say I'm surprised at the philosophical heights you are scaling. I would have thought it was far more a question of utility and feasibility. Without pretending to any knowledge of all these ingenious psychological theories it still seems to me to be useful and sensible to try to "tune in" to the attitudes and the language habits of my patients. I can't choose my patients on the basis of the kind of language they use. I wouldn't talk the same way to a factory owner as I would to a laborer or to a farmer as I would to a Turkish immigrant worker. If I want to be able to make any kind of diagnosis, or if I want them to follow any of my prescriptions, I must communicate with them in their own language and must consider the context in which they live. I must say I hadn't seen it as a moral problem before. But possibly all this excitement is just the expression of your search for intimacy. . . . If my diagnostic powers haven't forsaken me altogether, your relationship has just reached the pseudohostility stage. . . . ''

The Second Day

Breakfast Chit-Chat

The next day the weather was fine, with Heidelberg looking more than ever like a picture postcard of itself. There was a good deal of pushing and shoving to get to the breakfast table; everyone was in a hurry, and there was no time for talking shop. Things still seemed rather tense between Theo and Maria, but after a while they too succumbed to the general atmosphere that was taking hold of the participants, an atmosphere that one normally finds only on pilgrimages or at evangelical meetings. This was one of the reasons why Doc decided to miss the official proceedings that morning and do his shopping instead.

The Paradoxical Nature of Grief

Norman L. Paul[1]

Where there is no paradox there is no life.

Saul Bellow
To Jerusalem and Back (2)

Because one cannot look at and talk about everything at the same time (a most unfortunate human predicament), a conceptual scheme says "look here," instead of (or as well as) "there." And in a certain sense, persons who use it will find what they are looking for.

F. J. Roethlisberger
*Contribution of the Behavioral Sciences
to a General Theory of Management* (24)

Paradox—Properly neuter of *paradox-us*, adj. contrary to received opinion or expectation, past, beyond, contrary to opinion.

1) A statement or tenet contrary to received opinion or belief; often with the implication that it is marvelous or incredible; sometimes with unfavourable connotation, as being discordant with what is held to be established truth, and hence absurd or fantastic; sometimes with favourable connotation, as a correction of vulgar error. (In actual use rare since 17th century though often insisted upon by writers as the proper sense.)

b) A conclusion or apodosis contrary to what the audience has been led up to expect.

2) A statement or proposition which on the face of it means self-contradictory, absurd, or at variance with common sense, though on investigation or when explained, it may prove to be well-founded (or according to some, though it is essentially true).

---

[1]Editorial Review by Betty Byfield Paul, L.I.C.S.W., Counseling Associates, Lexington, Massachusetts

b) Often applied to a proposition or statement that is actually self-contradictory, or contradictory to reason or ascertained truth, and so essentially absurd and false.

3) Paradoxical character, condition, or quality: Paradoxy.

4) A phenomenon that exhibits some contradiction or conflict with preconceived notions of what is reasonable or possible; a person of perplexingly inconsistent life or behaviour.

Oxford English Dictionary, 1971

MEANINGS HAVE LOST THEIR WORDS

The interest in the use of paradox in family psychotherapy has been fostered by such investigators as Don Jackson, Mara Selvini Palazzoli, Paul Watzlawick, and Jay Haley. It has been viewed as an effective avenue to jam and alter dysfunctional transactional circuitry in a variety of discordant marital and family situations. Its development has been occasioned by the appearance of almost cultlike adherents who appear polarized against equally intense antagonists. Such discord precludes the kind of reflective and collaborative synthesis necessary for future progress (this presumes we have the probability of a future and can know what constitutes progress).

One might ask, is there anything that can be synthesized with a paradoxically oriented psychotherapy (27)? In the structural systemic orientation to the family, there appears to be an aversion—some call it an allergy—to the sense of a past historical process and aspects of the introspective life of the individual. In using this orientation affects are considered to be unimportant and thus are ignored by the structuralists. The question has been for me what to do with affects.

If paradoxes can be employed effectively in selected family situations, one might consider the context out of which such paradoxical prescriptions or injunctions are derived. It does seem that the living process can be viewed as essentially paradoxical in most if not all respects. The life, death, living, and dying features of human existence are essentially paradoxical.

The quote "In the midst of life, we are in death" from the Book of Common Prayer (3), "Burial of the Dead" is a most powerful and persuasive presentation of the reality of all our lives. One difficulty with the reality of death is that we have all gotten to that time where our individual and collective arrogance and pretensions do not serve us in coping with this reality.

The earlier quotation from Roethlisberger (24), an eminent organizational psychologist, confronts us with the fact that what we see is fore-ordained by the limited, almost monocular nature of our seeing apparatus. Our seeing apparatus in symmetry with the manner in which we develop and cultivate language helps us in achieving languaged distortions of experience. Beginning with learning the alphabet, we evolve a sense of means of transforming experience into words from which the essence has been squeezed much like dehydrated frozen foods, which often cannot be identified.

A languaged linearity commences which renders us believing that events occur in linear fashion and are disconnected as one word is from the next. Added to that, we learn that unpleasant affects are not to be shared and are regarded generally as troublesome to most of the people with whom we come into contact. For many, the energies associated with such unpleasantness unacknowledged and unneutralized are channeled and redirected toward socially constructive and useful activities and occupations.

We learn well to achieve; for whom and at what cost are generally ignored. And if we get into the helping professions, the acme of which is medicine, we learn that mistakes can be acknowledged in words and that death is the enemy to be avoided. If it can't be avoided, we call in the mortician and the clergyman. The clergymen take over the death experience and medical men revert to the living.

Those of us interested in a holistic approach to life may develop an orientation called general systems theory as related to psychiatry. In the volume edited by Gray, Duhl, and Rizzo (10), there are no indexed references to the death of a person or to grief. This suggests that general systems cybernetics thinking views human beings like machines without affects, without a sense of history, and certainly without intrapsychic lives. General systems theory was to be a bold development that would enable its adherents to "pretend" without appropriate acknowledgment that the words were either the way the real world is or close to the way life is really lived. The spirit of science is violated by a conceptual frame, general systems theory here, which ignores by avoidance the experiential aspects of life. Whitehead's germane comments about this are:

> But, for the purpose of science, what is the actual world? Has science to wait for the termination of the metaphysical debate till it can determine its own subject-matter? I suggest that science has a much more homely starting-ground. Its task is the discovery of the relations which exist within that flux of perceptions, sensations, and emotions which form our experience of life. The panorama yielded

by sight, sound, taste, smell, touch, and by more inchoate sensible feelings, is the sole field of activity. It is in this way that science is the thought organisation of experience. The most obvious aspect of the field of actual experience is its disorderly character. It is for each person a continuum, fragmentary, and with elements not clearly differentiated. . . .

I insist on the radically untidy, ill-adjusted character of the fields of actual experience from which science starts. To grasp this fundamental truth is the first step in wisdom, when constructing a philosophy of science. (28, pp. 108–109)

The ringing clarity of Whitehead's comments demands that one focus on the interface between the continuous natural events one is experiencing, then observe what one processes in sensory terms of that experience, and then finally take note of how the original four-dimensional experience becomes in rhetoric two-dimensional. This imperfect field is always happening, simply and with imprecision and uncertainty. Michael Kammen in his masterful Pulitzer Prize–winning book, *People of Paradox: An Inquiry Concerning the Origins of American Civilization* (12), elaborates the thesis that the United States evolved through an interplay of governmental and cultural paradoxes on all levels. The ubiquity of paradox challenged the capacity for compromise and accommodation and still does. His concluding paragraphs offer us an interesting vantage point and vision:

We should recognize, as Hawthorne did, the innocence as well as the evil in our natures. We should understand, as William James did, that Americanism is a volatile mixture of hopeful good and curable bad. We must maintain, as Carl Becker pleaded, a balance between freedom and responsibility. For freedom unrestrained by responsibility becomes mere license, while responsibility unchecked by freedom becomes arbitrary power. We must pursue, as we have at our best, the politics of "utopian pragmatism." (12)

What is essential in appreciating the ubiquity of paradox? It seems that an essential requirement is the acceptance that words and the natural world of experience operate on two separate tracks, related to one another and yet not one another. The words "a tree" refer to a tree one may witness or remember or think about and at the same time we know that the words cannot truly convey what a tree looks like. We need a picture besides, and even a picture cannot convey the true experience of seeing a tree. In "Writing for the Theatre" Harold Pinter focused on labels and words:

> We don't carry labels on our chests, and even though they are continually fixed to us by others, they convince nobody. The desire for verification on the part of all of us, with regard to our own experience and the experience of others, is understandable but cannot always be satisfied. I suggest there can be no hard distinctions between what is real and what is unreal, nor between what is true and what is false. A thing is not necessarily either true or false: it can be both true and false. . . .
>
> I have mixed feelings about words myself. Moving among them, sorting them out, watching them appear on the page, from this I derive a considerable pleasure. But at the same time I have another strong feeling about words which amounts to nothing less than nausea. Such a weight of words confronts us day in, day out, words spoken in a context such as this, words written by me and by others, the bulk of it a stale dead terminology; ideas endlessly repeated and permutated, become platitudinous, trite, meaningless. Given this nausea, it's very easy to be overcome by it and step back into paralysis. . . .
>
> Language, under these conditions, is a highly ambiguous business. So often, below the word spoken, is the thing known and unspoken. . . .
>
> You and I, the characters which grow on a page, most of the time we're inexpressive, giving little away, unreliable, elusive, evasive, obstructive, unwilling. But it's out of these attributes that a language arises. A language, I repeat, where under what is said another thing is being said. (23, pp. 80–82)

In a most provocative overview in *War with Words* Shands posits:

> Language prescribes for us a linear ordering of data in discursive sequence. Overwhelmingly and unconsciously influenced by linguistic method, we then decide and enforce acceptance of the notion that the universe is organized on a linear basis, in cause and effect patterns of general relevance. Since language demands subject and predicate, actor and acted upon, in many different combinations and permutations, we conclude that this is the structure of the world. But we soon learn, in any delicate and complicated context, that we

cannot find such a concretely defined order except by imposing it. (26, p. 32)

Correctly, Selvini Palazzoli et al. (25) along the same lines state that "language is not reality." However, they claim that reality is "living and circular." In point of fact, while appearing circular, it is really a spiral moving into time. That is why terms such as homeostasis are incorrect. In denying time, one can maintain a fiction of the timeless or of no time. The appropriate term for feedback systems is homeodynamism. *Time* is always present—whether perceived, considered, or denied:

The past is never dead; it is not even past. (9, p. 92)

This paradox focuses on a core problem in our orientation to events in the past and the illusion created as one reflects back in time that in recapturing such experience, one is transported "back" in time. In actuality, it is the past in the "now" in a recursive fashion. We are again compelled to conclude that words are not the experience; while attempting to convey the essence of same, words limit one's appreciation of experience. Poets among others seem to recognize and accept this difference readily.

A relevant cybernetic theory must encompass experience in chronology. A way of conveying that experience beyond words must be developed. The recursive past is in the present here and now. Ghosts must be reconciled so that unburied events/objects can be really "buried" rather than pretend buried. Herein lies the paradox that plagues the numbed individual, who while living another reality has at his back instead the false conviction that the past in the "present" is dead.

THE PARADOX OF THE PHYSICAL NATURE OF THE HUMAN BEING

The human being in many ways can be viewed as an ambulatory paradox with a variety of contradictions both important and seemingly confusing. Some of these follow.

1. In terms of one's physical being, each human is discrete, physically separate, and capable of autonomous activity as he or she develops physically, mentally, and socially. This contrasts with the person's invisible connectedness to and with others from whom he or she has interiorized or introjected images. These images influence and regulate his or her path or journey toward other relationships and activities. The physicalness is visible; the emotional connectedness is not; this is especially apparent when working with an individual client or patient alone.

2. Consciousness or awareness of one's self as experienced by the self is generally limited to feelings, thoughts, dreams, fantasies, or fears one might have. In addition, one's awareness may include whatever sense of self, continuity, and self-image are present. These fluctuate depending on stress experiences and supportive relationships in one's relational field. A sense of self, continuity, and self-image require validation by both others and one's self. This self-validation process includes both positive and negative connotations which are regarded as having been derived from and stimulated by validation responses from parental figures and siblings.

The limitation in each of us is that anatomically each of us is constructed so that one's perceptions of the present environment external to the self, both physically and human, coupled with past memories, represents the principle data base for one's experiences. The nature of the data contrasts sharply with an absence of data of the observable self. This lack of data on the observable self is in sharp contrast to the inner self-image each of us constructs during the general conduct of life. This observable self, that which is seeable by others, represents the basis of the other's perception, reaction, and judgment of one's self. An assumption dictating much conflict is that the way in which one regards one's inner self-image will be translated faithfully into equivalent outward behavior. This capability is often regarded as governed by one's will. That this doesn't occur is attested to by the ever present nature of interpersonal conflict, especially in families.

3. Another major paradox which is often discredited has to do with the difference between emotional experiences and the languaged attempt at translating that experience into words.

In Eugene O'Neill's *Strange Interlude*, Nina looks at her friend Charles, a college professor, and says:

> You look frightened Charles! Do I seem queer? It's because I've suddenly seen the lies in the sounds called words. You know—grief, sorrow, love, father—those sounds our lips make and our hands write. You ought to know what I mean. You work with them. Have you written another novel lately? But, stop to think, you are just the one who couldn't know what I mean. With you the lies have become the only truthful things and I suppose that is the logical conclusion to the whole evasive mess, isn't it? Do you understand me, Charlie? Say, lie—(*She says it, drawing it out*) L . . I . . E . . ! Now say life. L . . I . . F . . E . . ! You see! Life is just a long drawn out lie with a sniffling sigh at the end! (*She laughs.*) (17)

The dilemma is that we are all not only ambulatory paradoxes but also ambulatory projection machines, projecting images we do not know are there, filtering those images whose meaning cannot accurately be conveyed with language. So, of necessity, one functions as if the world will remain chronically stable and unchanging even though one knows that change will occur.

DEATH, GRIEF, AND MOURNING

That death seems to be a dilemma which is of central concern for all is something that is subject to debate, more so recently in the United States, or so it seems. The dilemma of words is particularly apparent in attempts to define grief and mourning. The total range and configuration of responses to a major loss, or death, is called "mourning." Mourning includes physical behavior, both formal and spontaneous, and psychological processes both observable and covert, which are set in motion by loss. "Grief" is a more restricted term applied to the subjective state of mourning and excludes all the ritualistic and behavioral elements of mourning. Grief usually consists of such feelings as helplessness, anger, despair, and bewilderment, which overlap and vary in intensity from person to person as well as within one person during the mourning process. I am concerned primarily with grief rather than with all of mourning because grief is entirely subjective and personal and so directly accessible to empathic intervention in grief work.

Part of the difficulty with grief as an entity is that it is regarded generally as reaction to loss by death, but the process can be expanded to include normal fantasies of the other person being dead, such as often occurs with parents whose anxieties escalate when their children first learn to drive an automobile. Often such anxieties are expressed in a cerebral picture of a child being killed in an automobile. This can be regarded as the parents' ambivalence to losing a child to itself and part of the natural developmental evolution to adult selfhood. Such parents can come to regard and understand that such fantasies, however graphic, do not create an actual death.

The quandary in grief has to do principally with intense, recurrent dissonant affects and emotions challenging all in knowing how to abide and help resolve the pain of the bereaved. There is a general tendency on the part of family members and others involved in the care of the bereaved to employ a sympathetic posture. This assists in the suppression of unpleasant feelings and fantasies. The empathic requirements are generally sidestepped. Empathy is often confused with sympathy, and words of solace often don't provide solace. Empathy is too complicated a nonverbal nutrient to be adequately addressed in this paper (20–22).

George Engel, in his attempts to develop an adequate classification of the phenomenology of affects, readily acknowledged the inadequacy of language:

> We still recognize not only that in nature affects do not exist in pure, unalloyed form but also that to deal with affects in written, verbal, or conceptual terms is fundamentally inconsistent with their nature and can succeed only at the expense of their *oversimplification* and *impoverishment.* (7)

Despite deceptive limitations and constrictions with which language hems us in, we must persist in the exploration and assessment of grief because of its understated importance in human experience.

One type of hidden internal reaction to death, which occurs especially in children who have lost a parent, is the nurturance of a grudge. Grudges usually are bivalent in nature, both expressed toward the lost figure and at the same time deflected back onto the self, and spiraling from the image of the deceased to the self over time. One man who came for treatment expressed his guilt-laden grudge toward his father, who had died suddenly from a heart attack when this man was 8 years old, by both tormenting himself for years with a great inner sense of inadequacy and fearing that he was a homosexual, and at the same time being unable to exhibit responsive fatherly behavior toward his responsive sons. Hitler's "Final Solution" seems to have been generated in part as a consequence of his own tremendous pain that his mother died and that a Jewish doctor had been unable to keep her alive. The presumed rage toward her for being vulnerable and finally dying had to be directed elsewhere, because in part there had been no effective institutionalized means of assisting individuals through their process of grief.

Bowlby's well-documented studies of mourning and the range of responses observed in association with different kinds of loss experiences provide an interesting cognitive account of what can occur (4, 5). These studies do not, however, assist the clinician in knowing what to do. They neglect any emphasis on the empathic requirements to assist one in the asymptotic resolution of grief. Bowlby's linear discursive description of the mourning process unfortunately cannot take into account the multiple and seemingly instantaneous eruptions and intrusions of powerful, vivid, intense scenes from a "past" where an important person, now dead for 5 to 50 years, is vigorously alive. One may feel a "lost" happiness or sadness or rage, related to this or that event. The related hidden and silent preoccupation about such a loss often is expressed in distancing behavior toward members of one's current family and the source is unknown and unknowable to anyone. Words in these circumstances too often avoid, ignore, neglect, and circumvent the actual emotional experience. The net result of this type of omission kindles myths which are dignified often with the mantle of authority as having *scientific validity* and *truth*. Thus the unrestrained belief in words can't help but contribute to an insidious form of lying, or denying.

Paraphrasing P. D. Ouspensky's focus on "What Is Lying?" taken from *The Psychology of Man's Possible Evolution* (18), I would like to ask, "What Is Denying?" As it is understood in ordinary language, denying means distorting or in some cases hiding the truth, or what people believe to be the truth. This denying plays a very important part in life, but there are much worse forms of denying, when people do not know that they deny. We cannot know the truth in our present state, and can only know the truth in the state of objective consciousness. How can we deny? There seems to be a contradiction here, but in reality there is none. We cannot know the truth, but we can pretend that we know. And this is denying. Denying fills all our life. People pretend that they know all sorts of things: about God, about the future life, about the universe, about the origins of man, about evolution, about everything; but in reality they do not know anything, even about themselves. And every time they speak about something they do not know as though they knew it, they deny. Consequently, the study of denying becomes of the first importance in psychology.

The denial mechanism when applied to death and grief frequently is regarded as capable of disqualifying such entities from active consideration. This can't help in a paradoxical fashion to magnify their contextual importance to a position that seems to threaten all of us with a new expanded version of the Final Solution. Believing that death and grief exist as real elements in an imperfect human world does not render one being viewed as a cultist or a deviant. How many more world wars are required to bring home the fact that every family has its own history of deaths by war, tragedy, and illness, and that every family in some ways must live with derivatives of thwarted aspects of a grief process?

Geoffrey Gorer, an English anthropologist, concluded his well-known survey published in 1965, *Death, Grief, and Mourning*, which is about reactions to bereavement in Great Britain, with a statement I believe to be equally relevant to the American people in 1985:

> I think that the material presented has adequately demonstrated that the majority of British people are today without adequate guidance as to how to treat death and bereavement and without social help

in living through and coming to terms with the grief and mourning
which are inevitable responses in human beings to the death of
someone whom they have loved. (11, p. 126)

Kübler-Ross and Becker each elaborated on this focus in their outstanding
books. In *Death and Dying* (14). Kübler-Ross in 1969 highlighted the
sequential and recursive phases of the process of dying that attracted the
attention of both caretaking professionals and the public at large.

Becker in *Denial of Death* (1) addressed the problems resulting from
one's heroic attempts to transcend death. That failure of denial touches
those of us who believe we have, in fact, transcended mortality. His book
won a Pulitzer Prize in 1973. Although there has been increased interest
and attention since these publications, the impact of loss through death
has barely begun to show up as a major contextual focus for the well-
intentioned and well-informed psychotherapist.

One has the impression, given the earlier works by Bowlby (4) and
Lindemann (16), that, coupled with the books just mentioned, mental
health professionals would have by now gone beyond merely reflexively
citing the import of loss issues as a key problem in both individual and
family dynamics. When it comes to the actual process of therapeutic
intervention, such applications of this intellectual knowledge wither in
the face of the challenge of using these notions experientially. Part of the
question involves not only the timing, but also the manner of inducing
and encouraging the grieving process. One of the things that working with
family systems has revealed is that grief work confined to an individual
and his or her therapist may actually deaden the relational possibilities
for the client in his family. This tends to happen when the effects of grief
are confined and excluded from the family.

An excellent example of the exploitation of death is in social medicine.
In an extraordinary exchange in *Social Science Medicine*, Colin Parkes
responded to Allan Kellehear's article "Are We a Death-Denying Society?"
Kellehear concludes this thesis, positing that:

> We are not a death-denying society. The arguments and examples
> to the contrary are unconvincing as sociological explanations. They
> ignore the organisational considerations that are basic to any descrip-
> tion of institutional behaviours—whether this is the funeral industry
> or medicine. They do not separate out the issues of individual moti-
> vations, from group behaviours, tending to see descriptions of the
> former as explanations of the latter. This confusion and projection
> of private ideas with public behaviours has led to an oversimplified

and reductionist view of the relationships between the individual, society and death. Individuals will and do deny death as they also will become angry, laugh or feel sorrow in relation to death. These individuals will, as far as possible, express these emotions or attitudes in organisational settings that permit this. Sometimes they will be disguised, but always they will be private expressions.

On the other hand, societies do not deny death but instead organise for it and around it; exert forms of social control through sanctioning different types of myths and rituals toward it; culturally determine the conditions, circumstances and sometimes the nature of death; set in motion processes of conflict, reintegration and adjustments of roles. It does these things, despite the rich variety of individual attitudes and values in relation to death, simply because the requirements of living together dictate that group goals take priority over individual ones. This is the societal response to death, always complex and historically unique. In the Middle Ages the essential sociological meaning of death was religious. Today this meaning is medical. There are signs already that tomorrow this meaning may be a legal one. (13)

Colin Parkes response was:

It is a brave man who denies denial, and Allan Kellehear's paper provides much food for thought. His attempt to sever sociology from psychology, however, leads him to some odd conclusions. Thus, he dismisses "denial, happiness, and guilt" as artificial and anthropomorphic and progresses to the absurd conclusion that "society will cope with all fears, not psychodynamically, but organisationally."

In the last analysis all organisation, be it at a personal or societal level, occurs for psychodynamic reasons, and the sociologist who thinks he can ignore psychodynamics makes the same error as the psychiatrist who thinks he can "treat" all unhappiness with antidepressants.

Having said that, I found his main thesis quite tenable. I see little reason to believe that our society is more death-denying than previous ones; it is, simply, dead ignorant about death. One might argue, that the decline in popular concern about and belief in a life hereafter is a sign that we are now less inclined to deny death than our forebears, but this may only be possible because we no longer confront it in our daily lives. We have reduced the infant mortality rate, relocated the dying outside the home and transformed "the dying role into a low status technology intensive situation in need of sanitising.'' Death has become less visible and hence, easier to ignore. ''Age has become the measure of our dying'' simply because young people are now more safe from death than they have ever been before. Yet we have the paradoxical situation of the safest society the world has ever known "scared to death" by its own fantasies! Out of sight is not out of mind, and the fact that people in our society are now rarely seen to die does not mean that there is not a social image of death. But our social image of death is derived from fiction and from the more dramatic and horrific forms of death which make news and appear daily on our television screens.

If there is nothing you can do about an unpleasant situation, then it makes sense to ignore it. When doctors felt they had nothing to offer to the dying, they were right to offer nothing. Dying patients and their families took their cue from the doctors and asked for nothing. But this is no longer the case. Sociologists, psychologists, psychiatrists and many others have provided a wealth of advice on the ways in which we can help the dying to achieve "death with dignity" and the dying are beginning to demand these new ways to a "good death." It seems likely that the death of the future will not be "religious," "medical," or "legal" but social psychological. (19, p. 127)

THE GRIEF PROCESS

It should be obvious at this point that the process of mourning, which includes grief, is a most complex linear and recursive sequence of internal states and external behaviors that words cannot adequately describe. Thus the references herein at best raise more questions than can be answered. The grief process is a vital intergenerational entity which when considered from a combined individual–family perspective can be regarded as a base for a reconsideration of the array of different affective states.

The degree to which this process is thwarted will affect and infect both the bereaved and their unborn progeny in ways too numerous to enumerate or even know. When Helene Deutsch states, "The process of mourning as reaction to the real loss of a loved person must be carried to completion" (6), she raises an important range of critical questions. How can one achieve "completion"? Is this a real possibility in life or is this another kind of languaged impossibility? What are the requirements in the therapist to assist one to move toward completion? How can a therapist know whether he or she is really assisting the client in moving toward completion? Finally, is it possible to move toward completion without including other family members? And if other family members are to be included, who and in what sequence? Can numbness related to death and grief ever be confronted directly and then dissolved?

T. S. Eliot in "Ash Wednesday" provides a paradoxical challenge:

Teach us to care and not to care. (8, p. 111)

And consider Milan Kundera, from *The Book of Laughter and Forgetting:*

We are all prisoners of a rigid conception of what is important and what is not. We anxiously follow what we suppose to be important, while what we suppose to be unimportant wages guerrilla warfare behind our backs, transforming the world without our knowledge and eventually mounting a surprise attack on us. (15, p. 197)

REFERENCES

1. Becker, E. (1973). *The denial of death.* New York: Free Press.
2. Bellow, S. (1977). *To Jerusalem and back: A personal account.* New York: Avon.
3. *Book of Common Prayer* (1945). "Burial of the Dead."
4. Bowlby, J. (1961). Processes of mourning. *International Journal of Psychoanalysis, 42:* 317–340.
5. Bowlby, J. (1980). *Attachment and loss* (Vol. 3). New York: Basic Books.
6. Deutsch, H. (1937). Absence of grief. *Psychoanalytic Quarterly, 6:* 12.
7. Engel, G. (1963). *Expressions of the emotions in man.* New York: International Universities Press.
8. Eliot, T. S. (1936). *Collected Poems 1909–1935.* "Ash Wednesday." New York: Harcourt Brace.
9. Faulkner, W. (1966). *Requiem For a Nun.* 4th Printing. New York: Random House.
10. Gray, W., Duhl, F. J., & Rizzo, N. D. (Eds.) (1969). *General systems theory and psychiatry.* Boston: Little, Brown.
11. Gorer, G. (1965). *Death, grief, and mourning.* Garden City, NY: Doubleday.
12. Kammen, M. (1980). *People of paradox: An inquiry concerning the origins of American civilization.* New York: Oxford University Press. (Originally published in 1972 by Vintage Press)
13. Kellehear, A. (1984). Are we a death-denying society? *Social Science Medicine, 18* (9), 713–723.
14. Kübler-Ross, E. (1969). *On death and dying.* New York: Macmillan.
15. Kundera, M. (1980). *The book of laughter and forgetting.* New York: Alfred A. Knopf, Inc.
16. Lindemann, E. (1944). Symptomatology and management of acute grief. *American Journal of Psychiatry, 101:* 141–148.
17. O'Neill, E. (1959). *Nine plays by Eugene O'Neill.* New York: Modern Library.
18. Ouspensky, P. D. (1962). *The psychology of man's possible evolution.* New York: Alfred A. Knopf.

19. Parkes, C. (1984). Comment on "Are we a death-denying society?" *Social Science Medicine, 18(9)*: 127.
20. Paul, N. L. (1967). The use of empathy in the resolution of grief. *Perspectives in Biology and Medicine, 11*: 153–169.
21. Paul, N. L. (1973). The need to mourn. In E. J. Anthony & C. Koupernik (Eds.), *The child in his family: The impact of disease and death*. Melbourne, Flikrieger.
22. Paul, N. L., & Paul, B. B. (1975). *A marital puzzle*. New York: Norton.
23. Pinter, H. (1964). Writing for the theatre. *Evergreen Review* (winter).
24. Roethlisberger, F. J. (1964). Contribution of the behavioral sciences to a general theory of management. In H. Koontz (Ed.), *Toward a unified theory of management* (p. 59). New York: McGraw-Hill.
25. Selvini Palazzoli, M., Cecchin, G., Prata, G., & Boscolo, L. (1975). *A new model in the therapy of the family in schizophrenic transaction*. New York: Jason Aronson.
26. Shands, H. C. (1971). *The war with words: Structure and transcendence*. The Hague: Mouton.
27. Weeks, G. R., & L'Abate, L. (1982). *Paradoxical psychotherapy: Theory and practice with individuals, couples, and families*. New York: Brunner/Mazel.
28. Whitehead, A. N. (1949). *The aims of education*. New York: Macmillan.

Coevolution and Coindividuation

Helm Stierlin

Evolution—its origins, conditions, sequences, laws—presents us with the greatest riddle, the greatest challenge to our scientific understanding. This holds true for the evolution of the cosmos, which began approximately 18 to 20 billion years ago; it holds true for the evolution of planetary life—including human life—which started 3 to 4 billion years ago; and, finally, it holds true for social as well as cultural evolution. We are constantly confronted with the same phenomenon: existing systems lose their equilibrium, their elements arrange themselves in new ways, and there emerge new and, as a rule, more complex systems with new forms, new qualities, new relations to their environment—and this, so it appears, in an ongoing, unending process. In this way whatever presents itself to us as material substance—as stars, as colors, as organisms, as consciousness, as species, as family, as society, as culture—emerged or is indeed still emerging.

This evolutionary process can be looked at from two major perspectives: first, that of selection. Here we focus on an individual, a species, a culture, and ask ourselves: What made it possible that these could assert themselves against other individuals, species, and cultures? If we put the question this way, the answer will present the history of the cosmos, of the earth, of all life as a ruthlessly waged battle for survival, evolution as unmercifully eliminating all that is unable to assert itself, to adapt itself, to find a niche.

The possibly most central aspect of such self-assertion is the setting of boundaries: boundaries between me and not-me, between inside and outside, through which I delineate my own life, my own body, my own needs, my own interests, marking them off from the lives, bodies, needs, interests of others, through which I individuate myself vis-à-vis these others.

99

Seen this way, evolution means, above all, *individuation*. From this vantage the evolution of the immunologic system may be viewed as an expression and consequence of a trend toward ever more differentiated individuation. Within planetary evolution the immunologic system developed for the first time in the vertebrates. This system allowed them to assert themselves as individuals in new ways: They acquired a demarcating bodily automatism that operated beneath the threshhold of consciousness. Their organism developed countless specific antibodies against foreign and potentially noxious substances. All these automatisms served the differentiation between me and not-me. That which the immunologic system defined as me (or as belonging to or being useful to me) it retained; that which it defined as not-me, it rejected and devalued radically.

However, evolution may also be looked at from perspectives other than those of self-assertion, boundary-setting, and individuation. This will be the case when we focus on how various elements in one ecosystem depend on and interact with each other. If we do so, we recognize not only that, as Hegel put it, "the doing of the one is the doing of the other" (Das Tun des einen ist das Tun des anderen) but also that the evolution of the one is the evolution of the other. When we adopt this second, "ecosystemic" perspective, we will be impressed not so much by the struggle for survival, self-assertion, and individuation, as by cooperation, interdependence, and interaction—in brief, by coevolution.

For a long time scientists as well as politicians could afford the luxury of giving preference to the first perspective, which stresses the struggle for survival and individuation. But not any more. We experience ourselves increasingly as elements of complex interlocking ecosystems. This applies to our relations to our nonhuman as well as to our human environment. Consequently we are faced with the challenge—if not the inescapable destiny—of participating in coevolution. At the same time, we find planetary coevolution as a whole jeopardized more and more seriously, for planetary evolution is today accompanied if not superseded by an accelerating devolution, which the dictionary defines as retrograde evolution or degradation. Such devolution proceeds, for example, through the relentless destruction of countless species that have evolved over millions of years, a destruction due to an ever-increasing overpopulation, shrinkage of natural habitats, cutting down of forests, and planting of monocultures. And possibly such devolution may be brought about by the sudden advent of a nuclear winter, a prospect that seems only too realistic today.

Let us, with these considerations in mind, look now at so-called social and cultural evolution, and with that at the evolution of ideas and models, especially at those which we find relevant as psychotherapists. If we do this, we realize that ideas and models, too, may be viewed as living beings, as organisms, a view that has been elaborated by Edgar Morin (2), Jürg Willi (4), and others. Ideas and models, too, are elements, manifestations, and consequences of evolutionary processes. They, too, grow up, have their childhood, youth, and adulthood, their times of strength and maturity; they, too, have progeny, dry up, and die, while some continue to exist as mummies and fossils. And here, too, the evolution tends to produce a plethora of species with very varying life spans ranging from flies that live as "one-day wonders" to long-lived pachyderms.

This life of models and ideas, too, can be looked at either from the vantage of a struggle for survival, that is, of individuation, or from that of mutual dependence, mutual conditioning, and coevolution. In the first instance we look at how models or systems of ideas will individuate and assert themselves, possibly by expanding and incorporating other models and ideas (up to the point of indigestibility) or by condemning these latter to an impoverished existence by taking away the necessary air and light, that is, the public interest. Psychoanalysis and Marxism can be viewed as such expansively voracious systems of ideas. (However, we might well ask whether by now they may not have passed their zeniths.)

If, in contrast, we view the lives of models and ideas from the vantage of coevolution, it becomes less a matter of importance who wins or loses, who eats up others or will be eaten, but rather we are concerned with how models and ideas owe their existence to each other, how they support and nourish one another, how they emerge out of each other, turn into each other: how they coevolve. This then brings us close to a view which Hegel elaborated more than 150 years ago.

But that is not all. Today, in the context of accelerating technological and sociocultural change, we also find the evolution of models and ideas accelerating—so much so that we might almost speak of an explosion of models. At the same time we notice, here too, a worldwide trend toward devolution, that is, a flattening of the landscape of ideas and models, facilitated, among other things, by ever more perfect—and especially in totalitarian societies ever more realizable—possibilities for channeling and controlling information.

However, as psychotherapists living and working in the Western world we are mostly affected by the acceleration of the evolution of models and ideas. We are affected because we—especially—need models that permit us to reduce the complexity of a world that is becoming ever more complex—without running the danger of losing access to that complexity. And we are affected because we need models which determine our view of what constitutes sickness and health, of what is therapeutically helpful or harmful, and what accordingly should guide our therapeutic endeavors. By this I mean primarily all those models which try to grasp human relationships or, more exactly, try to grasp human relational reality, while at the same time opening up possibilities of influencing that reality.

First of all, we will note that we are negatively affected. We see in the accelerating cultural evolution essentially a battle for self-assertion, for survival, that pressures the spiritual fathers and mothers of models—the therapists, theoreticians, and author-gurus everywhere—to seek recognition through an ever-accelerating output of concepts and ideas, with the consequence that the flood of publications, particularly in our field, grows unabated. Not surprisingly, there now appear in the field of family therapy and family research worldwide several dozens of journals, in themselves only a small percentage of the plethora of existing psychiatric and psychological journals (which, by the way, also deal more and more frequently with relational and systems aspects). Thus we have, along with our capitalist consumer and throwaway society, a consumer and throwaway society of ideas. Hence the rapid accumulation of "idea waste" and "idea garbage," hence the massive problems of environmental pollution, hence the increasing difficulties for all of us to keep our bearings and find our orientation. This applies to our patients and clients as much as it does to us as professional helpers.

What this may mean for the seekers of help—our patients—was recently demonstrated by a family which approached our department for consultation. The family consisted of two parents, both in their late fifties, and two sons, both in their late twenties. All family members had collected diverse psychiatric diagnoses. Most pressing, though, was the problem of the sons: they were unable to finish their studies, had hardly any outside contacts, spent almost all of their time in apathetic brooding at home, and accused their parents of having failed as parents. All family members had individual therapies or psychoanalyses of up to five years or longer behind them. However, since—at least in their own view—nothing had changed, they had consulted various psychiatric or psychotherapeutic experts over the last six months. From these they had received the following recommendations (among others): further psychoanalytic or intensive psychotherapeutic treatment for all family members; further psychoanalysis for the sons only; psychiatric in-patient treatment for both sons or only one son; medical treatment, that is, medications for the sons and also for the parents, especially for the mother (who in the past had been treated for "depression"); group therapy of various kinds for the sons; couple therapy for the parents; and, finally, family therapy for all.

The likelihood of floundering hopelessly in the confusing psychiatric scene grew no less common in the United States than in Germany. On the occasion of my last stay in the States I heard about a family whose members had all in all accumulated 68 years of psychotherapy among them. Yet in so doing they had at least—and this is in itself an important systems aspect—helped to secure the economic survival of an important professional group in financially insecure times—that of our own group of professional helpers.

These problems of disorientation, however, affect the professional helpers hardly less massively than they affect those who are seeking help. And they especially affect those among us who are still seeking training, that is, those who are still ready, able, and willing to learn and to orient themselves anew. On the occasion of a similarly large family therapy congress in Heidelberg six years ago I mentioned that an astute American journalist and observer of the American psychoscene claimed to have counted several thousand psychotherapeutic schools, groups, and subgroups after he had differentiated among them as conscientiously as possible. Today he might have to put this figure even higher.

And yet this accelerating evolution and simultaneous proliferation of theories, models, doctrines, and therapeutic schools are moving us increasingly toward a point where in a certain sense quantity will turn into quality, a quality of awareness that encourages on its own the adoption of a coevolutionary and ecosystemic perspective. And we are likely to arrive at this point the sooner the more we are ready to expose ourselves to a cybernetic point of view, a vantage from which the many definitions, demarcations, models, and concepts will again be "liquefied." They present themselves in such a perspective as expression and consequence of an evolutionary stream, as shaped by relations, definitions, and constraints—particularly the constraints of language—all of which themselves need to be viewed as being in flux.

This applies in particular to concepts such as "drive," "self," "dependency," "the unconscious," as expounded by widely quoted psychotheoreticians past and present. Gregory Bateson (1), for one, reminded us again and again that these concepts, too, are mere reifying constructs that offer at best an illusion of stability, clarity, and comprehensibility. However, once such reifying concepts have become liquefied, we should not have much difficulty in reaching the conclusion that there exist for humanity well-nigh unlimited possibilities of arranging concepts and perceptions, hence unlimited possibilities of ordering data, punctuating sequences, establishing causal connections, and hence of allotting or exonerating from guilt, of marking out contexts, of constructing models, creating meaning. In sum, there exist nearly unlimited possibilities of constructing our reality, or, more exactly, our relational reality. At the same time, this view opens up an intrapsychic as well as interpersonal "multiverse," which at any point in any time may be changed by the introduction of new points of view, of new classifications, new perspectives, and new criteria of evaluation. And with that—and this makes us again think of Hegelian dialectics—there emerge new qualities of individuation, as the scope for human autonomy, for human freedom widens.

However, such widening of the intrapsychic and interpersonal margins for human freedom appears also as the central concern in those two trends (or, perhaps more correctly, movements) within the field of psychotherapy which, as this congress has shown, are now arousing the greatest interest. I have in mind radical constructivism and Ericksonian hypnotherapy. Both of them, we might say, are concerned with the study and utilization of our potentials for widening the margins of human freedom and autonomy. However, they do this from different vantages. Representatives of constructivism such as Ernst von Glaserfeld, Heinz von Foerster, and Francisco Varela have more epistemological, hypnotherapists more practical theapeutic interests at heart. The constructivist authors alert us to the many possibilities, inherent in any human being, of computing, constructing, negotiating individual reality in accordance with his own needs and interests. Francisco Varela, who has been called the biologist of freedom, wrote, for example, in 1982, "The sharpened sensibility for the full power of autonomy and the feeling of richness and expansion accompanying it are the most important thing I have ever learned in my life." And Milton Erickson and his disciples deliver a similar message. They too, in the final analysis, are concerned with enlarging the margins of individual autonomy by bringing their clients into contact with inner resources that so far have not been recognized and/or utilized, for example, by redefining as positive and as a covert strength that which these clients until then had devalued and rejected as symptoms, as pathological factors, or as character deficits.

Therefore, we may say that the very proliferation of ideas (which we viewed as an expression and consequence of accelerating individuation within sociocultural evolution) is part of a development that gives psychotherapy its big chance, the chance to extend the margins of individual freedom by introducing new perspectives, new information, new evaluations, by, if need be, a turning around of the whole point of observation (durch ein Drehen der ganzen Betrachtung), as Ludwig Wittgenstein once said.

This may then, as the practice of family therapy shows, result in the quick disappearance of even stubbornly persistent symptoms (e.g., those of anorexia nervosa or psychosis). Suddenly the blocked family-wide coevolution seems unblocked; all at once the evolutionary stream is free to flow again, as it were.

However, widening of the margin of individual freedom by the introduction of new perspectives will in itself not suffice. In addition, it will be necessary to accept more responsibility for one's decisions and actions. This is a point stressed particularly by radical constructivists: The more we can view ourselves as constructing our unique relational reality, the more likely it will also be that we view ourselves as responsible for the reality we have constructed, that is, for our behavior, our communication, and even our symptoms, as all these have come to codetermine this reality.

However, our very attempts to adopt a consistently ecosystemic and coevolutionary perspective may make it difficult to recognize this point. Mostly, these difficulties will attach themselves to the concepts of an ego, a self, an individual, and the related concept of individuation. These concepts, more than any others, seem suited to convey that someone experiences himself as a person who has his own value, who perceives, expresses, negotiates, and asserts his own needs and rights, who accepts responsibility for his actions, who takes charge of his life—that is, who demarcates himself from others, who individuates himself. However, these very concepts—ego, self, individual, and individuation—are more susceptible than other concepts to becoming reified, fixed, frozen and thus of being torn out of the context of living relationships. Therefore, it should not surprise us that precisely those psychiatrists and thinkers who pioneered a systemic and coevolutionary approach looked at these concepts with suspicion. Harry Stack Sullivan (3), for example, in many respects a pioneer of such an approach in psychiatry, spoke in 1950 of the "illusion of a personal individuality." And Gregory Bateson, our great ecosystemic guru, wrote in 1977:

> To draw a boundary line between a part which does most of the computation for a larger system and the larger system of which it is a part, is to create a mythological component, commonly called a "self." In my epistemology, the concept of self, along with all arbitrary boundaries which delimit systems or parts of systems, is to be regarded as a trait of the local culture—not indeed to be disregarded, since such little epistemological monsters are always liable to become foci of pathology. The arbitrary boundaries which were useful in the process of analyzing data become all too easily battle-fronts, across which we try to kill an enemy or exploit an environment. (1, p. 53)

Bateson appears here as the spokesman of a radically ecosystemic, coevo-lutionary perspective. Yet at the same time he blocks out a problem area that is becoming ever more central for family therapists. I have in mind the fact that family-wide coevolution must develop hand in hand with family-wide coindividuation.

Elsewhere I have spoken of the necessity for a family to find, again and again, new levels of "related individuation." I defined "related individua-tion" as a general principle according to which a higher level of indi-viduation will always presuppose as well as require a higher level of relatedness. But if this is the case, there emerges one central question: How can the members of a closely knit social system—such as a marriage or a family—consistently demarcate themselves from (or individuate them-selves against) each other in such a way that nobody will be a loser, that nobody will be left behind, that nobody need have the feeling of having been exploited—without there resulting an endless struggle of attrition and demarcation which nobody will be able to win?

To approach this question let me return to the image of a battlefield which Bateson evokes with the preceding quotation. This image seems particularly pertinent to what family therapists experience. It suggests that instead of a joint development of family members in synchrony with their individual and family life cycles, instead of the emergence of ever new and ever more complex forms of relatedness, there is a blockage of over-due, family-wide coevolution and coindividuation. We then observe what we have come to call (perhaps none too precisely) homeostatically fixed, massively bound-up, rigid, or enmeshed family systems. And many such blocked and bound-up systems do indeed give the impression of battle-fields where individual members (or selves) who are blind to their mutual dependence are fighting for every inch of ground, fighting with the most varied arsenal of weapons and strategies. For example, in a number of families and marriages the partners attempt, again and again, to disquali-fy what the other says, they try to avoid defining their relationship to each other, become engaged in war games, as it were, in which the only valid rule is a metarule that there is no rule. We observe such "war games" typically in families in which at least one member has been diagnosed as schizophrenic. In these instances we also speak of "schizo-present" fami-lies.

In other families the war game presents itself rather as a "victim game": Each of the partners, again and again, attempts to operate the guilt lever on the other by showing himself or herself as more sacrificing, as more self-renouncing than the other, thus asserting his or her "moral superiori-ty." Typically, this kind of family battle remains hidden from the observer for long stretches of time. Rather, we frequently find a leaden pseudo-harmony under cover of which ruthless trench warfare is being waged. We observe this most frequently in families whose members are suffering from a serious and chronic psychosomatic illness.

To sum up, in both kinds of families here sketched as ideal types we find the blockage of an overdue family-wide coindividuation, occurring, however, in a different form each time and with differing consequences for therapy. In the case of schizo-present families such blockage essentially reflects the fact that the jointly negotiated relational reality—the reality of jointly shared basic assumptions, values, meanings, and the like—has become excessively "softened." Therefore, there is a lack of anchoring points, of clear and consistent meanings that would allow one person (particularly important for a growing child) to delineate his position as against that of others, to individuate himself with respect to those others.

In contrast to the schizo-present family, we find in "psychosomatic families" that the common relational reality is excessively "hardened." There exist iron-hard family values and family rules, as it were, frequently transmitted over the generations, which every member must obey. Such rules may require that one has to renounce one's own needs in favor of those of others, one must never slacken, no family member must be left behind, and so on. The very hardness of such values and delegations will then thwart any attempts to break away, to adopt other values—to individuate one's self against the other(s).

In sum, we find in schizo-present as well as psychosomatic families a blockage of family-wide coevolution and coindividuation, differing, however, in that, on the one hand, we have the context of a too "soft" and on the other that of a too "hard" relational reality. Yet should this blockage persist, there is an equal risk of devolution and degradation in both cases. Such a course of events seems inevitable, once the partners fail to see that—to paraphrase a well-known dictum by Marx and Engels—the conditions of the individuation of the one are also the conditions of the individuation of the other. However, to realize and change such a plight there is usually need of a "jump" in one's perception, a new view of things, as well as new concepts that imply new links, new punctuations, and new relations.

An example from present-day politics may illustrate what this means. The FRG (Federal Republic of Germany) and the GDR (German Democratic Republic) find themselves at present in a situation that reflects maximal (even though, in the main, one-sided) demarcation, as evidenced by walls, barbed wire, and death zones. If we define individuation essentially as self-demarcation and self-assertion, then we may also speak here of an individuation that has been pushed to its limits. And yet even this individuation shows itself to be increasingly inseparable from relatedness, so that even here the concepts "related individuation" and "coindividuation" could be applied. However much the two German states, due to historical and societal factors, may confront each other as hostile brothers, they are still forced into a "jump of perception" which causes them, too, to see their own individuation as dependent on the individuation of the other, that is, which makes them aware of their interdependence and coevolution.

Recently the historian Rudolf von Thadden from Göttingen coined a concept that expresses a central element of this state of affairs: the concept of a "community of responsibility" (Verantwortungsgemeinschaft) which, in the meantime, has been adopted by Genscher, the German Secretary of State, and Honecker, the President of the GDR. In sum, even in situations where we demarcate or individuate ourselves against each other radically, we need to recognize our joint responsibility for ensuring that our individuation does not negate the conditions necessary for the individuation of others, as otherwise the common basis for the survival and evolution of both sides will be destroyed.

Families and couples (like other human systems) can be viewed as "communities of responsibility"—that is, as communities whose members are responsible for constantly negotiating and shaping a joint relational reality which, again and again, both requires and facilitates family-wide coevolution and coindividuation. And such negotiating and shaping should—either with or without therapeutic help—become easier the more their awareness of the full power of their autonomy, the full scope of their freedom, sharpens.

REFERENCES

1. Bateson, G. (1977). The birth of a matrix or double bind and epistemology. In M. Berger (Ed.), *Beyond the double bind*. New York: Brunner/Mazel.
2. Morin, E. (1977). *La Methode: Vol. II. La Vie de la Vie*. Paris: Edition du Seuil.
3. Sullivan, H. S. (1950). The illusion of personal individuality. *Psychiatry, 13*: 317–332.
4. Willi, J. (1985). *Koevolution*. Reinbek: Rowohlt.

The Emergence of a Comprehensive Systems Approach: Supervisor and Team Problems in a District Psychiatric Center

Mara Selvini Palazzoli

This paper[1] is one of a series in which I describe our effort to apply the systemic model not only to the field of family therapy. Starting in 1981 we fostered the emergence of a comprehensive system approach in psychiatric institutions through our common effort to transform a biomedical psychiatric center into a systemic one.

This paper focuses on a specific acquisition. It aims to demonstrate how the systems model provides new instruments to understand and change the dysfunctional families but also the dysfunctional team (supervisor included).

THE TRANSFORMATION OF A DISTRICT PSYCHIATRIC CENTER

In the spring of 1981, the politico-administrative authorities nominated me part-time supervisor of the team running the District Psychiatric Centre at Corsico, a built-up area bordering on the southern suburbs of Milan. The Centre had been set up in 1973 on strictly biomedical lines: Its main function was to keep an eye on, and to assist, patients discharged

[1]This paper appeared previously in *Journal of Family Therapy* (1985) 7: 135–146; it is published here with the editor's kind permission.
I wish to thank Brian Cade once again for his help in improving the English text.

from the local psychiatric hospital, as well as to dispense free medication. In 1980, a new team of professionals took over and persuaded the authorities to appoint me supervisor. I accepted without hesitation, knowing that this Centre enjoyed an exceptional situation: The two psychiatrists and two psychologists in the team had adopted the same conceptual (systemic-relational) model as I had, and they had all been trained in family therapy. Moreover, the team had not been forced to carve out a niche in an indifferent or hostile institution but had been allowed to effect a peaceful revolution in relative autonomy. At the time I was appointed, the psychiatrists and psychologists had already begun to transform the Centre by the gradual implementation of two related decisions:

1. To concentrate on so-called new-users, that is, people who had not been subjected to biomedical psychiatric procedures and for whom family therapy would therefore be the first form of treatment;
2. to win over the other staff members (four nurses and a social worker), all of whom had been trained in traditional psychiatric methods, to the systems approach.

In 1981, when I began my work at Corsico, the situation was as follows. The nurses were in process of being drawn into cooperating in the application of family therapy to new users by being entrusted with two important tasks. The first of these was the filling in of record cards of the new users that concentrated primarily on information of a relational type; the second was the explaining of our methods of work to the new users, showing them the room reserved for interviews and the equipment in it, and inviting to the interview all family members living under the same roof as the client in such a way as to ensure that they really did turn up, with a consequent falling off of "deserters." However, the gradual nature of the transformation inevitably created an incongruous situation: side by side with being drawn into the systems approach, the nurses and the social worker were also expected to continue their traditional duties with the chronic patients (about 150) we had inherited from our predecessors. Most of these lived with their families, but a small number with no family to take them in after their discharge from mental hospitals (which were closed by law in 1978) had been housed in small, low-cost apartments provided by the local authority. This burden of "chronic" patients, one might almost say this jetsam from a deplorable past, was a permanent source of worry to the psychiatrists and psychologists. Unable to fit them into their plans for the Centre, they tended to leave them as much as possible to the care of the nurses and the social worker, who dealt with their sickness and unemployment benefits.

However, that situation was understood to be purely temporary. All of us agreed that we must avoid transforming the Centre into a family therapy outpatients' clinic—we intended to meet all the needs and demands of our clients in keeping with our chosen model, and not necessarily with family therapy. As far as the chronic patients were concerned, it was agreed to hold a weekly meeting of all the staff during which the whole staff team could discuss current problems and possible solutions. Soon after I was appointed to Corsico, I offered to act as supervisor for the nurses, leaving it to the team to fix the precise dates.

The team as a whole made a very positive impression on me; the relational climate seemed excellent, and all members seemed eager to further the common plan by making the maximum personal contribution. In 1982, after having worked there for a year, I described the situation in Corsico in that article, in which inter alia, I mentioned the advantages of working with a transdisciplinary team (2).[2] For instance, we had been able to save the team from the many pitfalls inherent in the adoption of various conceptual models. However, looking back on this period with the wisdom of hindsight, I realize that I had exaggerated the importance of that achievement, believing as I did that the act of sharing the same model (and especially the same systemic model) tends to diminish conflictual attitudes by itself. The subsequent experience might have helped to guard me against the illusion that the path of a team like ours is always a smooth one. Conflict is inherent in institutions and in them, as in everything that is alive, it can either give rise to stagnation or act as a spur to progress.

However, all this should become clearer in what follows.

---

[2]Various people have asked me to explain the difference between interdisciplinary and transdisciplinary. I shall try to do so with the help of an example. A government decides to lay a pipeline and asks a team of experts to prepare the necessary plans. These experts are engineers, geologists, geographers, lawyers, economists, etc., and each of them will apply his particular model. They constitute an interdisciplinary team. In the recent past the spread of the systems approach and its adoption by students of a host of different disciplines has enabled ecologists, biologists, economists, chemists, physicists, sociologists, town planners, and therapists to share and apply the same model. In that case we speak of a transdisciplinary approach. In a transdisciplinary team, the various members share the same model and perform various tasks to reach a common objective.

THE BLACK PERIOD:
SEPTEMBER 1982–MARCH 1983

In September 1982, when I resumed my work at Corsico after the summer vacation, I found that the psychiatrists and psychologists were deeply uneasy about their family work: The "new" cases treated by family therapy had produced some highly frustrating failures. Some of these cases, in particular, were of special interest to me because the type rarely turns up in my private Centre. It would have been a great pity had I not taken advantage of the occasion, the risk of other failures being what it was. Thus it happened that, step by step, I fell into the trap of becoming a family therapy supervisor above all else. It was then that I noticed to my regret that the greater my own readiness and acumen, the slower and more obtuse the therapists became, which persuaded me all the more that they needed my supervision—a vicious circle that made all of us unhappy. That trap was already there, it was in the very nature of the project of transformation of a traditional psychiatric center. Because, if our Centre should transform itself according to the systemic model, our therapists had to be able not only to avoid labeling clients as mental patients, but also to approach the families in crisis in such a manner as to induce rapid change and consequently the disappearence of the symptoms. Otherwise, it would have become inevitable to send the identified patient to the hospital. But our therapists could not be different from how they were, young and of limited experience.

As for the regular meetings of the whole team, at the time we were almost solely occupied with the supervision of one of our nurses who was trying to help a chronic young schizophrenic with frequent domiciliary visits. After a very successful phase, her efforts ended in failure following a clumsy intervention by the young man's family, which we could do nothing to stop. As a result, the young nurse had been placed in an impossible position. This unfortunate period made me feel increasingly ill at ease, the more so as I had to admit to myself that the planned transformation of the Centre was making no progress. Indeed, there were signs of regression. Moreover, I myself seemed to have taken on the role of a supervisor of uninspired family therapy in an atmosphere of general discontent. But I could see no way out. I brooded a great deal and wondered if it would not have been better to set a date for the end of my supervision at Corsico.

During the last few weeks of that period, some comments about the weekly meeting also reached my ears. These meetings had taken place in my absence, and in them the entire team had discussed the nurses' and the social workers' problem with the chronic patients. It appeared that these meetings had been demoralizing because not a single concrete decision had emerged from them. Fortunately, we were on the brink of an incident that was to prove providential.

THE INCIDENT

At the beginning of April, during my afternoon at the Centre, I joined the psychiatrists and psychologists who were waiting for me to arrange a family session. We read the records and discussed them. Everything was just the same as usual. After some time, I left the room to make a telephone call, walked down the corridor and passed the nurses and the social worker. "How's everything?" I asked. "Not too good," they replied. "Pietro, one of our chronic cases, has smashed all the glass in the door and the windows that give onto the street. It happened this morning, and we had to call the ambulance to take him off to the hospital." I had no time to find out more because I was expecting a family and was due at the session.

At the end of the afternoon, I called the whole team together and told them what I had decided to do about the incident. At my next visit, we would hold a full meeting and devote it entirely to Pietro. The team would have to provide me with full details of Pietro's story and also of his relations with them.

PIETRO

The youngest of four sons of a peasant family from Corsico, Pietro was introduced early on to a "deviant" way of life. From his records, it appeared that between the ages of 7 and 12 he had been kept in a home for retarded boys. At 14, he had lost both his parents. At 16, for no precise clinical reason that could be found in his file, he had been admitted to a psychiatric hospital and transferred after a year to an institute for chronic patients where he remained for the next 20 years. Somehow he must have adapted himself to institutional life for he had been allowed to work in the institute's factory and also, at intervals, on the land.

In May 1978, following the law closing psychiatric hospitals, Pietro, then 39, was discharged and referred to the Corsico Centre. Because his brothers, all married and with children, refused to take him in, he was placed, some months after his discharge from hospital, in a small, low-cost apartment reserved for cases like him by the local authority. He lived there under the supervision of the staff of the Centre, sharing the apartment with another seriously ill patient who was subsequently moved, so that from January 1981 Pietro lived alone. He had a total disability pension and also a savings account book, in which, over the long years of his stay in the institution, he had set aside what little pay he had earned for his labors, now amounting to several million lire. When he was placed in the charge of our Centre, the control of his money was given to the social worker who drew Pietro's pension every month and managed his savings book. Every other day Pietro would be given money for his daily needs, as well as, from time to time, an extra amount for special expenses, like shoes and clothes. His rent, gas, and electricity bills were paid directly by the social worker.

In time, as Pietro's records revealed, an interesting development occurred: Pietro was gradually but unmistakably adopted by all our staff at the Centre. The home visits paid him by some of the nurses to check if he was clean and properly fed became more prolonged; often a nurse would stop with him for several hours keeping him company and playing cards with him. Once a week one of the psychiatrists and the local social worker would also call on him, unannounced. On these occasions, Pietro would give them small presents, pipe tobacco or toffees.

Gradually the ties became closer. Pietro would be given lifts home from the Centre by the psychiatrists: he would turn up regularly at the canteen and have lunch with the staff. At the same time he also started to make greater demands. In particular, he kept asking for more cash, and for withdrawals of excessive sums from his savings book. If he was refused, he would become aggressive, get drunk, and start breaking ashtrays, medicine bottles, and the like. To prevent worse, the staff member concerned at the time would generally do as he asked. Moreover, this escalation of undesirable effects was accompanied more and more frequently by a redundancy: whenever Pietro managed to go beyond tolerable limits, the psychiatrists would propose sending him to hospital:[3] Pietro would accept and, welcomed as an old friend, would spend a few pleasant days and behave very well. He would then be discharged and the cycle would recommence.

From January 1983, as the records showed, this repetitive game increased in intensity, and the intervals between successive admissions to hospital grew shorter. The exasperated nurses and social worker asked the doctors to intervene. But no one knew what to do. Each one alternated between random concessions and refusals, between permissiveness

---

[3]After the official closure of the psychiatric hospitals, Italian general hospitals opened wards to which acutely ill mental patients could be admitted for the shortest possible periods.

and strictness. (At the same time, as subsequently emerged, the psychiatrists and psychologists became annoyed with the nurses for bothering them with matters of no moment, while the nurses felt they had been left in the lurch by "those four who are always barricading themselves in their room to discuss family therapy.") It was at this point that Pietro had picked up a chair and smashed the windows at the Centre and was sent to the hospital.

During the telling of this story, with each member of the team making a contribution, I would interrupt now and then with a question. I was particularly interested in the period between Pietro's discharge from the home of chronic patients and his move to the low-rent apartment under the supervision of our Centre. A number of facts then came to light that had been completely overlooked: During that period, which had lasted for three months, Pietro had managed pretty well (and this after 35 years of institutionalization!); he had regularly taken his meals in a public canteen (open to both the administrators and the public recipients of public assistance) and had slept in a public dormitory. He had been drunk on only three occasions (in the company of a friend). Hence it seemed clear that his ties with members of our Centre had caused him to regress.

In view of these facts, I felt certain about what had to be done. There was no time to lose. Pietro would not be kept in a hospital for long.

THE INTERVENTION

In particular, I realized that the incident that Pietro had instigated provided a welcome opportunity for uniting the team round the solution of a burning problem. Moreover, this particular episode had another great advantage: like a fresh spring breeze, it could blow away the "elitist" barriers that were apparently dividing our team. This time family therapy did not come into it at all; all members were on par—all had committed the same mistakes, and no one had anything to boast about.

At the end of that meeting, I decided to say nothing at all about what had happened, not one to link the episode to the problems of the team. Instead, I would profit from the favorable wind and steer our ship toward a concrete goal, that of Pietro's extrication from an impossible situation. I accordingly made the following proposal: While Pietro was still in hospital, the team would assemble for a full meeting, and if necessary for more than one, and draw up a written set of rules. In this, the members of the team would lay down how each one of them should behave toward Pietro and, conversely, what behavior Pietro would have to adopt toward them. Upon his discharge from hospital, which we would be told about in advance, Pietro would be escorted back to the Centre where the rules would be read out to him by the psychiatrist in charge, preceded by a full explanation. In substance, Pietro would be told that the team had come to appreciate that it had held him back for too long from assuming the responsibilities that were properly his.

THE RULES

I have since been told that the whole team found the drafting of the rules a distressing chore. All alike were reluctant to cut the apron strings: They were worried that Pietro might not eat enough, would not clean his rooms, would give himself up to debauchery and dissipation. . . . Finally the team agreed on a document with the five following points:

1. The team will end all domiciliary visits to Pietro and stop interfering in his private life.
2. All members of the team agree to treat Pietro like any other user, and will cease to be on familiar terms with him (no more meals taken together, lifts in cars, etc.).
3. Pietro will be taught to take full charge of his financial and other affairs within six months. During the first two months, a sum of money sufficient for his weekly needs (a quarter of his disability pension) will be sent to the porter's lodge of his building once a week. For the following two months, the money will be sent once every two weeks, and for the two months after that, every three weeks. At the end of six months he will receive his full pension and will also take charge of his savings books.
4. Since Pietro will be expected to behave like every other user of the Centre, he will be seen by appointment only.
5. Violent behavior will no longer be considered a symptom to be treated by hospitalization but an antisocial act to be reported to the adjoining police station (with whom, in fact, an understanding was reached).

On the day Pietro was discharged from hospital, he was escorted to the Centre and received by the psychiatrist in charge in the presence of the whole team. The psychiatrist (that, too, had been agreed by the team) addressed him gently but very firmly. He told him, in essence, that the team had realized that for far too long the team had treated him as a baby, incapable of taking on his own responsibilities, thus preventing him from becoming an adult. The team had accordingly decided to adopt a set of rules that would help them avoid their old mistakes. For the same reasons they had also drawn up regulations for Pietro. The psychiatrist then read out the rules.

Pietro's immediate reactions were considerably less dramatic than we had feared. For a few moments he put on a pitifully dejected air and produced a few tears. When he recovered his composure, he agreed to cooperate, adding in a low voice that it was perhaps too late.

Over the next few days, while the team waited with trepidation for Pietro's every move, he surprised us all. He asked for an appointment with the psychiatrist and spoke to him about his plans. He had been saving up for a second-hand bicycle (in Corsico, public transport leaves much to be desired) and even knew at what market stall in Milan he would be able to find one and at what price. After that he planned to save some more money to buy a tape recorder. He had also made some friends, and had even become involved in an amorous relationship that was causing him some grave problems, though not of the kind that had troubled him before.

TOWARD A THEORY OF THE INCIDENT

Let me now offer some theoretical reflections on the events I have been describing.

If we look at what I have called the black period of my work in Corsico, it becomes clear that it sprang from the division of the team into components: a "first-class" sector made up of the supervisor and the psychiatrists and psychologists engaged in family therapy, and a "second-class" sector made up of the nurses and the social worker. Now it is clear that when we tried to involve the second-class staff in our new approach by having them do little more than collect and record information of a relational type, we were not doing really enough to maintain the unity of the team. Seen in retrospect, the divisions were not at all the result of the difficulties we had anticipated, namely the use of distinct conceptual models, but of the inability of the first-class members and of the supervisor to go beyond the compass of family therapy and to seek other applications of the systems approach. The same short-sighted attitude also resulted in the tendency to delegate the care of chronic cases to the nurses because with chronic patients, in fact, family therapy cannot be applied either because many of them have no family left or because the family refuses to cooperate. It must be stressed that this development had taken place despite our clear determination—and our declared intentions—to avoid the "familiocentric" label at all costs.

The explanation seems to lie in an elementary fact: While it is extremely simple to make decisions of this type in the abstract, this was practice. I must underline the word **concrete**, because it is the golden thread, the main path, to be followed through our work.

To drive this point home, I shall return to the end of the black period, to my direct intervention as supervisor immediately after the incident. I did not make speeches or comment on what had happened in the past. Instead I made a concrete proposal that was entirely forward-looking: I asked the team to compile the greatest possible amount of data on Pietro's case and on his relations with the Centre. That was the first step, and indispensable for the next. In fact, in the absence of adequate information no adequate decision is likely to be made.[4]

Once the necessary information had been gathered, I proceeded to the actual prescription: the drafting of the set of rules governing their relations with Pietro and his with them. *The prescription was an authentic systems intervention inasmuch as, in order to change Pietro, the team had to change itself.* And in fact the prescription worked in precisely that sense, with numerous positive consequences. During the meetings held to draw up the rules, the psychiatrists and psychologists heard at first hand of, and learned to profit from, the concrete and detailed information that the nurses and the social worker were able to give them of Pietro and their experiences with him. In fact, it appeared that they had enough such information to explain his behavior and to arrive at new directives and decisions. The nurses and the social worker felt appreciated for once and released from their corner. The common task of drawing up the rules was accompanied by a positive reintegration of the whole team, helped subsequently by Pietro's unexpected and touching feedbacks. The whole experience inspired us to take a fresh look at our chronic cases and to start a research program that is beginning to bear fruit. Being a new field to all concerned, the successful treatment of chronic patients gives scope to creativity by one and all. As for the supervisor, she was able, once she had escaped from the trap of acting as supervisor, to resume the true role of supervisor of a team. The family therapists, as they resumed the supervision of each other, not only made good use of what they had learned, but found again inventiveness combined with growing therapeutic success.

There is yet another concrete factor on which I wish to dwell here,

---

[4]Here I would like to emphasize that this approach is isomorphic with family therapy. In the latter, too, the collection of information precedes the intervention aimed at producing a change. The effectiveness of that intervention also depends on the adequacy of the information obtained.

the "incident" itself. In fact, the incident introduced into the team, which had by then become rigid and repetitive, an explosive element, a disturbance, and hence a grave problem that could only be settled with a different organization.

At the same time, the incident, being the result of a feedback from the previous organizational modality, not only highlighted its malfunction but also provided a key for the new organization. In other words, inasmuch as the incident was Pietro's reaction to the incongruous behavior of a disunited team, the organizational modality to be adopted could not be a collaborative one.

What could we have done if the incident had not occurred? In the private Centre of which I am the director, the coordinator of research on relationships in large systems has recently put forward a new method for the gradual unification and collaboration of the heterogeneous component of a group or team engaged on a common project (1). Although that method is preventive rather than therapeutic, it is relevant to our discussion. Pisano believes that the progress of team collaboration can be gauged with the help of forecasts "about the integration of the team's attitudes (to the users), the adoption of a common strategy of intervention, unanimity with respect to the objectives, and the positive appreciation of the competence of each member (of the team). If the predictions prove correct, they can be used to gauge the development of the organizational process involved and its level."

In the Corsico team, signs of closer collaboration reappeared after the Pietro incident, and more precisely after the whole team had managed to draw up and to adopt the set of rules. Only after that had happened was it possible to discern a clear integration of the team's attitude to the various users; an acceptable division of the tasks involved in an agreed strategy; a unanimous determination to reach the set objectives; and acceptance, free of elitist overtones, that each member was making an essential contribution of his own to the job in hand.

By contrast, during what we had called our black period, no prediction of the development of a collaborative process could have been fulfilled. The malfunctioning of the team was already patent. Moreover, my own position had become shaky in that I too was a participant in a game to whose adoption I had actively contributed and which I was continuing to play despite myself. In that situation a supervisor who, while involved in the game, tries to make helpful comments on an impasse in order to resolve it has very poor prospects of success.

I am convinced that the right road to positive change is another road: taking advantage of a concrete event. Thus past experience, over and above the present one, leads me to think that any incident (not necessarily a dramatic one!) is likely to prove auspicious. For when an incident occurs, it is no longer the supervisor who tries to impose his will, but the incident itself which drives home to everyone involved the urgency of the problem to be resolved. This conviction gives one the patience to wait for an incident to happen and the readiness to take advantage of it, as one might leap onto a bus that passes by at an awkward or dangerous moment. The incident is an occasion not to be missed; it is the concrete element that, in allowing us to act, saves us from the perils of having to talk.

In conclusion, to treat (i.e., change) a disturbed team the supervisor should behave as a family therapist who knows very well, and from long experience, that a prescription works much better than the most eloquent explanation.

REFERENCES

1. Pisano, I. (1984, July). *Sous Systèms Scolaires: Effect catalysant du Psychologue sur la Communication*. Paper presented at Colloque International des Psychologues Scholaires, Orléans.
2. Selvini Palazzoli, M. (1983). The emergence of a comprehensive systems approach. *Journal of Family Therapy, 5*: 165–177.

Lunch Chit-Chat

In the balmy sunshine of a beautiful day in May, two participants of the conference ran into each other around midday (quite by chance) and decided to have lunch together. Their names? Theo and Maria. (Whoever would have guessed?) And of course they had nothing better to do than embark on another argument about what they had heard that morning. (After all, that's what they were invented for!) The "warming-up session" (or whatever one might care to call the first few exchanges before really getting down to business) we can safely draw a veil over (as with so much in the relationship between these two). In medias res, then!

Theo: A fabulous woman, that Mara Selvini. The way she gets her message across, brilliant! She could read out of the telephone directory and I'd still listen to her all day!

Maria: A clear case of an idealized mother substitute. And it obviously makes it impossible for you to try to come to grips with her ideas rather than anything else. The enormous influence she has had on the family therapy scene isn't the result of how she puts things but of what she says.

Theo: She's a charismatic personality, that's all. And that's probably what makes her such a successful therapist. After all, being a good therapist is far more a matter of personal qualities than of the theories one happens to espouse.

Maria: You see? Just as I thought! You find her "fabulous" as a person and that's the end of it. In other words, what she does can only be done by her and by her alone. It can't be taught and it can't be learned. And that's all there is to it.

Theo: All right then, what did you think of what she was saying?

Maria: Pretty good, but nothing special. She just described the picture that emerges when one looks at an institution from a systemic perspective.

Theo: Well, I thought it was very good.

121

After this, the discussion became ever more trivial so that we can safely leave them to it for a moment. It wasn't in fact until they got round to Helm Stierlin's impossible performance that things livened up a little.

Theo: Psychoanalysis as a voracious mummy, isn't that how he put it? I would never have thought to hear him say such a thing. I had always been of the opinion that he was at pains to reconcile the systemic approach with psychoanalysis, and there he was laying into analysis like nobody's business. Did you notice? It got some people's backs up so much that they got up and left!

Maria: But I bet they didn't leave for the reason you suggest. To my mind he goes much too far in that direction. This constant concern of his to show that one position can be reconciled with another borders on the obsessive! All the controversies in the evolution of family therapy haven't been able to dislodge it one bit. In the end one just doesn't know where he stands.

The conversation had now taken an interesting turn. To get to the crux of the matter we can summarize the next few stages of it as follows: The criticism of an integrative approach was made more concrete and questions of the therapeutic relevance of all kinds of integration concepts came up for review (along the lines of "fish is good, chocolate sauce is good, just think how good fish with chocolate sauce must be"). Apart from ideological differences the main point at issue was how to deal with affects in therapy and how the influence of the past is to be evaluated.

Theo: I simply refuse to look upon man as nothing but a kind of thermostat-regulated heating system. That's what I don't like about your systemic approach. It's downright reductionist; for you, people are just machines. What about the affective aspect, what about history? This big thing of yours about circularity is just a negation of the past. The past is never over and done with, it is ever-present, in every moment of our lives. And the more you try to keep it at arms length instead of facing up to it squarely, the stronger that influence becomes. And that's what Norman Paul said very clearly in his lecture.

Maria: Systemic models aren't that, you know! Nobody would dream of denying that the past has an effect on the present. But what very often tends to get ignored is the fact that the present has an effect on the past as well. To put it more precisely, the effect of the past on the present is the effect of our image of the past. And it is an image we are constantly reshaping and reevaluating in the present. That's why history is always being rewritten, individual history, family history, social history. So it's not a question of an objective past, which nobody can claim to know anyway, but of various subjective views of the past. All our discussions seem to gravitate in the last resort around the question of how real reality is. And anyone who assumes that there is such a thing as a reality that exists objectively, independently of the observer, is bound to find most systemic therapy strategies mechanistic.

Theo: For me the approach to the affective element, how this is dealt with and integrated, is one of the central problems of human development, both individually and collectively. And that means that this element must be an essential factor in any kind of therapy. The only way that change can be achieved is via insight into the conditions of one's own development. If the processes involved in mourning and bereavement, say, are negated or suppressed, then there can be no delimitation, no individuation, no development, in individuals, families, or society.

Maria: Very impressive your profession of faith! "Ex cathedra," as it were. If that's your view and your definition of therapy, then you're bound to pursue a therapeutic approach in which your main concern is with the past. But if one happens to see therapy as a joint quest for and development of problem-solving strategies in crisis situations, then it usually makes more sense to concentrate on the present. If you spend all your time struggling to remember, then it's going to blind you to the possibilities of shaping the future.

By this time, Doc, laden with parcels, had joined the other two. His commentary was laconic: "It looks to me like you mean two different things when you talk of therapy. And you're probably after different things as well—the one affects, the other effects!"

"How Can I Make My Patients as Chronic as Possible?" A Science Fiction Fable

Fritz B. Simon and Gunthard Weber

Once upon a time, in the dim and distant future, all the people working in the field of psychotherapy and psychiatry were family therapists. Systemic thinking was part of their basic training. Everybody knew that so-called psychic illness could always be correctly understood and properly treated in a systemic context.

The upshot of this was that therapy was disconcertingly successful, "disconcertingly," of course, because therapists, just like anybody else, have got to earn a living somehow.

When it became obvious for all concerned that the future of the whole profession was at stake, the Chamber of Family Therapists, the association of doctors working in this area, appointed a scientific commission to analyze the situation and also present proposals as to how the disaster facing the whole body of therapists might best be averted.

We should like to outline the central proposals made by the commission. As it was a commission made up entirely of family therapists, there is presumably no need to emphasize that their proposals were founded above all upon considerations of a systems-theoretical nature.

The members were unanimous that all individual measures should be geared to the major ultimate objective: ensuring that there would always be an adequate number of patients available. They were equally unanimous in their verdict that the best thing would be to try to devise a kind of dearth-prevention scheme that would ensure that families developed in such a way as to guarantee patient-production. As the possibilities of exerting direct influence on the families themselves appeared restricted, it was necessary to concentrate on the context of social institutions surrounding the families.

As much as sports clubs encourage talented children and promising young performers from an early stage, it should be equally feasible to systematically train individual children who differed from the norm in any way in their early youth so as to prepare them for a career as patients. Like the skiing institutes that exist in Alpine countries to nurture gifted young skiers, it should be possible to establish boarding and finishing schools for children and young people of special aptitude, providing them with the very best in patienthood training that could be made available. And thus the idea of clinics for child and adolescent psychiatry was born. To achieve as broad a spread as possible in these training activities, the establishment of so-called educational advice centers as well as youth and school psychology services was proposed. The ulterior motive here was to ensure an adequate "labeling effect." The existence of such centers would make it possible for an official body, that is, an authority from outside the family, to allocate to the relevant member of a given family the role of patient. This official conferring of patient status would then have a long-term intrafamiliar effect.

And yet all these dearth-prevention measures still seemed inadequate. The only real solution was to create a form of institution that would guarantee chronic patienthood to as reliable a degree as possible.

If one regards the acute symptoms manifested by a patient as the expression of a family crisis which cannot be resolved by the family itself with the help of its own conventional resources, then one has the choice of two strategies for tackling that crisis. One of these is to attempt to change the family structures in such a way as to enable all members of it to develop without producing symptoms of any kind and without any one member being saddled with the role of "sick person" for the duration. This strategy was dismissed out of hand by the commission as being patently unsuitable. The second way of tackling the family problem was that of singling out one member of it and declaring him or her to be the problem, that is, defining that member as the patient. Putting the person in a so-called psychiatric clinic would then of course offer a number of advantages. The therapists would be seeing the patient alone and in isolation only. His behavior should not need to be related to family structures and those family structures themselves would not have to be called into question. This in itself was a powerful argument. But the objection that was quickly voiced was that liberation from the family might lead to the clinic proving to be a successful "therapeutic milieu" for the patient. If that were the case, the whole operation would have been pointless. This was a substantial objection that obviously could not be dismissed out of hand. And it led logically to the next proposal: structuring the clinic in such a way that it matched the structures within the family as nearly as possible. At all events, the clinic must provide *no* reason whatsoever for the patient to change.

Schooled as it was in circular and systemic thinking, the commission found it an easy task to make concrete proposals. All that was necessary was to apply what was already known about dysfunctional families to the planning and organization of psychiatric institutions. But this was where the trouble started. After all, it wasn't as if dysfunctional structures were all more or less identical. Should one take families with particularly rigid structures as a model or rather those in which total confusion reigns because there aren't any halfway permanent structures detectable at all? Which was better, regimentation or anarchy?

As usual when there is disagreement, both were tried out. Some clinics were organized with a very rigid set of structures. They presented a well-defined hierarchic pattern and clearly prescribed roles. Attempting to cross the frontiers erected by this allocation of roles was strictly prohibited. At the apex of the hierarchy were the senior ward attendants and doctors, presenting an approximate counterpart to authoritarian fathers in families. One rung lower on the ladder were the caring, understanding mothers, that is, the younger nurses, male nurses, and medical staff. And at the very bottom of the hierarchy were those cast to play the role of irresponsible children—the patients. Whether they were genuinely ill or just being naughty was really beside the point. One way or the other they had to be watched over. This model was termed custodial psychiatry; its guiding principle was rigidity. Isolation from the outside world was a further feature of this model, just as in families that have organized themselves into fortresses. They were far away from all contacts that might cause disturbance or disruption, hedged off, secluded, fearful of any kind of nearness or proximity, splendid in their isolation. They were similar in many ways to families in which individual members were very clearly separated from one another, where the generation gap was uncrossable and the emotional involvement between the members was almost non-existent. In the literature on family therapy there were plenty of terms in currency to describe such families: disengagement, emotional divorce, expelling, distance-sensitivity.

The contrasting model (which, incidentally, fulfilled its function equally efficiently) was the so-called social-psychiatric approach. The first commandment, to be observed at all times in clinics organized along social-psychiatric lines, was: There shall be no rules. Here was thus no clear-cut hierarchy, all role patterns were called into question, demarcation was declared to be a betrayal of the common cause, the motto "We'll always stick together" was the guiding principle of all activity. Accordingly, it was never clear who was a patient and who a therapist, who was a healer and who a sufferer. The role of the doctor and his opinion had as much influence—and no more—than that of anybody else on the ward. Being nice to one another was a value and an end in itself, one that was not allowed to be queried by reference to such profane questions as what use it was supposed to be. In short, it was the image of a family where relationships are strongly intertwined, mutual binding is thought highly of, and individual needs are looked upon as something immoral. To make the anomie complete, demarcation of a spatial character was also jettisoned. The wards were not supposed to look as if they were part of a clinic. Cafeterias, tearooms, and sitting rooms were taken as a model. The clinics were brought into the community, all the better to replace such petit bourgeois trappings as livingrooms or bedrooms. The clinic was the ideal, a superior home away from home.

Of course, as interpersonal relations are considerably more complex and ambivalent than can be accounted for by such simple organizational designs, pseudo-hostility was an immediate feature in the clinics modeled around the first approach. For despite all the clarity of demarcation and separation, everybody knew that mutual dependence was unavoidable. With the second model, with its emphasis on the harmony aspect, precisely the opposite occurred—pseudo-mutuality. As nobody can ever do nothing but good to his fellow men, the staff working on this highly demanding and involving model began to develop a clandestine resentment vis-à-vis their own patients. In both cases, conceding the existence of such ambivalence would have been tantamount to calling the respective models radically into question. It was obvious that in the custodial model the positive feelings that the staff had for their patients had to be denied, whereas in the case of the social-psychiatric approach the same was true of the negative feelings. The contradictory functions of psychiatric institutions caring on the one hand and controlling on the other were given a different emphasis on either side.

It was thus possible, without too much trouble or any specific initiation, for the clinics to bring about successfully the same kind of communicative disturbances that are found in dysfunctional families. Communication had to take place simultaneously on various levels. On the one level hostility (or harmony) was the basis of communication, on the other just the opposite. On the one level attempts were made to control, but this was largely doomed to failure because everyone was trying to be caring at the same time. The same thing held vice versa: The attempt to be caring was torpedoed by the necessity of control.

The real advantage of the whole thing was, according to the family therapy experts who made up the reform commission, that after a while nobody would be able to remember how these clinics had originated. The patients, once safely excised out of their family context, would be regarded as individuals again, their madness traced back to factors located within themselves (schizococcus infection, Vitamin C deficiency, etc.). This development would succeed best if the patients would keep things at such a pitch (via tantrums, attempted suicide, etc.) that the therapists would never have the time to sit back and think things over quietly. Habitual overstrain would ensure that nobody would start reflecting on the conditions prevailing in a system that keeps patients' symptoms constant despite all efforts to the contrary. Paradoxical as it may sound, cutting down on staff would in the long run lead to the creation of more jobs in the therapy work. If there were sufficient staff, someone somewhere might start asking questions and—perish the thought—rediscover the old family therapy strategies. Unless, that is, new areas of activity could be opened up.

And, indeed, restricting activity to the institutions meant curtailing the possibilities of achieving optimum chronicity. Worse still, it involved very real dangers for the whole program. In some way there was obviously going to have to be cooperation between families and psychiatrists, to keep the revolving door in motion. Only as long as psychiatry could convincingly claim to be therapeutic, that is, to institute change, would families refrain from resorting to their own resources for change. Again a paradox on the face of it: Only the reputation for bringing about change could ensure absolute stability in the long term. The idea that something is changing must trigger ambivalent feelings. Change is an opportunity and a risk at one and the same time. As long as the therapists were on the side of change, the patients could stay on the side of resistance. Thus ambivalence was preserved and things stayed as they were.

At this point in the debate, the commission came up with a proposal of pure genius. Some way must be found of fudging the difference between the context "family" and "psychiatry," some way of making therapists into family members and family members into therapists. Thus was born the idea of Relatives' Groups, which would also be defined as the psychoeducational approach. It brilliantly united the optimum chronicity of custodial psychiatry with the advantages of social psychiatry. As, in terms of the social functioning of the individual, family and psychiatry have very similar roles to play anyway, it was not too difficult to train relatives to behave like deputy therapists. This ensured that the patients were never sure whether they were dealing with normal people or psychiatrists. Is this nurse my sister or is my sister only a nurse? In this way it was possible to consistently prevent clear definition of relationships, and all in the name of so-called relapse prophylaxis.

But even after much care had been taken to prevent things from changing too fast in psychiatric institutions and in families as well, the commission continued to be worried. After all, there could still be some psychiatric patients who might successfully apply for jobs and, notwithstanding all the precautions taken, secure their financial independence and autonomy.

Therefore, a subcommittee concerned with matters of work and employment proposed to apply also in the work domain the strategy of "tiny steps" that had made the psychoeducational approach so successful. Accordingly, besides the network of therapeutic institutions, day clinics, halfway houses, therapeutic communities, and the like, there came to exist a chain of rehabilitation outfits, occupational therapy centers, and protected workshops. The government that was in charge at that time supported this scheme wholeheartedly. In this way, the number of the unemployed could be made to appear smaller than it was, and additional jobs for therapists could be created.

The commission closed its endeavors with one essential insight. Whatever institutional form was selected for implementation of optimum chronicity strategies—custodial, community psychiatry, relatives' recruitment, rehabilitation, or whatever—a medical illness model or a concept of deficiency was always an essential basis. It would be in the interests of all those involved as it would not only absolve the families of guilt but—far more important—the patients and therapists as well. Being free of guilt means being free of responsibility. And if you have no responsibility, then you can't have any influence either, and above all you can't change anything. And that's the moral of this fable, one which by the way closes like they all do. Everything happened just as the commission said it should and they all (therapists, relatives and patients, institutions and families) lived happily ever after, some more so, others less so. And if they haven't died out by then, that's what's really going to happen. Or should one say that's the way things are going to stay?

Family Environment and the Etiology of Schizophrenia: Implications from the Finnish Adoptive Family Study of Schizophrenia

Pekka Tienari, Anneli Sorri, Ilpo Lahti,
Mikko Naarala, Karl-Erik Wahlberg, Tuula
Rönkkö, Juha Moring, and Jukka Pohjola

The notion that disordered family relationships may be a significant factor in the development of schizophrenia is not new. The mother–child relationship in particular has been hypothesized to be disturbed, and early clinical studies of the mothers of schizophrenics seemed to confirm this hypothesis of the "schizophrenogenic" mother, as it was subsequently termed. Further research broadened the concept of parental influence to include the father as well. But with the appearance of more sophisticated views of family relationships, notions of single parent–child relationships were considered oversimplified conceptualizations, and the emphasis was placed on disturbances in the total family system instead.

Most works have uniformly studied family interaction patterns only after the diagnosis of schizophrenia in an offspring and, in many instances, following treatment. Only a limited number of studies have employed control groups permitting the direct linkage of family variables with schizophrenia as opposed to other forms of pathology. And many of those did not involve direct observations of family interaction but instead made inferences about interaction on the basis of observations of the behavior of family members in individual test situations (6).

The difficulty of establishing an etiologic role for family variables in the development of schizophrenia was considered evident by Reiss (8) in his summary of the scientific requirements for such a demonstration. First, the hypothesized variable must be clearly defined and measured by a reliable and objective method. Second, the causal role of the variable must be assessed by demonstrating that it (1) is specifically linked with schizophrenia as opposed to other conditions and states, (2) has an impact on the individual before the onset of schizophrenia, and (3) is not confounded with a covarying or concomitant variable that is a "true" etiologic variable.

We agree that the study of differences between the families of schizophrenic patients and other families provides an important starting point for identifying family variables, but we cannot answer questions about the position of the family variables in causal sequences. The recent trend to incorporate family studies within a risk research paradigm stems primarily from the recognition of this point (3). Earlier, before the risk research studies were begun, the question of the direction of effects was discussed by Mishler and Waxler (7). They distinguished an "etiologic" interpretation, in which the family patterns existed prior to the development of schizophrenia; a "responsive" interpretation, in which the family behaviors followed and appeared to be adaptive to the illness; and a "situational" interpretation dependent on differential orientations of families to the hospital, the investigator, or the research setting. The three interpretations all involved a linear concept of causality and need to be differentiated from the transactional theory, in which causality is understood in terms of reciprocal determinants and feedback models viewed within an unfolding developmental context (2).

Two main alternative strategies for sampling data on family relationships at a given time have been used. First, some studies have called for the examination of communicational patterns of key relatives (parents or spouses of the schizophrenic). This strategy is based on the hypothesis that the enduring patterns of communication and relationships sampled in the tests and interviews of key relatives can be inferred or will be significant indicators of the relatives' behavior when they are with the identified patient or the subject at risk. This work emphasizes two constructs: "communication deviance," thus far studied as a possible parental precursor of schizophrenia in an offspring; and "expressed emotion," studied as a parent or spouse predictor of later relapse of schizophrenia. Second, members of the entire family or at least the triad of the parents and the identified patient offspring have been in direct interaction and communication with one another (21).

Wynne et al. (21) showed that the frequency of communication deviances as scored in individual Rorschach records of parents was significantly greater in families with a schizophrenic offspring. This relationship varied directly with severity of disorder in the offspring. Interestingly, the communication deviance scores of the offspring (who were overtly psychotic) were lower than those of their nonschizophrenic parents. If one hypothesizes that communication deviances in one family member may engender similar deviances in the other family members, this finding suggests that the primary direction of effects could be from the parents to the offspring, not the reverse. This finding is in contrast to the common assumption that the disturbed communication of schizophrenics may induce deviance in parental communication. At any rate, the findings do underline the important point that the communication deviance measure is not identical with measures of clinical psychopathology (21).

Studying the communication of families at varying degrees of risk for the development of schizophrenia in an offspring constitutes another method for examining the role of parental communication deviance in the development of schizophrenia. The primary question addressed by such analyses has typically been: Are the disorders that have been found in the communications of the parents of schizophrenics also present in the communications of the parents of children or adolescents who are at high risk for schizophrenia? By studying families before the onset of schizophrenia, the investigator attempts to minimize the effects of the schizophrenic child on the family system and thus to rule out the responsive hypothesis as an explanation for the existence of parental communication deviance in families where schizophrenia has already been diagnosed in the offspring. Several high-risk studies have recently been reported that make use of data collected at the first stage of an extensive longitudinal investigation of the family and schizophrenia (17).

Prospective longitudinal designs offer the greatest advantage for examining the temporal relationship between the characteristics of family interaction and the development of schizophrenia in children. As Reiss (8) pointed out, however, to establish an etiologic role for the family in the development of schizophrenia, it is not simply enough to demonstrate that deviant family interaction precedes the onset of the disorder in the child. It must also be shown that family variables and psychopathology in children are not spuriously related. For example, it has been suggested that the common finding of the relationship between parental communication deviance and the presence of schizophrenia in an offspring may be genetically determined: both the degree of parental communication deviance and the risk for schizophrenia in the child are products of a common genetic heritage. A study of adopted children makes it possible to differentiate between genetics and environment, because the biological parents give the genetic properties and the adoptive parents the rearing environment.

MATERIAL AND METHODS

A nationwide sample has been collected of all women in Finland hospitalized because of schizophrenia. The sample, which includes both consecutive admissions and resident population, consists of 19,447 schizophrenic women (16). Through registers it has been found that 289 offspring of 263 schizophrenic women were officially adopted away. Of these 289 offspring, 196 were placed in Finnish nonrelative families before they reached the age of 5 years (143, or 73% before the age of 2 years). Our clinical study has been focused on the offspring (and their adoptive families) who were born in 1970 or earlier; in other words, those who are now at the age of risk for schizophrenia.

These subjects were blindly compared with matched control offspring and their adoptive families, that is, adopted-away offspring of biological parents who had not been hospitalized because of psychosis. The matching was made by people from outside our institute who were given the matching criteria and who carried out the procedure independently. The adoptive index and the control series were numbered randomly in such a way that the four psychiatrists conducting the personal interviews were blind as to whether this was an index or a control family (11, 14).

The adoptive index and control families were investigated in their homes directly and intensively with procedures that usually take two days (14–16 hours). The family relationships are studied through family and couple interviews as well as the Consensus Rorschach and the Interpersonal Perception Method (4). Both the adoptive parents and the offspring are interviewed personally and the Individual Rorschach is given after the Consensus Rorschach. In the adoptive families, the MMPI (Minnesota Multiphasic Personality Inventory) is given only to the adopted offspring. An abbreviated version of the WAIS (Wechsler Adult Intelligence Scales) is used for screening intellectual deficiencies, various visual and other perceptual disorders, and organic difficulties. We have also started personal interviews and testing of the biological parents. Of the biological index mothers (hospitalized because of schizophrenia) 85 have already been interviewed as well as given the Present State Examination, the Individual Rorschach Test and the MMPI (14, 15).

All the interviews and the test examinations are tape-recorded. This makes it possible for other investigators to carry out blind ratings later.

PRELIMINARY RESULTS

We had by May 1985 contacted about 270 adoptive families for field-work, and 249 had been preliminary scored. We must point out that all the preliminary results at this phase are very tenuous, because not all the families have been interviewed yet.

Mental Health Ratings of Adoptive Offspring

The mental health ratings of the offspring are shown separately in the index group and in the control group for the 102 pairs in which the index cases and their matched controls had been investigated (see Table 1). We see that of the 8 psychotic cases 7 are offspring of schizophrenics and only 1 a control offspring. One of the psychotic index cases received the diagnosis of manic-depressive psychosis, 5 are schizophrenics, and 1 has paranoid psychosis. There is hence an overall trend for the offspring of schizophrenics to be more disturbed than the offspring of controls (one-tailed sign test .0377). The total number of severe diagnoses, 31.4% in the index group and 15.7% in the control group, corresponds to the findings of Rosenthal et al. (9).

Family Mental Health Ratings

The total interview material was used on ratings of the mental health of the families as well. We used five classes based on global ratings:

1. *Healthy:* In healthy families anxiety usually is slight and the boundaries between individuals and generations and to the outside world are clearly defined. Primitive transactional defenses are not used and interaction is unambiguous and mutual. There is no overt or chronic transactional conflict in the family. Receptiveness is open and empathy consistent.

2. *Mildly disturbed family:* There may be transient transactional conflicts and observable mild anxiety or depressive moods. Primitive transactional defenses are seldom used. The boundaries between the generations and to the outside world are clear. The reality testing of the family is good.

3. *Neurotic family:* There exists an unresolved transactional conflict of mild or moderate severity. The interpersonal patterns in the family are clear but to some extent restricted and repetitive. The boundaries between the generations and to the outside world are clear. Reality testing by the family is good.

4. *Rigid syntonic families:* Analogously to the ego-syntonic functioning

Table 1

MENTAL HEALTH RATINGS OF OFFSPRING
(Matched Pairs, as of 5/85)

Clinical Ratings of Offspring	Biologic Mothers	
	Index—Hospital Diagnosis of Schizophrenia	Controls
Healthy	1	9
Mild disturbance	45	44
Neurotic	26	33
Character disorder	14	10
"Borderline"	9	5
Psychotic	7	1
Total	102	102

One-tailed sign test .0377

of individuals, the family that is syntonic feels its way of coping is adequate, but others see it as disturbed or dysfunctional. A major family conflict is unresolved and unacknowledged. Overt anxiety is usually low. Family members draw a sharp boundary between experience within the family and outside the family. The boundaries *within* the family (between the generations and between individuals) are blurred. Family patterns do not change despite major life events and role changes (rigid homeostasis).

5. *Severely disturbed families:* Conflict is open and often chaotic. The level of anxiety is high and basic trust low. All boundaries are unstable and unclear between individuals, between generations, and between the family and the outside world. Agreement on reality (reality testing) is low. Primitive "transactional defenses" (such as projective identification and splitting) are common. Family patterns are seldom in stable equilibrium.

These features constitute an attempt to describe the most common characteristics of the families with the different ratings. We consider the following factors to contribute to our ratings: anxiety and its level; boundary functions between the individual members, between the generations, and to the outside world; parental coalition; quality of interaction; flexibility of homeostasis; "transactional defenses" (1); conflicts, empathy; power relations; role; reality testing; and basic trust.

If we look at those cases (Table 2) where both the index case and his

Table 2

MENTAL HEALTH RATINGS OF ADOPTIVE FAMILIES
(Matched Pairs Only, as of 5/85)

	Biologic Mothers	
Clinical Family Rating	Index	Control
Healthy	3 $\rbrace$ 40	9 $\rbrace$ 36
Mild disturbance	37	27
"Neurotic"	21	29
Rigid-syntonic	23 $\rbrace$ 40	30 $\rbrace$ 36
Chaotic	17	6
Total	101	101

Two-tailed sign test .4158

or her matched control family has been investigated (101 pairs), we can see that the number of severely disturbed families is higher in the index group, but the rigid syntonic families and "neurotic" families are slightly more common in the control group. The difference between the index and control families is not statistically significant ($p = .4158$, two-tailed sign test).

At this phase we can hardly make any interpretation of the possible differences in rearing environments. We wish to point out that in less than one third of the cases the mother had had her psychosis before the adoption. In most cases the psychotic symptoms of the mothers became manifest much later. It is therefore not likely that the biological mother's psychosis was a selective factor for the placement. One might, of course, also ask whether the vulnerable child might have an impact on his or her adoptive parents.

If we look at all of the 112 index cases thus far rated (Table 3), 7% have been diagnosed as psychotic, 16% as being either psychotic or borderline, and a total of 30% have received a severe diagnosis. In the subsample (43 offspring) that has been reared in seriously disturbed (rigid, syntonic, and severely disturbed) adoptive families, the figures are doubled: 16% for psychotics, 37% for psychotic and borderline together, and 65% for those having a severe diagnosis. In striking contrast, there is no psychotic, no borderline, and only three character disorder offspring reared in the 49 healthy or mildly disturbed adoptive families. This supports the hypothesis of interaction between heredity and environment.

In Table 4 the mental health ratings of the 112 index cases (offspring of schizophrenic mothers) are shown in relation to their adoptive families. The ratings of the children and the family ratings are not independent. The result is highly significant. We can see that of the eight psychotic subjects, one (manic depressive) grew up in a neurotic family, four in rigid syntonic families, and three in severely disturbed (chaotic) adoptive families. Also, all but one of the borderline patients grew up in seriously disturbed families. Note that there are no borderline or psychotic offspring who were reared in healthy or mildly disturbed families and only three mildly disturbed offspring who were reared in rigid-syntonic or severely disturbed (chaotic) adoptive families.

Our hypothesis that family rearing appears to be a protective factor is supported by the data showing that none of the 49 offspring of schizophrenic mothers who were reared in a healthy family environment or in a mildly disturbed family environment had schizophrenia or a borderline state, whereas 7 (16.3%) of the 43 offspring of schizophrenic mothers who were reared in the severely disturbed (rigid, syntonic, or chaotic) families became schizophrenic and 16 (37.2%) became psychotic or borderline when reared in a severely disturbed adoptive family.

The preliminary data on the adoptive families could be regarded as a result of this procedure, in which the same psychiatrist interviewed and

Table 3

INDEX ADOPTEES

(As of 12/84, Total $N = 112$)

Disturbed Offspring	(Total $N = 112$)	Percentage	Adoptive Family Rearing Environment			
			Seriously Disturbed ($N = 43$)		"Healthy" ($N = 49$)	
Psychotic	(8/112)	7.1%	(7/43)	16.3%	(0/49)	0%
Psychotic + "border-line"	(18/112)	16.1%	(16/43)	37.2%	(0.49)	0%
Psychotic + "border-line" + character disorder	(34/112)	30.4%	(28/43)	65.1%	(3/49)	6.1%

Table 4

CLINICAL RATINGS OF INDEX OFFSPRING AND THEIR ADOPTIVE FAMILIES

(All Index Cases Studies as of 12/84)

Clinical Ratings of Offspring	Clinical Ratings of Adoptive Families					
	Healthy 1	Mild Disturbance 2	"Neurotic" 3	Rigid, Syntonic 4	Severe 5	Total
1. Healthy	1	1	0	0	0	2
2. Mild disturbance	5	32	9	3	0	49
3. Neurotic	0	7	8	6	6	27
4. Character disorder	0	3	1	6	6	16
5. "Borderline"	0	0	1	5	4	10
6. Psychotic	0	0	1*	4	3	8
Total	6	43	20	24	19	112

*Manic-depressive adoptee.

Collapsing levels 1 + 2 and 4 + 5 in the adoptive family data, and levels 1 + 2 and 4 + 5 in the offspring data, $\chi^2 = 59.321$, df = 6, $p < .00005$.

tested both families as units and the individual family members. To obtain permission to see these families, the condition was that there was not to be more than one person to see each family. A question can therefore be raised as to whether the family interviews and ratings that were conducted first may have influenced the later ratings of the offspring. Several procedures can be used to evaluate this possibility of a halo effect that may have biased the rating of the offspring.

One methodological check was carried out using the MMPIs obtained from the adoptive offspring. The MMPI ratings were assessed blindly by a psychologist who was not aware of the clinical data on the families or the mental health ratings made for the offspring themselves. The offspring who were individually classified as severely disturbed in their MMPIs had been reared significantly more often in disturbed adoptive families. The MMPI ratings of the offspring varied according to the independent clinical ratings of the adoptive families. The result was highly significant (12). The MMPI ratings of the offspring correspond significantly to the clinical ratings independently made of them (12). Further assessment along these lines will be carried out using other MMPI scoring procedures as well as the Individual Rorschach assessments of communication deviance and of thought disorder, in order to assess the individual characteristics of the adopted-away offspring separately insofar as possible from the family system evaluation.

We then applied independently the Beavers–Timberlawn family evaluation scales (5) to the Couple Consensus Rorschach only. A psychiatrist who had had no clinical contact with the families made these ratings of their functioning by listening only to the audiotape conversation of the adoptive parents trying to reach agreement on Rorschach percepts. Her global ratings did correspond highly significantly to the clinical ratings made by the psychiatrists who interviewed the same families. She was also able to predict highly significantly the global ratings of the offspring independently made (12). Of the different Beavers–Timberlawn scales, closeness, empathy, overt power, and coalitions did correlate with the adoptee's mental health ratings made independently on the basis of the clinical interviews (Table 5). Invasiveness, closeness, receptiveness (permeability), and empathy did correlate significantly with the clinical ratings of the adoptive families. It is noteworthy that the offspring is not present in the Couple Rorschach, so that his or her behavior does not bias this Consensus Rorschach rating.

The IPM (Interpersonal Perception Method) (4) makes use of 60 dyadic issues, around each of which 12 questions must be answered. Each member of the dyad answers the questions separately. The issues are presented

Table 5

**BLIND SPOUSE INTERACTION RATINGS VERSUS CLINICAL RATINGS
OF ADOPTIVE FAMILIES AND ADOPTEES**

Beavers–Timberlawn Scales for Rating Spouse Interaction	Adoptee Mental Health Ratings*	Clinical Ratings of Adoptive Families*
Closeness	.0007	.008
Empathy	.004	.025
Overt power	.035	.135
Coalitions	.045	.134
Invasiveness	.054	.001
Receptiveness	.055	.024
Range of feelings	.065	.143
Unresolved conflict	.245	.093
Mythology	.096	.061

*p values of χ^2 for each Beavers–Timberlawn Scale (trends in 9 of 13 scales).

as phrases that express interaction and interexperience. All can be used with self and self–other reference. Each point of view is directed to relationships. In the test the individual is asked, in some central matters, to express his own direct view of the matter, to postulate the way in which his partner experiences the same matter, and to conjecture what the other thinks his view of this matter to be. When reciprocally matched comparison is used the profile that the technique discloses is the profile of the relationship between two points of view: (1) the comparison between one person's view and another's on the same issue tells us whether they are in agreement or disagreement; (2) if one person is aware of the other's point of view, we say he understands him, and if he fails to recognize the other's point of view, we say he misunderstands. Several IPM variables also correlated significantly with the mental health ratings of the adoptive families based on clinical interviews (12).

DISCUSSION

In earlier adoption studies, rearing variables were studied in a very limiting manner, focusing mainly on the hypothesis that the diagnosis of rearing parent is a rearing variable. Our results seem to support the hypothesis that even in families where one of the parents is severely disturbed, the other can balance the situation a lot (12). When Wynne, Singer, and their co-workers (19, 20) used the parental "communication deviance" measure with Wender et al.'s (18) Rorschach protocols, they were able to discriminate blindly the two groups of rearing parents (*both* the biological parents who reared their schizophrenic offspring *and* the adoptive parents who reared a schizophrenic) from the parents who reared normal adoptees. No adoption study of schizophrenia has thus far reported data using direct family relationship measures. Rosenthal et al. (10) assessed the quality of the relationship between the child and his or her adoptive parents on the basis of the individual interview data of the children. The degree of psychopathological disorder in the child was then correlated with the quality of the parent–child relationship.

Interaction of genetic and family environmental factors can be interpreted in several alternative ways. There is a possibility that genetic factors are specific and necessary and might interact with nonspecific environmental factors. Another possibility is that genetic factors are nonspecific and contribute to vulnerability not only to schizophrenia but also to a broader class of psychopathology. Genetically transmitted vulnerability may be a necessary precondition for schizophrenia, but a disturbing rearing environment may also be necessary to transform the vulnerability into clinically overt schizophrenia.

Healthy family rearing can also be a protective factor for a child at risk. There is a further possibility that the genetic vulnerability of the offspring manifests itself in a way that is disturbing to the adoptive family. The "direction of effects," that is, whether greater weight should be attributed to genetic vulnerability versus family disturbance, will need to be examined more definitively through the longitudinal combination of the adoptive family strategy and the risk research strategy for studying families prospectively, beginning before the onset of illness in the offspring.

The major goal of our adoptive family study is assessing genetic and family-rearing contributions to schizophrenia and other psychopathology. We are interested in seeing the extent to which genetic and family environmental variables interact to determine the outcome of the adoptees and their impairments and strengths during development. We would also like to elucidate whether the genetic risk is reduced by a protective family environment. And we would like to know whether the direction of effects between genetic and family-environmental factors can be clarified through prospective longitudinal study of adoptees at risk.

In the 102 pairs where both the index and control families have been investigated and rated thus far, the total number of severe diagnoses (psychosis, borderline, character disorder) is 31.4% (30/102) in the index group and 15.7% (16/102) in the matched control group. Of the eight psychotic cases, seven are offspring of schizophrenics and only one is control offspring. However, no seriously disturbed offspring has been found in a healthy or mildly disturbed adoptive family, and those offspring who were psychotic or seriously disturbed were nearly all reared in seriously disturbed adoptive families. This combination of findings supports the hypothesis that a possible genetic vulnerability interacts with the adoptive rearing environment.

REFERENCES

1. Alanen, Y. (1980). In search of the interactional origin of schizophrenia. In C. Hofling & J. Lewis (Eds.), *The family evaluation and treatment*. New York: Brunner/Mazel.
2. Dell, P. (1980). Researching the family theories of schizophrenia: An exercise in epistemological confusion. *Family Process, 19*: 321–335.
3. Goldstein, M. (1985). Family factors that antedate the onset of schizophrenia. The results of a fifteen year prospective longitudinal study. *Acta Psychiatrica Scandinavica, 71* (Suppl. 319): 7–18.
4. Laing, R. D., Phillipson, H., & Lee, A. R. (1966). *Interpersonal perception: A theory and a method of research*. London: Tavistock.
5. Lewis, J. M., Beavers, W. R., Gosset, J. T., & Phillips, V. A. (1976). *No single thread: Psychological health in family systems*. New York: Brunner/Mazel.
6. Liem, J. H. (1980). Family studies of schizophrenia: An update and commentary. *Schizophrenia Bulletin, 6*: 429–455.
7. Mishler, E. G., & Waxler, N. E. (1968). Family interaction and schizophrenia: Alternative frameworks of interpretation. In D. Rosenthal & S. S. Kety (Eds.), *The transmission of schizophrenia*. London: Pergamon Press.
8. Reiss, D. (1976). The family and schizophrenia. *American Journal of Psychiatry, 133*, 181–185.
9. Rosenthal, D., Wender, P., Kety, S. S., Welner, J., & Schulsinger, F. (1971). The adopted-away offspring of schizophrenics. *American Journal of Psychiatry, 128*: 307–311.
10. Rosenthal, D., Wender, P. H., Kety, S. S., Schulsinger, F., Welner, J., & Rieder, R. O. (1975). Parent–child relationship and psychopathological disorder in the child. *Archives of General Psychiatry, 32*: 466–476.
11. Tienari, P., Lahti, I., Naarala, M., Sorri, A., Pohjola, J., Kaleva, M., & Wahlberg, K. E. (1985). Biologic mothers in the Finnish Adoptive Family Study: Alternative definitions to schizophrenia. In P. Pichot, P. Berner, R. Wolf, & K. Thau (Eds.), *Psychiatry* (Vol. 1). New York: Plenum.
12. Tienari, P., Sorri, A., Lahti, I., Naarala, M., Wahlberg, K. E., & Moring, J. (1985). Interaction of genetic and psychosocial factors in schizophrenia. *Acta Psychiatrica Scandinavica, 71* (Suppl. 319): 19–30.
13. Tienari, P., Sorri, A., Lahti, I., Naarala, M., Wahlberg, K. E., Moring, J., Pohjola, J., & Wynne, L. C. (1985). The Finnish adoptive study of schizophrenia. *Yale Journal of Biology and Medicine, 58*: 227–237.

14. Tienari, P., Sorri, A., Lahti, I., Naarala, M., Wahlberg, K. E., Moring, J., Pohjola, J., & Wynne, L. C. (1985). Interaction of genetic and psychosocial factors in schizophrenia. The Finnish adoptive family study: A longitudinal combination of the adoptive family strategy and the risk research strategy. *Schizophrenia Bulletin* (in press).
15. Tienari, P., Sorri, A., Naarala, M., Lahti, Boström, C., & Wahlberg, K. E. (1981). The Finnish adoptive family study. Family-dynamic approach on psychosomatics. A preliminary report. *Psychiatric and Social Science Review I:* 107–115.
16. Tienari, P., Sorri, A., Naarala, M., Lahti, I., Pohjola, J., Boström, C., & Wahlberg, K. E. (1983). The Finnish Adoptive Family Study: Adopted-away offspring of schizophrenic mothers. In H. Stierlin, L. C. Wynne, & M. Wirsching (Eds.), *Psychosocial intervention in schizophrenia*. Berlin: Springer-Verlag.
17. Watt, N. F., et al. (1984). *Children at risk for schizophrenia: A longitudinal perspective*. New York: Cambridge University Press.
18. Wender, P. H., Rosenthal, D., & Kety, S. S. (1968). A psychiatric assessment of the adoptive parents of schizophrenics. In D. Rosenthal & S. S. Kety (Eds.), *The transmission of schizophrenia*. London: Pergamon Press.
19. Wynne, L. C., Singer, M. T., Bartko, J. J., & Toohey, M. L. (1977). Schizophrenics and their families: Recent research on parental communiction. In J. M. Tanner (Ed.), *Developments in psychiatric research*. London: Hodder & Stoughton.
20. Wynne, L. C., Singer, M. T., & Toohey, M. L. (1976). Communication of the adoptive parents of schizophrenics. In J. Jorstad & E. Ugelstad (Eds.), *Schizophrenia 75: Psychotherapy, family studies, research*. Oslo: Universitetsforlaget.
21. Wynne, L. C., Toohey, M. L., & Doane, J. (1979). Family studies. In L. Bellak (Ed.), *Disorders of the schizophrenic syndrome*. New York: Basic Books.

The Family in
Individual Therapy

Theodore Lidz

I am very pleased and proud to have been invited to celebrate the tenth anniversary of a department that has had not simply a broad but a profound influence on psychotherapy. I assume that a major reason I am here, even though my contributions to the techniques of family therapy have been minimal, is to represent the fathers—perhaps more properly the grandfathers—of family therapy. In the beginning there were Nathan Ackerman, Don Jackson, and me—there probably were others, but we were the ones who were writing and exploring—all psychoanalysts whose interests in families and promulgation of family therapy were not very well received by our psychoanalytic colleagues. I believe that Nathan Ackerman initially had the most profound influence and though I often disagreed with his therapy, I am sorry indeed that he and Don Jackson are not alive to be with us today.

My own interest in the importance of the family to psychodynamic theory and psychotherapy goes back to my work with schizophrenic patients and their families in 1940. The first systematic research on the families of schizophrenic patients was carried out by Dr. Ruth Lidz and me but was interrupted by World War II and not published until 1949 (16)—but my interest at that time was that of a psychopathologist as much as of a psychotherapist. When, however, our group at Yale started our intensive study of the families of schizophrenic patients, we became involved in family therapy almost immediately. Family therapy need not be conjoint family therapy, and I still believe that it can sometimes be more effective when the family members are treated separately or in pairs, depending on the circumstances. Indeed, as I shall discuss presently, I have come to believe that all psychotherapy, including psychoanalysis, should involve a major focus on the patient's family of origin, for all patients have emerged from a family that guided or misguided their development, and whose ways, loving care, rejections, conflicts, styles of communication, and parental models for identification and internalized parents remain an essential part of them for better or worse, even beyond their own lives on into those of their children. Perhaps the first, but surely one of the first, formal conjoint family therapy sessions was carried out in 1952 with one of the initial families in our schizophrenia project. The patient—the designated patient, if you will—was a young woman in her first semester of college who was truly hebephrenic—giggling, muttering a sort of word salad, and often rolling on the floor asking to be "fucked" (20, pp. 181–182, 319–320). Today, from the work of Brown and colleagues (3, 4) and Vaughn and Leff (28) that has demonstrated the prognostic value of hostile and critical remarks of parents, we would know that the young woman's prognosis was grim. At the admission interview, her mother could not recognize her daughter's pathetic and desperate condition, for she said, "There's nothing really wrong with her, she's just a little stinker. She thinks she's a queen and wants everything her own way."

Nevertheless, with a very good therapist, a good therapeutic milieu, and the absence of neuroleptic drugs, the patient soon emerged from her hebephrenic state and talked about how her mother refused to recognize her problems or even listen to her when she sought advice. The patient would weep with despair as she talked about her mother's aloofness, indifference, and lack of guidance. We decided to set up a meeting between the patient and her parents—her older sister refused to participate— together with the patient's psychiatrist and the family's social worker. I watched from behind a one-way mirror. Aided by her therapist, the patient poured out her feelings very coherently, telling about her problems with roommates at college, her confusion about sex, and her parents' refusal to listen to pleas for guidance. It was a very moving session, until in the midst of the patient's anguished pleas and tears of despair, the mother nonchalantly tugged at her waist and said to her social worker, "My dress is getting tight, could you have someone here place me on a diet?" I witnessed an instantaneous relapse into hebephrenia. We did not give up; the patient improved and we had another family session. This time, under similar circumstances, the mother looked out of the window and said, "I think it will rain tonight," and we witnessed another relapse. The patient did not recover, and it took a year until we recovered and tried conjoint therapy again. We were then inexperienced and unprepared to counter the mother's defensive need to ignore and even less prepared to utilize it beneficially.

My basic interest was the study of schizophrenic disorders from which

I would not let myself be diverted into explorations of techniques of family therapy. However, we believed that effective treatment of schizophrenic patients—and we were having considerable success—required modifications of the patient's family as well as the patient's attitudes toward the family. However, we found these families difficult to modify greatly or even sufficiently, and considerable effort went into releasing the patient from the family—not simply to be able to live away from the family, but to escape a parent's symbiotic needs and double-binding and to have the patient recognize that the parents' ways of perceiving and relating were confused and confusing, and were not the necessary way of living—a task complicated greatly by what Nagy (2) has termed the patient's "invisible loyalties."

Family therapy, particularly when used in combination with individual and group therapy, could be not only useful but critical in freeing the patient. A very chronic schizophrenic young woman had a "perfect mother" about whom she would not speak to her therapist, who had become aware that the mother had provided a fictitious picture of the family situation and fended off efforts to explore the real state of her marriage by her attitude of professional superiority. A critical change in the patient's understanding of her mother came during a family therapy session. The patient had spent a weekend at home for the first time in several years. When the therapist asked how the weekend had gone, the father replied, "Not too bad—only Eve spent too much time watching TV, and she wouldn't phone her brother." When the therapist turned to the patient, she said, "It was good to be home but it would have been nicer if my father hadn't criticized me so much," at which point the mother interrupted: "Your father never criticizes you!" The patient said nothing for a moment and then said, "You know, Mother, somehow I always feel tense when I'm with you." Her mother responded, "If you are, you're the only person I know who is uneasy when with me!" The patient remained silent, but on the basis of her experience in group therapy, recognized the bind in which her mother had placed her, as well as her mother's efforts to deny the validity of the patient's feelings. With her individual therapist, she ceased maintaining her silent loyalty to her mother and her acceptance of her mother's version of reality and began to trust her own perceptions and feelings. Thereafter, her progress was steady and after years of chronicity she went on to a virtual recovery.

The very apparent deficiencies of the families we were studying turned my attention to a simple question: Why does the family exist in all societies and what are its essential functions? And as we were finding that the communication in all of these families was difficult to understand, if not grossly aberrant, my attention turned to the study of the role of language in psychosocial development, and whether the family's problems in communicating might predispose an offspring to become schizophrenic. It seemed to me that before we went off in search of better and briefer ways of changing the family or its transactions, it would be useful to know the family's functions for both the spouses and children and what requisites a family needed to fulfill in order to form a suitable milieu in which its children could develop into reasonably integrated persons.

My first attempt was published in *The Family and Human Adaptation* (1963) published in German as *Die Familie und Psychosoziale Entwicklung* (1971) in which I pointed out that for children to develop into competent adults a number of prerequisites have to be fulfilled that had been largely overlooked because everywhere they were carried out almost unknowingly by the ubiquitous family. Of course, the child requires adequate nurturance, and parents had to change the nature of the nurture they provide in accord with the child's changing needs, which include fostering felicitous separation from the family by the end of adolescence, as Helm Stierlin (26) has examined so thoughtfully. Less obvious was the relation between the family structure and the child's personality integration; and I suggested that to provide the proper structure, the parents need to form a coalition in regard to their children, adhering to the generation boundaries and their respective gender-linked roles.The family also has the task of socializing the child, by conveying, largely through the behavior of its members, the basic social roles and the worth of the social institutions, along with what behaviors the society prescribes, permits, and proscribes. Fundamental, too, is the enculturation of the child through transmitting the adaptive techniques of the culture including its system of meanings and logic. The parents also properly provide models for identification to serve as guides into adulthood, and both of whom are internalized to a greater or lesser degree. Although the family has these and still other important functions for its children, it must be remembered that the family also subserves essential functions for the parents and for the society, both of which can, and to some extent always do, interfere with its child rearing. It also is obvious that parents often lack the emotional stability, knowledge, or a suitable marriage to provide these essential requisites for rearing children adequately. The orientation proposed can change profoundly the understanding of the etiology of psychiatric disorders and provide a firmer base for psychotherapy, including family therapy; indeed, it requires that a family orientation become central to all psychotherapy including psychoanalysis.

Critical to my orientation has been the recognition that the emergence of the human species depended largely on the acquisition of language, which, aside from improving collaboration with others and enabling reflective thought and foresight, gave humans the capacity to transmit what they learned across generations, so that learning became cumulative and peoples developed different sets of customs and techniques—different cultures—to live in different environments or under different social conditions. Like all other organisms the human physiological makeup permits existence only under certain environmental limits, but *Homo sapiens* can alter environments to meet these physiological limits. In brief, though the human species has been defined in many ways—as the talking animal, the symbolizing animal, the tool-bearing animal, and so on—the human is, in essence, the organism that cannot survive without assimilating a culture. The family is the primary conveyer of the society's culture, and its shortcomings in preparing its children to live in the society constitute a major source of psychopathology.

When our group at Yale related schizophrenic disorders to what we termed schismatic and skewed families (18), and Wynne's group (30) at the National Institute of Mental Health described closely related pseudo-mutual and pseudo-hostile families, and both of these research groups, as well as Bateson, Jackson, and colleagues (1), emphasized the abnormal communication patterns in these families—whether the pervasive irrationality (19), the amorphous or disruptive styles (24, 25, 31, 32), or the habitual double binds (1)—a new phase in psychopathology opened that related the type of psychopathology a person manifested to the transactions in the family in which the individual grew up, rather than primarily to fixation at and regression to a specific developmental phase. The orientation was not altogether new. Robert Knight (15) as well as Joseph Chassell (6) had previously related "essential alcoholism" to a fairly specific family background; Johnson and Szurek (14) linked sociopathy to superego defects in parents; Bruch and Touraine (5) traced the cause of marked obesity in children to a family configuration that developed over two or more generations. Later Cohen and a distinguished group of psychoanalytic colleagues (7) found a family pattern that gave rise to severe depressions. Both Minuchin's (22) study of families of the slums and Pavenstedt and Malone's (23) study of Boston housing project families revealed how disorganized families propagate themselves by producing children bereft of the culture's techniques of adaptation, including adequate linguistic capacities for self-direction or sufficient object constancy for relating to others meaningfully. Then, too, other such connections between a specific type of family milieu and a given psychopathology had been described: Hendin (12) for suicides among blacks in New York;

Stoller (27) for transsexuals; Wurmser (29) for narcotic addicts; Lidz et al. (21) for female amphetamine addicts; as well as still more recent studies of families of obsessive-compulsives (13).

The awareness that patients with these various psychiatric syndromes are very likely to have grown up in families with characteristic patterns should be critical to family therapists as well as individual therapists, but thus far, aside from those working with one or another of these specific types of patients, little attention has been given to the guidance these studies can provide.

I wish to turn now more specifically to the topic of the family in individual therapy. You will recall that Freud abjured treating patients who were still dependent on parents for he found he could not keep the parents from intervening or even disrupting the analysis. He did not, of course, consider working with the families—except in the case of Little Hans (10), or after he turned away from his seduction theory of focusing on the family as the source of a patient's problem as can be noted most clearly in his mishandling of Dora's therapy (9) and his misunderstanding of Schreber's schizophrenic condition (11). Anna Freud (8), however, clearly warned that psychiatrists, and particularly child psychiatrists, should not consider that all problems arise from purely intrapsychic conflicts but should pay attention to the environment, that is, family problems.

Family therapists have often tended to disregard the individual patient and have termed the patient who comes or is brought for therapy as the designated patient while considering the entire family as the patient. This orientation has advanced psychiatry in some ways, but in the opinion of conservatives like me has tended to overlook the fact that whereas changing the family transactions often can alleviate an individual's psychopathology, by the time most patients come to therapy the family transactions with which they grew up have become an integral part of their personalities and they have "internalized"—to use a questionable term—not just the parental figures but often the divergent directives of conflicting parents, and their personalities have been distorted by failures of the family to provide some of the requisites I have cited. Moreover, with many adult patients the family of origin is not available, and therapy with the family of procreation—the marital family—though it can be helpful, may miss the essential problems.

To overcome the problem that disheartened Freud, therapy with children and adolescents should often, perhaps usually, involve family therapy for the formative influences are still active and cannot be countered by working with the designated patient alone. Several years ago I was asked by a colleague to see a patient and her parents. The parents wished another opinion and the psychiatrist wished to know if I considered the patient—clearly borderline or, according to DSM-III, schizotypal—to be schizophrenic. Ellen was then 20 years old, seriously obsessive, and almost paralyzed by mysophobia and a handwashing compulsion as well as agoraphobia. She had made little progress in a year of therapy but was developing a trusting relationship with her therapist. Some six months later I saw the patient and her parents for a second time. When I went to the waiting room to bring the parents to my office, I was struck by the way they were sitting—as far apart as possible and oblivious of one another. When I spoke with them, they reluctantly admitted that they remained married primarily for the sake of the children. I informed Ellen's psychiatrist that I had the impression that the psychotherapy would make little progress without concomitant family therapy. I agreed to see the patient and her parents together (a sister was in another city).

The first session was illuminating. The father sat himself in the most comfortable chair, the patient in the other chair and closest to me—and the mother was left to sit in an uncomfortable position on the couch. The patient kept her head turned away from her parents and emanated resentment but said little while her parents spoke of their concerns about her—the father obviously desparately concerned. When I tried to have Ellen give her views of the family situation she refused; she insisted that there was nothing she could say, but her demeanor and tone expressed profound bitterness. Her mother said that Ellen looked and acted this way day after day, at least when she, the mother, was around. I commented that I could not speak for the parents, but I would think that they would prefer to hear why she was so angry rather than live with her sullen, silent resentment. The parents agreed. After Ellen demurred for a few minutes she burst out, "I hate her, I hate her," looking at her mother. "I'm afraid I'm going to kill her. She hates me, and why shouldn't she. My father has no use for her and avoids her. He never talks to her or tells her anything—but takes me for rides in his car and tells me about his business—you'd think I was his wife." After a pause and her mother's denial that she hated Ellen, the young woman complained that her mother had never really paid attention to her, she was too attached to her own mother and sister, that she preferred Ellen's sister, and so on and on.

The father tried to insist that Ellen was wrong—of course, they all loved one another—but the mother intervened and said that her husband thought only of Ellen. When he came home from work, his first question was, "How is Ellen, has she done anything today?" He never asked how his wife was feeling, even though he knew she had been depressed. The father insisted that Ellen was sick and naturally was his major concern.

And so it went. It did not take long to learn that the mother had always been phobic about driving a car, obsessive in her care of the home, and had been taking antidepressive medication given her by the family physician. The father, a rather tough-looking character, revealed, much to his daughter's surprise, that like his daughter he had left college because he could not stay away from home, and when in the army had been court-martialed three times for running away to return home. One reason he was so oversolicitous with Ellen was his concern that she had inherited her condition from him. There was much more, of course, but I am sure you are familiar with similar situations—the patient, the so-called scapegoat, with her illness the only common interest of the parents, parentified by a father, jealous of the attention her mother paid her sister, fearful that if she left home her parents would separate, and filled with unbearable hostility to a parent she needed.

In this instance, the patient was still deeply involved with her parents and sibling and each day fueled new resentments and predicaments. Efforts to change the parents' attitudes and feelings toward the patient and each other seemed essential before the patient could overcome her fears of killing her mother or of leaving her home.

Now let us consider a 28-year-old woman who has been married to a pediatric resident for two years and sought therapy because she had been unable to become pregnant. Unfortunately, I rapidly discovered that the couple never had sexual relations when she was likely to become pregnant, and she conceived before we had an opportunity to solve some deep-seated problems, which may have caused the pregnancy to end in a stillbirth. The patient had been a highly capable person who had made a successful start as a journalist, but since her marriage had been virtually paralyzed by anxiety and was becoming phobic about attending the theater or concerts where she would have a sense that people were staring at her that was not, or not yet, delusional. She was anorgasmic though not quite frigid during sexual intercourse, despite knowledgeable attempts by her husband and herself to overcome her difficulties. When she and her husband had engaged in sexual play prior to marriage, she remained completely passive and sometimes almost rigid while her fiancé stimulated her in various ways.

Since her parents lived on the Pacific coast and her two younger sisters in different distant cities, family therapy with her family of origin would not have been possible. Moreover, the difficulties seemed to focus on her sexual relations with her husband, so marital therapy seemed appropriate. Her husband was eager to start marital therapy but the patient absolutely refused. If it had been undertaken, it would probably have also led to the pregnancy, and though it might have improved the marital relationship, in light of the subsequent individual therapy, it probably would not have changed matters appreciably. The patient's sexual inhibitions were, as she was at first only dimly aware, deeply rooted in her development. Her physician father had "eloped" with her mother, taking her not from her family but from a close woman friend whom she loved and who strongly opposed the marriage. The patient's early years were spent in an isolated foreign community where, she believed, her father had an affair with the only white woman, the attractive and seductive wife of the head of the industry that employed her father. They moved to a city in the United States at the time the patient entered school. When she started to mature sexually, her father constantly admonished her, as he later did her two sisters, to pull her skirt down, button up her blouse, and not expose her chest, saying he wasn't raising his daughters to become whores. He was fond of the patient but awkward and unable to be affectionate. Although there was only a year and a half step in age between successive sisters, they shared little. She was certain that she had never seen her sisters naked and recalled one sister hiding in a closet to see how she looked when undressed. There was little communication between any of the members of the family. She puzzled a great deal about her parents' backgrounds. She knew that her father had been disowned by his father but did not know why, and she knew virtually nothing about her mother's family.

Her mother died while the patient was in therapy. She left a letter for the patient, her oldest daughter—a letter to be read after the mother's death. It was an apology for not having been a better mother. It said she had loved the patient deeply but had not been able to express it, and went on to say that she had been unable to love her husband, for the only real love in her life had been the woman from whom her father had "rescued" her, much against her true feelings. The letter clearly conveyed that the mother had been a lesbian who had feared any intimate contact with her daughters, and had been unable to be a satisfactory sexual partner to her husband. It is of interest that the patient did not realize the major purpose of the letter, until she reread it a month or so later, and then asked in therapy, "My mother was telling me she had been homosexual, wasn't she?"

Then, some months later, while working at the interpretation of a dream, the patient suddenly stopped and exclaimed, "That is what I have blotted out!" When she was 13 or 14, she alone had a room on the third floor of their home. Her father would come and sit beside her bed and masturbate her, while she, in order not to embarrass him or to stop him, would pretend to be asleep. Now she understood her vague but terrible anxiety about having sexual relations, and her passivity in sexual play prior to marriage as well as her functional night blindness. There was much more about her parents and their relationship with each other and their daughters. The patient overcame her anxiety, had a child, and eventually resumed her career. All that I have sought to convey here is that for this woman, marital therapy would have been unlikely to enable the patient to uncover, relive, and gain an understanding of her strange parents and their effect on her marriage and sexual life.

I have sought to illustrate primarily that the patient's family of origin is critical in most if not all individual psychotherapy. I would like to be able to say how we can tell after an initial interview whether the problem is better suited to family or to individual therapy. Perhaps all we can do is be sufficiently open and flexible to shift from one approach to the other as we learn more about a patient or a family. There are some of us who believe that most children and adolescents require family therapy, but also that many adolescents and young adults with anaclitic borderline or schizophrenic disorders will require both individual and family therapy. However, I also believe that individual psychoanalytically oriented therapy and particularly classical psychoanalysis can be futile if it seeks to understand a psychiatric disorder in terms of problems in the oedipal or preoedipal periods or through understanding of intrapsychic problems derived from aberrant drives or fixations. Individual therapy can be—and in psychoanalytic practice in contrast to psychoanalytic theory, very often is—family oriented, with a major focus on how the family transactions led to both intrapsychic and interpersonal impasses as is apparent in the case I just presented in a fragmentary way.

REFERENCES

1. Bateson, G., Jackson, D., Haley, J., & Weakland, J. (1956). Toward a theory of schizophrenia. *Behavioral Science, 1:* 251–264.
2. Boszormenyi-Nagy, I., & Spark, D. (1973). *Invisible loyalities.* New York: Hoeber & Harper.
3. Brown, G. W., Birley, J., & Wing, J. K. (1972). Influence of family life on the course of schizophrenic disorders: A replication. *British Journal of Psychiatry, 121:* 241–258.
4. Brown, G. W., Monck, E., Carstairs, G. M., & Wing, J. K. (1962). The influence of family life on the course of schizophrenic illness. *British Journal of Preventive Social Medicine, 16:* 55–68.
5. Bruch, H., & Touraine, G. (1940). Obesity in childhood. V. The family frame of obese children. *Psychosomatic Medicine, 2:* 141–206.
6. Chassell, J. O. (1938). Family constellation in the etiology of essential alcoholism. *Psychiatry, 1:* 473–503.
7. Cohen, M., Barker, G., Cohen, R., Fromm-Reichmann, F., & Weigert, E.

(1954). An intensive study of twelve cases of manic-depressive psychosis. *Psychiatry, 17:* 103–137.

8. Freud, A. (1965). *Normality and pathology in childhood.* New York: International Universities Press.

9. Freud, S. (1953). Fragment of an analysis of a case of hysteria. In J. Strachey (Ed. and Trans.), *The standard edition of the complete psychological works of Sigmund Freud.* (Vol. 7). London: Hogarth Press. (Original work published in 1905.)

10. Freud, S. (1957). Analysis of a phobia in a five-year-old boy. In J. Strachey (Ed. and Trans.), *The standard edition of the complete psychological works of Sigmund Freud* (Vol. 10). London: Hogarth Press. (Original work published in 1909.)

11. Freud, S. (1958). Psycho-analytic notes upon an autobiographical account of a case of paranoia (dementia paranoides). In J. Strachey (Ed. and Trans.), *The standard edition of the complete psychological works of Sigmund Freud.* (Vol. 12). London: Hogarth Press. (Original work published in 1911.)

12. Hendin, H. (1969). *Black suicide.* New York: Basic Books.

13. Hoover, C., & Insel, T. (1984). Families of origin in obsessive-compulsive disorder. *Journal of Nervous and Mental Disease, 172:* 207–215.

14. Johnson, A. M., & Szurek, S. A. (1952). The genesis of antisocial acting out in children and adults. *Psychoanalytic Quarterly, 21:* 323–343.

15. Knight, R. (1937). The dynamics and treatment of chronic alcohol addiction. *Bulletin of the Menninger Clinic, 1:* 233–250.

16. Lidz, R. W., & Lidz, T. (1949). The family environment of schizophrenic patients. *American Journal of Psychiatry, 106:* 332–345.

17. Lidz, T. (1963). *The family and human adaptation.* New York: International Universities Press. (Die Familie und Psychosoziale Entwicklung. S. Fischer Verlag, 1971).

18. Lidz, T., Cornelison, A., Fleck, S., & Terry, D. (1957). The intrafamilial environment of schizophrenic patients: II. Marital schism and marital skew. *American Journal of Psychiatry, 114:* 241–248.

19. Lidz, T., Cornelison, A., Terry, D., & Fleck, S. (1958). Intrafamilial environment of the schizophrenic patient. VI. The transmission of irrationality. *A. M. A. Archives of Neurology and Psychiatry, 79:* 305–316.

20. Lidz, T., Fleck, S., & Cornelison, A. (1965). *Schizophrenia and the family.* New York: International Universities Press.

21. Lidz, T., Lidz, R. W.. & Rubenstein, R. (1976). An anaclitic syndrome in adolescent amphetamine addicts. *Psychoanalytic Study of the Child, 31:* 317–348.

22. Minuchin, S. Montalvo, B., Gurney, B. G., Jr., Rosman, B. L., & Schumer, F. (1967). *Families of the slums.* New York: Basic Books.

23. Pavenstedt, E. (Ed.) (1967). *The drifters: Children of disorganized lower-class families.* Boston: Little, Brown.

24. Singer, M. T., & Wynne, L. C. (1965). Thought disorder and family relations of schizophrenics: III. Methodology using projective techniques. *Archives of General Psychiatry, 12:* 187–200.

25. Singer, M. T., & Wynne, L. C. (1965). Thought disorder and family relations of schizophrenics: IV. Results and implications. *Archives of General Psychiatry, 12:* 201–212.

26. Stierlin, H. (1974). *Separating parents and adolescents: A perspective on running away, schizophrenia, and waywardness.* New York: Jason Aronson.

27. Stoller, R. (1968). *Sex and gender: On the development of masculinity and femininity*. New York: Science House.
28. Vaughn, C. E., & Leff, J. P. (1976). The influence of family and social factors on the course of psychiatric illness: A comparison of schizophrenic and depressed neurotic patients. *British Journal of Psychiatry, 129:* 125–137.
29. Wurmser, L. (1974). Psychoanalytic considerations of the etiology of compulsive drug use. *Journal of the American Psychoanalytic Association, 22:* 820–843.
30. Wynne, L. C., Ryckoff, I., Day, J., & Hirsch S. (1958). Pseudo-mutuality in the family relations of schizophrenics. *Psychiatry, 21:* 205–220.
31 Wynne, L. C., & Singer, M. J. (1963). Thought disorder and family relations of schizophrenics: I. A research strategy. *Archives of General Psychiatry, 9:* 191–198.
32. Wynne, L. C., & Singer, M. T. (1963). Thought disorder and family relations of schizophrenics: II. A classification of forms of thinking. *Archives of General Psychiatry, 9:* 199–206.

Dinner Chit-Chat

Exhausted from listening to so many papers and taking part in their various work groups, pale, haggard, and with rings under their eyes, our three friends met for dinner. They had very little inclination to talk about what they had been doing. In fact, if the editors of this book hadn't kept on at them, they might not have mentioned the conference at all. It took Doc's complete bafflement at the psychiatric "chronification fable" to inject some life into the proceedings.

Doc: If I understand the fable and the discussion of it correctly, the idea was that psychiatric institutions function in exactly the same way as the patients' families. Was that it?

Maria: No need to be so deprecatory. You've hit the nail on the head first time!

Doc: But that's a scandalous argument! And it's a vicious slur on the attempts of all those who do their best to help their patients, day in and day out!

Maria: Intention and effect just happen to be two different things, that's all. It's not as if the problems that families have mean that they lack the necessary good intentions. In fact, it very often seems that all the misery that exists in the world is the fruit of good intentions. Every family has its own ideas about how to solve the problems it encounters, about what's to be done for the best. And if it finds it cannot rid itself of its problems along those lines, then it starts looking for an institution that has similar ideas about the nature of the problems in question. Calling in such an institution is nearly always the application of the "more of the same" maxim. The patient finds his view of the world confirmed in the institution. It is a world where he fits best if he is disturbed.

Theo: Another of your way-out systemic hypotheses!

Doc: But things can't be that one-sided! After all, such institutions offer a kind of shelter in which individual development and specific aid are possible. You're surely not going to deny that lots of patients leave the clinic in a much better condition than they entered it.

Maria: True. The only question is whether their condition has improved because they are in the clinic—or in spite of it!

Theo: Let's look at the hard facts for a moment, the Tienari study, for instance. This study is the most comprehensive large-scale attempt so far to determine to what extent schizophrenic disturbances are genetic and to what extent they can be traced back to the environment, in other words, to the family surroundings the patient has lived in. And Tienari and his assistants have managed to avoid most of the methodic shortcomings that have made the so-called Danish adoption studies so controversial. While suggesting that there is such a thing as a genetic predisposition for schizophrenic disturbances (albeit probably a nonspecific one) they don't stop there. In fact it appears that in all cases where the adoptive families doing the upbringing are anything like functional, that is, if they are flexible and clear in their communicational strategies, then this genetic factor was unable to assert itself. And that seems to me to be the most convincing argument so far produced in favor of a family-oriented approach to the prevention and treatment of schizophrenic disturbances.

Doc: Hm!

Maria: And so we come full circle. For me, these three days here have been something like a crash course in the history of family therapy. All the founding fathers and mothers seemed to come alive again in Theodore Lidz' paper. It's a funny feeling, I find, when one suddenly realizes that the books one has read were actually written by real living people you could put your hand out and touch. What courage and pioneering spirit must have been required in the fifties to pursue family-oriented research into schizophrenia at a time when family therapy congresses attended by thousands of devout pilgrims were still unheard of!

Doc: Cheers!

The Third Day

Breakfast Chit-Chat

Maria: Today's the big free-for-all. I'm looking forward to seeing the gladiators in the arena. The panel discussion on the video of the first interview with a family should be a real cut-up!

Doc: And who gets butchered?

Theo: Who do you think? Those poor saps of therapists who were silly enough to let themselves be observed practicing their handiwork. Who else?

Maria: If you ask me, I think the participants in the discussion are more likely to go for one another. After all, we've got representatives of the whole range of family-therapy approaches together in the same cage.

Doc: I wouldn't be that optimistic if I were you. I can't see one member of the family-therapy confraternity sticking a knife into another one in public, however different their opinions may be.

Theo: Still, the mixture is a very explosive one. We've got psychoanalysts and systems fanatics, multigeneration archeologists, bereavement buffs, and technocrats of the here-and-now all sitting at the same table arguing about what they think they've discovered in this outsize Rorschach Test.

Doc: But in my experience there's always some soothing, smoothing moderator only too ready to live up to his title and keep things from getting too extreme, making sure that no real conflicts arise and that nobody gets hurt. What's the lucky fellow's name? Jürg Willi. Anybody know anything about him?

Theo: A pretty logical choice for the part, a Swiss couples therapist. "Collusion" is his hobby-horse, the dividing up of a common conflict among various positions. Perhaps he can get the participants to see things that way. It can hardly be a coincidence that so many UNO institutions have their headquarters in neutral Switzerland.

Maria: If you ask me, the most promising controversy is going to be the one between the historically oriented therapists on the one hand—Ivan Boszormenyi-Nagy, Norman Paul, and Eckhardt Sperling—and the therapists who concentrate more on the rules and regularities obtaining in the here-and-now—Mara Selvini Palazzoli, Gianfranco Cecchin, and Luigi Boscolo.

161

Theo: Whose side do you think Luc Kaufmann and Lyman Wynne will be on?

Maria: Hard to say. I've always seen Lyman Wynne as the researcher and integrator par excellence, the man who knows it all, who's seen it all. And Luc Kaufmann is another specifically Swiss blend of solid experience and innovative uninhibitedness, the whole topped off with a good deal of understatement.

Theo: And what's the point of having three representatives of the so-called Milan model on the panel, all proclaiming the same convictions?

Maria: I wouldn't be so sure of that. Don't forget that the men and the women in the Milan group have been going their different ways for some time now.

Doc: Then let battle begin!

Transcript of Panel Discussion

Willi: Nowadays it is common knowledge that in panel discussions like this women should have a say equal to that of men. Therefore, I am a little surprised to notice that on this panel of family therapists there is only one woman, Mara Selvini, in a round of seven men. *(Enthusiastic cheers from the auditorium.)*

At a time when men are trying to emancipate themselves the organizers of this Congress have probably been thinking: Let's find out whether seven men are enough to offset the weight of one Mara Selvini. I am not at all sure they have succeeded in this. Possibly, next time even more men will have to be seated in this round. *(Laughter in the auditorium.)*

Well, our plan for this panel discussion is as follows. We have a videotape which we will discuss together. The therapists are Gunther Schmidt and Fritz Simon from the Department for Psychoanalytic Basic Research and Family Therapy here in Heidelberg. First Dr. Schmidt will give a brief summary of the family interview, then we will watch together some excerpts from this videotape, and then we will discuss them. Dr. Schmidt, will you please start.

Schmidt: Perhaps I should tell you first why we have chosen just this family. We thought that we had heard by now much about families with anorectics, schizo-present families, and similar rigid family systems. However, these families are not representative of those whom our colleagues who are gathered at this conference are likely to meet in their daily practice. Also, these families do not reflect those with whom all the participants of this panel are dealing in everyday life. Therefore, we thought we should present a family with a problem which you are more prone to encounter in your own practice. Further, this family offers an interesting basis for the discussion of the different concepts of the panelists.

At this point I shall not tell much about the family in order to avoid influencing the ensuing discussion. We shall watch some segments from an initial interview. First of all, let me present the genogram of the

163

family. At the same time, let me show you the seating order obtaining in the interview.

As you can see, this is a family with four children. The oldest, Karl, sits on the left side. He is 32 years old. He was the one who contacted us and initiated the interview. He is married and has two small children. Karl is a merchant, running a small food store. His sister Anita is 30 years old. She is also married and has one child. His younger sister, Lotte, is 21 years old. She, too, is married and is also mother of one child. Then there is Walter, 13 years old. Walter is the identified patient. I try to indicate this, obviously not very skillfully, as you can see, by drawing two squares around him. I guess you are familiar with this kind of notation. The women are drawn in round circles and the men are drawn as squares—obviously, just as this corresponds to nature. The mother is 53 years old. The father died approximately half a year before the family came to see us. He was then 59 years old. The interview took place in 1983; it was the first interview with this family. Thus the nuclear family seen by us consisted then of the mother and her four children.

As I mentioned earlier, the initiative for the interview came from the oldest child, Karl. He was the one who called us for an appointment. At first he wanted to come only with his mother and his 13-year-old brother, Walter. He reported that Walter had become a big problem during the last months. About half a year ago his father had died and since that time Walter had appeared very nervous. He had also developed problems in school. Karl had assumed that his little brother could not cope with the death of his father. Frequently, so Karl told us, Walter would behave very strangely toward his mother. Sometimes he would say "Mama, Mama, Mama" 20 or 30 times in a row, saying nothing else.

The family had met with little success in trying to cope with the situation. His mother would frequently try to show empathy with Walter, sometimes she would argue with him, or she would repeatedly ask him for the meaning of his monotonous statements. But nothing would help. Walter would not say anything else besides "Mama, Mama, Mama" and would not explain anything. Sometimes he would also say his mother was a witch and he believed that she was not his real mother. As a result, mother now was approaching a nervous breakdown. I got this preliminary information from the telephone call Karl had made.

As a rule, the first telephone contacts in our institute are not made through one of the therapists. Rather, a secretary who is given special

Genogram of the family (presented at the panel discussion)

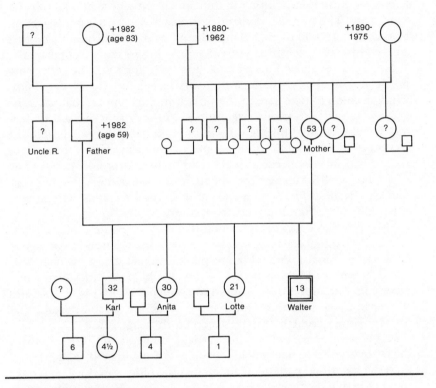

Seating order during the interview:

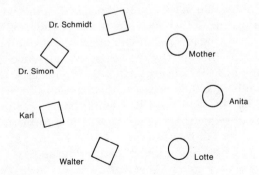

criteria for the gathering of information takes the phone calls. Karl told her on the phone that he lived in his own house, not in the house of the mother and the nuclear family. Karl is married, as I said earlier, but lives very close to his mother in the same town where he also runs his food store. The two sisters also live in this town. This is a town of approximately 15,000 to 20,000 inhabitants. At the moment, only mother and Walter, the identified patient, are living in the parental house.

Since Walter started his problematic behavior Karl, the older son, has been visiting mother and Walter very frequently. He is there almost every evening to take care of the situation. Karl reports that when he is there and tries to take charge things will sometimes go a little better. We also learned through the phone call that father had died half a year ago of a carcinoma of the stomach. About a year before his death he had had surgery because of this carcinoma. After his operation he was quite well for some time but then his condition worsened very quickly. He died finally in a special hospital for carcinoma patients situated about 300 kilometers from home.

Usually we ask also for information about the context of the referral. We heard that Karl had gotten the recommendation to contact us from a gynecologist with whom he plays handball at a sports club. Karl had asked him to whom he could turn for help and the doctor had given him our address. He wanted to come only with his mother and Walter but when we told him that we thought it was important that his two sisters come he finally accepted this suggestion.

A few more words about the seating arrangements: Mother sits on the far right, next to her the older daughter, Anita, then daughter Lotte, then the identified patient, Walter, then the older son, Karl, and next to him the two therapists. Also a few more words about the genogram. In the genogram that you have in front of you, it may look as if the father is the only child in his family of origin. But this we do not know for sure. At the time of the interview we were still lacking relevant information concerning this point. Our guess was that father was not the only child. Before the start of the initial interview we always ask the parents to fill out a special sheet that will provide us with information about the family. We then use this information to form some first hypotheses about the family. In this family there was only one living parent. As a consequence, we have only the information the mother gave us about her family of origin.

So much as a first report. With that let me stop.

Willi: Thank you very much. We shall now see an excerpt from the videotape. Following this, the panelists will have the opportunity to put further questions to Dr. Schmidt.

TRANSCRIPT: EXCERPTS FROM A FIRST INTERVIEW

Scene 1

Karl: Dr. X had just stated that my father had turned completely yellow. He was terribly skinny and weak, and then he was sent to the hospital and had surgery . . . ah, during surgery they also diagnosed a kidney problem, and anyway he was so weak. Right from the beginning the doctors had said that the illness had already progressed and that the operation was risky. But there was no other chance, and this was the only possibility left to prolong his life. And my father, our father, had surgery on Monday morning and then he was in intensive care until Wednesday. That same day he died . . . and I wondered should or shouldn't one call now. . . . So we got our things together, so that Walter wouldn't be alone when he'd get the news. We went home, first I called my wife and told her not to say anything. We got to the house, Walter opened the door and asked: "Where is Daddy?" . . . the father?

Dr. Schmidt: He expressed this loss clearly in words?

Karl: Yes.

Dr. Simon: And Anita, when did she get the news?

Karl: She . . .

Anita: I found out, when I, well, I was working and I had a feeling because he had had the kidney problem during surgery and because they had said that if anything changed they would inform us. And since nobody had called I was pretty sure that something had happened. I had this strange feeling that they'd come home and say "Daddy has died."

Karl: And so it went on. Anita got upset 'cause we had said that Daddy was doing badly and that we had to be prepared for everything. They wanted our mother to be present when they told Walter the whole story.

Dr. Simon: Offhand, the mother is the one who can best comfort him?

Karl: Yes.

Dr. Simon: Altogether, who was best in comforting whom in this situation?

Karl: I don't think that any one of us was able to comfort 'cause we all were occupied with ourselves.

Dr. Simon: Walter, where did Karl go when he felt like being comforted? Who was able to comfort him?

Walter: To uncle Robert.

Dr. Simon: Who is Robert?

Walter: He's a brother to my father.

Dr. Simon: Did he go to see him or did Robert go to him?

Karl: He . . . came.

Anita: Karl had a nervous breakdown, shortly before. . . .

Karl: When I rode home from T., I had to pull myself together in order to concentrate, 'cause back home I got dizzy all of a sudden. And then the doctor gave me some injection. . . . (directed to Mother) Do you remember what sort of injection that was?

Mother: Some tranquilizer, I guess. He was completely down. Imagine what he had experienced and then he had to drive home in the night. And that was . . .

Anita: And he had also been sitting at father's bed.

Mother: . . . and this had been too much for him, for three days he had been sitting there, was in the hospital and in the intensive care unit.

Dr. Schmidt: Naturally, when Karl breaks down under this sort of pressure, his body must relax. Well, when he suffers a breakdown, what is it that can best help him in such a situation?

Mother: Well, he has a family and kids; he cares a lot for them and that gives him strength, 'cause they need him.

Dr. Schmidt: In other words, you are saying that he regains strength because he is aware of having responsibility and because he is in a position to help them?

Mother: Yes, sure.

Dr. Simon: And then the uncle came?

Walter: Well, Mom also went to see him.

Dr. Simon: Hm, so he, the uncle, was the one who could best comfort your mother. Or did your mother . . .

Walter: Mama went to Karl.

Dr. Schmidt: Ah.

Lotte: . . . and worried about Karl, after all he had to go through.

Mother: That was all too much for him, what we had to go through during those days.

Dr. Schmidt: In other words, does this mean that Karl was stressed even more than mother was?

Lotte: Well, he had already known about it . . .

Dr. Schmidt, asking Lotte: Hmhm, we already heard, ah, Walter might have worried or might have asked: "Are you going to die?," ah, "Won't Mom die too?" Or something like that. This would then express some anxiety with regard to your mother's well-being. As I said before, is there someone in the family who had worried that it might be too much of a strain . . . on Karl?

Lotte: I think all of us.

Dr. Schmidt, asking Lotte: All of you. About whom did you worry more, about Karl or about your mother?

Lotte: About both of them.

Dr. Schmidt: . . . if at all, did you worry as much about Karl as about your mother?

Lotte: . . . I guess a little more about Karl since he had that nervous breakdown, and then broke down at work.

Dr. Schmidt: What in particular were your worries? Naturally it's not easy to talk about this matter, I understand that. What could have happened to him if he hadn't pulled himself together. What were you worrying about most?

Anita: An electrocardiogram had to be made. The result was rather bad, and therefore we really worried, mother too. At times, we were a little distracted, but then the anxieties were there again.

Dr. Schmidt: From what were you distracted?

Anita: From our father, I mean we all were terribly shocked, but we knew also that something had to be done about the house. . . .

Dr. Simon: That life then goes on.

Anita: How it'll go on.

Dr. Schmidt: Hmhm. In other words, he could have had a physical breakdown.

Anita: Yes.

Dr. Schmidt, asking Anita: If Walter hadn't caused you any trouble, if he had continued to be the same . . . if you would not have had to concentrate so much on him. What do you think would have been stronger— worrying about Karl or the pain caused by your father's death?

Anita: I think father's death.

Dr. Schmidt: The pain caused by his death would have been stronger?

Anita: Because . . . things had calmed down.

Dr. Schmidt: The problems with Karl?

Anita: Yes.

Dr. Simon: Going back to the comforting . . .

Dr. Schmidt: Yes.

Dr. Simon: I realize that you are a family that needs a lot of comforting and that has suffered a big loss. Therefore, I am certainly interested. . . . You said that in this situation no one was really able to give comfort to the others because you all suffered a big loss and you all suffered to an equal extent. And that you all feel the same about it. Well, Karl has his own family who is comforting him, so you said. But what is the case with the other children?

Mother: It might be similar for her (Lotte), she also has a family, she's married, has a kid, a small one. They both have to take care of their families. He can take comfort from the fact that we know he is responsible.

Dr. Simon: Hmhm. That means that this is a family that is comforting,

that shows one that life has to go on; that I do have responsibility.
Mother: Yes; it is so, life has to go on.
Dr. Simon: In other words, worrying about their own families will also distract your daughters a bit from their suffering?
Mother: Yes; 'cause life must go on somehow.
Dr. Simon: Hm. That's the case with both of them . . .
Dr. Schmidt: Tell me . . .
Karl: Over there someone's stomach rumbled.
Dr. Simon: How about Walter? Who was able to comfort him?
Mother: Well, it seems as if Walter was afraid to lose me; lately he has been behaving rather strangely. He keeps on saying: "You're not my mother anymore," "I want to go away to an orphanage." And lots of such things. I told him: "You are my son, my boy," just like he is my son and that is my girl. I don't discriminate. No, I don't do that. No one will be able to say that I make a distinction between them.
Dr. Simon: I want to go back to the question. Walter, who's the best in comforting your mom? Is there anybody outside the family to whom she can turn?
Walter: Yes . . .
Dr. Simon: A sister or someone, a friend?
Walter: Ha.
Dr. Simon: Well, what do you think? Is there anybody? If there was a person, who could it be?
Walter: Maybe Karl.
Dr. Simon: Karl, hm.
Dr. Schmidt: Would she go to him by herself when she needs comforting? Or wouldn't she?
Walter: I don't know.
Dr. Simon: Karl, if Walter wanted to comfort your mother, how would he best do this? What would help her most to get over her pain?
Karl: I think the best way would be not to bother her with all those questions.
Dr. Simon: Would she suffer more if she had to worry about Walter or if she didn't have to worry about him?
Karl: Do you mean regarding our father?
Dr. Simon: Yes.
Karl: My mom was terribly distracted by this, that's correct. But when . . . one really cannot . . .
Dr. Simon: So it's no comfort, but it's distraction.
Dr. Schmidt: Would he be able to comfort her at all? I mean, is there anything at all that could comfort your mother?
Karl: Yes, I do think so . . .

Scene 2

Dr. Schmidt: How old does he (Walter) appear when judged by his behavior?

Karl: Right now he's six or seven years old.

Dr. Schmidt: Six or seven. I'm trying to imagine the whole situation; if Walter behaves like this and your mother and he are so close together and fight, what does she do then? To whom does she turn to get these problems off her chest? Or does she try to manage by herself?

Karl: No, most of the time she calls me and I have to . . .

Dr. Schmidt: Ah, most of the time Karl, to whom else does she turn?

Mother: If he isn't at home, I call her . . .

Dr. Schmidt: You call Anita and then . . .

Mother: . . . 'cause he doesn't do what I tell him to do.

Dr. Schmidt: If Anita and Karl weren't at home, would you then turn to Lotte?

Mother: He doesn't listen to her as well.

Dr. Schmidt: Well, most of all these people he respects most of what Karl is telling him to do. In other words, Walter does something wrong and your mother calls Karl.

Karl: Yes.

Dr. Schmidt: And Karl . . .

Karl: I don't know how to explain this, but I feel like a kind of avenger, one who . . .

Dr. Schmidt: So Karl shows up . . .

Dr. Simon: Lotte, if Walter didn't cause that much trouble, do you think that Karl would stop by that often in the evenings?

Anita: Yes.

Lotte: I don't think so . . . not that often.

Karl: I think he wouldn't stay that long.

Mother: But he would visit me no matter what.

Dr. Schmidt: So he'd come. Does he stop by every evening?

Mother: Almost every evening.

Dr. Schmidt: Does Anita visit you more than Karl?

Lotte: Yes, Anita.

Karl: I think one can . . .

Anita: I think . . .

Lotte: . . . 'cause Karl has his job and then during lunch hour he can stop by easily.

Mother: Yes.

Lotte: . . . in the evenings he has . . .

Mother: . . . after work he comes to see me.

Lotte: We stay longer and when Anita doesn't have to work then she stops by in the morning and afternoon, it depends . . .

Dr. Schmidt: And Walter, he rings the bell, so to speak, and Karl comes. Well, the order seems to be like this: Walter rings, mother informs Karl, and Karl hurries to see Walter.

Karl: Yes (*Walter is laughing*).

Dr. Schmidt: And then he is laughing.

Dr. Simon: Well, whenever Walter thinks that Karl should come it's the best for him to call his mother a witch or something like that.

Anita: . . . no . . .

Walter: I haven't done this in a long time.

Dr. Simon: No? Hm. What's the most effective thing you can do to make your mom call Karl? What would you have to do? You've had experience by now.

Walter: To walk into the woods.

Dr. Simon: To ride there with your bike?

Karl: Don't know.

Dr.Schmidt: What was most effective until now? Going into the woods, or . . . ?

Lotte: And to bother her . . .

Dr. Schmidt: What was more effective, running to the woods or upsetting her? . . .

Lotte: That . . .

Mother: Naturally, I get nervous when he runs to the woods.

Dr. Schmidt: You became afraid.

Karl: That's only natural.

Dr. Simon: When you are upset. . . ?

Mother: No, when he goes away.

Dr. Simon: And when he tells you something crazy, are you then more afraid than when he runs away?

Mother: No, this doesn't frighten me. The worst is his getting on my nerves; when he feels like fighting with me, I can't stand it 'cause I'm still shaken by my husband's death.

Dr. Schmidt: Lotte, how does your mother react when he is being obnoxious?

Lotte: She's trying to keep him calm, so that he won't freak out, but then we all lose our . . .

Dr. Schmidt: You lose your temper?

Dr. Simon: And what happens when you lose your temper?

Lotte: Then he gets beaten . . .

Dr. Schmidt: Then he gets angry . . .

Lotte: He starts screaming . . . once he fell.
Mother: He locks himself into his room or into the bathroom.
Dr. Schmidt: He screams?
Anita: Yes, lately he's been arguing with her all the time.
Dr. Schmidt: He argues with your mother?
Anita: Yes. As if he wanted to tell her how to behave.
Dr. Schmidt: As if he was your father?
Lotte: Yes.
Mother: Right.
Walter: Yes, 'cause you are not listening to me.
Mother: I'm always listening to you.

Scene 3

Dr. Schmidt: Hm. I have one more question, Lotte. Your mother is be-
    coming irritated and "explodes." Let's assume all this wasn't true:
    Walter will go to school as usual, will behave well, very well—in that
    case, what will be the most important thing for your mother? What will
    she dedicate herself to, mentally and physically? Will she work on try-
    ing to get over your father's death?
Lotte: I guess she would.
Dr. Schmidt: How will she feel then? Will she become sad or will she be
    able to manage?
Lotte: When she's alone she might worry. I don't know for sure, but then
    at night, lonely, she definitely feels bad.
Dr. Schmidt: Do you mean that then she will feel even worse?
Karl: Yes.
Dr. Schmidt: Would she worry more?
Karl: I ought to say that my mother has not gotten over our father's death
    even though she felt it was a relief because he had suffered so much.
    He couldn't have been saved and because he died he didn't have to
    suffer anymore. This might have given her some comfort . . .
Dr. Simon: That's very charitable reasoning. I mean that this was the best
    for your father in this situation; it comforts. But you are missing him.
    How did she manage, how does she manage without him?
Karl: It causes her a great deal of trouble. As I said before, the best would
    be if she had some sort of distraction and . . .
Dr. Simon: Do you think she might say: "I don't want to live anymore"?
Karl: No, no I don't think so. She has to worry too much about Walter . . .
Dr. Simon: . . . about Walter?
Karl: Yes.

Dr. Simon: . . . all children are grown up.

Karl: . . . since he is her child she is responsible for him. Even if he didn't cause problems. She also cares for her grandchildren.

Dr. Simon: And when Walter is grown up, when he leaves the house, would she grieve for your father? I mean then she won't be responsible anymore for Walter.

Karl: Sure, but I think time is a great healer.

Dr. Simon: Will she find something else worth living for?

Karl: I think so; she is already working in the garden again . . .

Dr. Schmidt: You mean she's trying to orient herself, trying to face the new situation? Lotte, your mother seems to have started to reorient herself toward life. Who has gotten best over your father's death by now? Well, it has not been long since he. . . . Who has gone back to normal life?

Lotte: Well, I don't know for sure. When I lie down at night I start to cry once in a while but then I tell myself that life has to go on. It's better if one isn't reminded too often.

Dr. Simon: And what do you think?

Karl: I think I can say that I was the first in getting over it. Already a year before he died the doctor let me know that there was no hope. That moment back then was surely as terrible as his actual death.

Dr. Schmidt: You mean when they notified you about his condition?

Karl: Yes.

Anita: And a couple of months earlier our grandma had died . . .

Dr. Schmidt: Your father's or your mother's mother?

Mother: His mother.

Dr. Schmidt: Hmhm, many important . . .

Mother: Eight weeks earlier.

Dr. Schmidt: Eight weeks prior to your husband's death?

Mother: Yes.

Dr. Simon: Did she live in the same village in which you live?

Mother: Yes, on the other end.

Dr. Schmidt: Was she an important person in your family?

Mother: Yes, she always came to see us.

Karl: I have to admit that her death didn't affect me that much. I knew that soon she was to be 80 years old and that she had to die sooner or later. When she finally passed away I felt that she had lived a long life and that also our father could live so much longer. Therefore I wasn't sad.

Dr. Schmidt: So you were distracted by your father's illness?

Karl: Yes.

Dr.Schmidt: Did the others feel the same?

Lotte: Yes.

Dr. Schmidt: Who is missing grandmother most? Lotte, what would you say?

Lotte: I don't know.

Karl: I think none of us had time to think about this.

Dr. Schmidt: No one had time. . . . I'd like to ask one more thing. What about the future? Let's assume . . . the question is whether you want to continue the family interviews. . . . What are your expectations? What will be in five years? Karl, what would you say? Do you think that Walter will change his behavior, or that everything will come out all right anyway?

Karl: By himself he won't change. Lately he has gotten worse. Therefore I insisted in having this interview.

Dr. Schmidt: What do you think would happen if it continues to get worse?

Karl: For that we are here; we don't know what to do anymore.

Dr. Schmidt: Let's assume that there was no solution to your problem. What would happen?

Karl: I don't know, as I said we want to get rid of the problem.

Dr. Schmidt: Hmhm. What do you think, Anita?

Anita: I would say that mother cannot go on like this, her nerves wouldn't stand it any longer, and the same would hold true for Walter.

Dr. Schmidt: And what would happen?

Anita: I don't know.

Dr. Schmidt: What do you suppose . . .

Anita: I imagine that one day he might go mad.

Dr. Simon: And what will the family do then?

Anita: It would be different for all of us.

Dr. Simon: How would your mother react, and Walter, what would happen with him?

Anita: I really don't know.

Dr. Simon: You are definitely no prophets, but you know the two . . .

Dr. Schmidt: Everyone has his fantasies and suspicions . . .

Dr. Simon: In what could it result? It doesn't, it shouldn't happen, but . . .

Karl: I imagine that both have to be hospitalized.

Dr. Schmidt: Hmhm. In a psychiatric hospital?

Karl: Yes.

Dr. Simon: Together or separately?

Karl: Separately.

Dr. Simon: Who would be the first?

Karl: I think my mother.

Dr. Schmidt: Which would be the symptoms? Would she be depressed, sad, or . . . there are a lot of possibilities.

Karl: I think there would be a nervous breakdown, 'cause she wouldn't be able to manage anymore.

Dr. Simon: What would it look like?

Karl: Well, despair.

Dr. Simon: Desparate.

Karl: Yes, somehow. If you don't see a solution.

Dr. Simon: No outbursts of rage or the like?

Karl: Well, rather resignation.

Dr. Simon: Hmhm. And he . . . ?

Karl: I could imagine that Walter would have outbursts of rage . . .

Dr. Schmidt: What do you think should happen during these family sessions?

Karl: He should be brought to a point where he will only ask questions when he really has a question. He has to learn how to ask them instead of saying Mama hundreds of times. If he gets lost in saying "Mama" he will soon have forgotten what he wanted to ask her in the first place.

Dr. Schmidt: What might help, what would have to happen?

Karl: I had hoped that you'd address Walter more often today, so that his problems might become clearer.

Dr. Schmidt: Well, that's another question. Someone could perhaps say that Walter should be put in individual therapy. There are child and adolescent therapists. That will be a possibility. But that's also something which would affect the whole family.

Karl: . . . yes.

Dr. Schmidt: . . . what would then be the case with the whole family? What would have to . . .

Karl: My mother ought to relax more. Maybe this would help him. I already suggested it, but I don't know whether it's right. Therefore we need your advice. Maybe I should move in with them for a while.

Dr. Schmidt: With your entire family, or . . . ?

Karl: Maybe with the whole family. I then already. . . . If that does not work out. I may move in by myself . . .

PANEL DISCUSSION

Willi: This is definitively the end of the video presentation. I hope that our English-speaking panelists could understand the English translation. I hope also that you could pick up the emotional quality of the session.

Now I would like to suggest that at first the panelists ask Dr. Schmidt for further information, if they wish to do so. However, Dr. Schmidt should only give such information as he had himself at the time of the interview. That is, he should not give any information relating to further developments. Otherwise, we would lose the thrill of the thing and we could not jointly speculate about what followed afterward.

Boszormenyi-Nagy: I would like to ask a question because I lost a fantastic amount of process here and because I could not read the transcript beforehand. Could you say what you think you were doing, what was the therapeutic intervention, how would you define it?

Schmidt: I could talk a lot about that but I think if I talked too much now that might create a problem.

Boszormenyi-Nagy: No, I don't mean too much now. What I mean is: Why did you select this particular tape, is there something in your mind critical to this?

Schmidt: Well, we thought a family such as this one could open up different kinds of therapeutic realities in the sense that its problems could be attacked with different concepts and different therapeutic approaches could be elicited. Therefore it was our plan to give you the opportunity to discuss what you would have done in this case, what might be important for you. With this in mind, we selected some sequences that we thought might offer a good basis for a discussion among these panelists. Also, we thought that there are important things in this family's dynamics and coping style, as reflected in these video excerpts.

Boszormenyi-Nagy: I feel like wanting to get some help, but maybe it's not easy for you. It's difficult for me to truly respond to this material, I . . . shoot in the air. My impression was that this is a kind of information gathering from a psychological point of view without my seeing the intention of the intervention.

Schmidt: I would like to talk to this point later because we might have different points of view as to what is or could be an effective intervention.

Willi: I would like to suggest that we only ask for information relating to the family situation in the beginning of the interview—just in case somebody did not understand everything.

Boscolo: Just one question. Before father's death was there talk about the son having to go to an orphanage? And if so, how long before father's death?

Schmidt: There was no such talk. We learned, though, that he, Walter, was the son who was closest to father up to the time when the carcinoma was discovered. Then the father changed his behavior.

Selvini Palazzoli: How?

Schmidt: Well, in a sense he withdrew above all from this son, from Walter. His rationalization, his explanation was something like this: Maybe I have to die, therefore I want to make it easier for him to say goodbye. In this sense one could say he rejected him in order to spare him pain. After the operation he seems to have stuck to this plan of helping him with the impending loss. This we heard from Karl.

Wynne: What did the mother say before the death? Did she also withdraw from Walter?

Schmidt: No, she didn't withdraw. This, I think, is important information about the coping mechanisms in this family. We heard that for a very long time Karl, the oldest child, was the only one who knew about father's carcinoma. The father was in a hospital when it was discovered. I think he knew about the diagnosis, but I'm not sure about this. Anyhow, the doctors told Karl about the diagnosis and then Karl decided not to tell anybody in the family about it because he believed it would be too hard on them. He kept this to himself for more than half a year, I think almost up to the death of the father. Only then did he tell his mother and later his oldest sister. Walter was kept uninformed just up to the death of the father.

Paul: Was there a time lag between the time that Karl knew about his father's carcinoma and the father knew it? Was the father told the same thing Karl was?

Schmidt: I don't know anything about that.

Paul: Do you know anything about what the father knew and at what point?

Schmidt: As far as I remember the father knew. Also, he went to a hospital where usually only carcinoma patients are being treated. But Fritz Simon has a different opinion. According to him, the father didn't know. Since we couldn't find out, I can't tell you.

Wynne: But father must have known at least when he was withdrawing from Walter in order to save Walter.

Schmidt: That's right. I think the implication of this decision was then that he knew about his carcinoma.

Paul: But you don't know when that happened, in advance of his death? Do you know what had happened in advance of father's death? When did father begin to withdraw as a way of caring for Walter?

Schmidt: Approximately six months before his death.

Sperling: I would like to ask, did Walter change his behavior when father entered the hospital? Or did he change only after the death of father?

Was there any change in the family while father was away or did its functional dynamics remain the same? Does that mean that Walter acted as always until the news came that father was dead?

Schmidt: So we heard it in the interview. But I have to add that father was not away all the time. After the operation he was at home for some months and he was then relatively well. His condition became better at first, then it became worse and he had to go to the hospital again. But the family says that Walter's strange behavior appeared only after the death of father.

Wynne: What was the nature of the changes in the relationship between Walter and Karl? . . . During the year that Karl knew about his father's impending death and knew that his condition was hopeless, was there any change in closeness, perhaps less closeness? What was going on between Karl and Walter?

Schmidt: Karl told us in the interview that he thought it was not a good decision by father to reject Walter. So he might sometimes have tried a little bit to compensate for that rejection. Therefore, it could have been that there was a little more closeness between Karl and Walter.

Willi: Are there any other questions?

Kaufmann: Was grandmother ill for a long time or did she die suddenly?

Schmidt: Do you mean the maternal grandmother or . . . ?

Kaufmann: The paternal grandmother who died about the same time.

Schmidt: No. As far as we got to know she just was very old. She was 83 years of age, she was also ill, but rather in the sense of a senile dementia. She didn't die from a long chronic illness but rather, as far as the family explained it, because of her advanced age.

Kaufmann: And did she live in the house of her son or nearby?

Schmidt: She lived nearby but that is not fully clear to us. They told us that she was there every day, that she always spent time with the family, but whether she lived there or not we do not know for certain.

Kaufmann: And during the time when father was back home again, has she been there also?

Schmidt: Yes.

Kaufmann: Thank you.

Wynne: Do you know anything about the interpersonal setting in which the father developed his cancer, particularly in relation to his mother? How was his relationship with his mother and what kind of a loss, if any, was it for him—a loss that he may not have been able to share with the rest of his family including Karl?

Schmidt: I think this is a very important question, but we have no infor-

mation at all about that, because in this initial interview the family came
to us with a different kind of presenting problem and we had not
enough time to elicit information about this issue.

Boszormenyi-Nagy: At the end of the first segment, just at the point when
there is a question about would he, Walter, be able to comfort mother—
and I think Karl says "yes"—the segment stops. To me that would be
the most crucial information. What happened after that sentence? What
happened after that?

Schmidt: Well, I must confess I don't remember exactly, because it's now
two years back. I think we didn't stay too much with this topic. What
we heard, so far as I can remember, was that he was somebody who
in a sense supported mother. For example, Karl told us that in order
to cope with the situation with Walter he had tried out various strategies. One of these strategies was for some time even to attack mother.
For example, he would come to the house and say: "Ah, Walter, it
could well have been that your mother lied to me, that she is a liar."
When this happened, Walter would always jump up and say: "Hey, get
away from my mother, she is not a liar, she's OK" and he thus defended
mother. That was one kind of support which could indicate that he was
very empathically tuned to mother's feelings, to mother's inner experiences. Otherwise, I have not much more to say.

Willi: Well, I believe, we can now close this part. At the end of the discussion Dr. Schmidt will give us some further information about what
went on later. Now it would be interesting for us to hear the hypotheses
of the experts on this panel, how they see this family, what they would
view as the most essential problem. As a starter, one of the experts
should present his point of view, and thereupon we will ask for dissent-
ing opinions. Well, who wants to present his point of view first?

Boszormenyi-Nagy: I have a comment on the same point I made earlier.
From the point of view of my approach the greatest immediate therapeutic resource lies right at that moment where they cut off. If this is
indeed the situation that the boy is comforting mother, then I would
like to really sort of enlarge the therapeutic focus from there. So, that's
my comment. Here, I think, is a major resource which I as a therapist
would utilize immediately in the first session with the most likely
immediate advantages for the family at the time.

Willi: Could you also tell us how you would go on developing this, that
means in which sense you would have proceeded with the exploration?

Boszormenyi-Nagy: Well, because this highlights the crucial level of family relationships, the level where people can rely on each other. Thus
even a seemingly sick child can be a resource who is available for the

mother in times of grief. And out of that could develop a capacity in the family to honestly face this important level of reliance on each other. But what I see here is a kind of jumping from question to question about descriptions of behavior but not grabbing the obvious thing that is there. That's my comment from my vantage point. From this vantage point mutual reliance is the most important dimension of therapy.

Boscolo: I was impressed by the way they sit and how the analogical communication during the session unfolds. We see three women sitting close to each other, then Walter sitting close to his brother. We might expect that he would be sitting close to his mother, but he is sitting close to the brother. Now we see the brother is crying; he seems like the most upset. This seems also to accord with the history which we heard. So, Walter's father has died. His older brother looks very sad, looks like the most upset in the family. And my impression is that mother is the woman between the two girls, who are close to each other.

Now, one point impressed me about this case. And that is the first complaint: We heard that when father died Walter started to say "You are not my mother anymore. I want to go away to an orphanage." At least that's what I heard the mother say. Now, I get the impression that she tried constantly to treat all of her children equally and that, I think, is certainly a common parental aspiration and goal. But it seems to me, particularly in terms of their ages, it would be quite inappropriate to treat them in the same way. Thus a 13-year-old boy might be regarded as having different needs, in other terms, a different entitlement than the adult offspring. This may then reflect something about what this relationship was like before and what makes it now so ambivalent and problematic. And this may also shed light on the question that everybody seems to have here: how to understand his behavior, his way of reversing the role of being the comforted one into that of a caretaker for mother; at the same time his own needs remain obviously very great. So there is this particular dimension of the caretaking and attachment between mother and Walter, this being probably the most problematic one. Karl has done what he could, I think, which has its limits, though, because he can't really replace father unless he moves in. I wonder also what kind of resource the two other sisters might be, what kind of mothering they could give, where they might fit into the picture as traditional resources. So, these are some of the questions rather than answers that I would have.

Willi: Thank you very much.

Cecchin: It seems that the therapist and also the commentators here are talking about caretaking and comforting. But this looks like a theme that perhaps the family didn't propose and that the therapist is proposing. There are, indeed, a lot of questions about comforting. But we can introduce another theme, for example, making sense in the relationship. I can understand Walter: The father didn't want to deal with him when he, the father, went to die, so Walter didn't feel a sense of relationship. He might have concluded: This might not be my father. When the father died the mother did not deal with him. When there is a problem she calls the brother, not him. Therefore, it makes sense to me when he says "You are not my mother. I don't exist here. I don't count." Accordingly, he has to escalate his behavior, and the more he has to escalate his behavior the worse the problem becomes. Because when Karl comes in all the time in order to take care of the relationship of mother and Walter, they cannot stop each other. They need always a third one, Karl, so Walter might have thought, had no right to come. Walter thought that he was the one who was supposed to comfort mother, that is why he responds with yes to the statement "Do you think he would comfort his mother?" My question would be: How come he was not permitted? How come the family does not permit Walter to exist, to comfort everyone and to mourn the father, to take care of his mother? Nobody permits it. Everybody lies. So everybody says something as if to try to protect him like he was a kind of a crazy boy. I think this is a more important theme—not caring, but making sense.

Willi: Thank you. Dr. Kaufmann, please.

Kaufmann: Some things I didn't understand. What comes to my attention is partially overlapping with things that have been discussed already. When one observed these people, how they were sitting, so well-behaving, one could notice that they didn't look at each other even when the loss of father was brought up as a topic. They seemed very inhibited in the way they related to each other. It seems to me that there was nobody who helps the father to work through his mourning for his mother. Obviously he would have noticed that she was at the end of her life. He himself was in so difficult a situation that he couldn't do that on his own. It seems that he was then not supported by his wife. And so it goes on to the next generation. I don't believe that this family has mourned together. For me this would therefore be a first goal in this phase of the treatment. This would not be in conflict with the way in which information is being gathered here. I assume that the father wanted to protect his son from the pain of mourning because he himself couldn't mourn for his mother. Unfortunately, it then turned out that the son was alone.

Willi: Dr. Sperling.

Sperling: I want to continue a little along the line which Dr. Kaufmann introduced, that they couldn't look into each other's eyes. In the present situation I can understand that very well. What, we have to ask ourselves, is going on in this group of people who are so afraid of each other, who are burdened by two deaths that just happened, who are so afraid of death that in the case of one death nobody is allowed to know of it for a long time? And here I would like to agree with Dr. Nagy in that at first there has to be built up trust. So far, they all have lied to this boy and he doesn't know from them anything other than that they also lie to each other. I wonder, who could be the one who could bring a little spark of truth into the situation? The boy, too, is playing a game with mother, in this sense: "Well, if father is not really dead or if he cannot die, if I didn't hear this before and now suddenly hear it, then I can also say my mother is dead. And if all reality is here distorted, then I can also say you are a witch." He seems to be in a phase in which he tries out how and whom he can trust under which conditions. I believe the therapists should look out for the person on whom one can rely the most. For me this would be Karl, simply because he had the relevant information from the very beginning. But also Karl is not trustworthy, because he didn't pass on that information. Karl took care that the whole family would not be surprised by something which, in fact, could have served as a kind of preparation for joint mourning, as a time of premourning, as it were. At the end, Walter was the most surprised.

Selvini Palazzoli: I described a game exactly like this one in an article which recently appeared in the *American Journal for Marital and Family Therapy*, under the title "The Problem of the Sibling as the Referring Person" (1985, Vol. 11, pp. 21–34). In this article I described the most salient characteristics of this type of family:

(a) The identified patient is diagnosed as psychotic; (b) the parents are not motivated to do family therapy but they come under the urging of a sibling; (c) this sibling is actually the referring person and in many ways the most "competent" and "prestigious" family member. In such a situation, a family therapist should not meet the request of the "prestigious" sibling because, in so doing, he would become involved in the family game, the very game which, by putting the identified patient in an intolerable inferior position, maintains his psychotic behavior. In the videotape that was presented the referring sibling is Karl, and

Karl is really the most competent member of his family. My hypothesis is that long before the father's cancer, there was a sort of secret "marriage" between mother and Karl. The problem, after the father's death, is not a problem of mourning, but one of succession: Who will become the "spouse" of the "Queen"? Karl or Walter? This is the problem! . . . The Queen is very ambiguous; her intentions are unclear. Before the death of her husband, in my opinion, she had promised something to Walter, in an allusive, nonverbal way. She persists now in this ambiguous behavior and leaves Walter confused with a painful feeling of a betrayal. But also Karl is not in a pleasant situation. Because it is not clear if mother likes his frequent visiting and counseling. Maybe she is fed up with "husbands," with men who control her life!

In order to test this hypothesis, I would need to ask many questions, to collect information concerning the history of the relationship between the two parents, between Karl and mother, between Walter and mother, sisters and mother, and so on. In the case of a positive testing of my hypothesis, my intervention at the end of the second session would be the following. I would turn explicitly to Karl. It was *he* who consulted us, it is *he* who deserves our conclusion. I would tell him that the team has decided to stop because family therapy would be very dangerous for him. For the time being he needs so much more to be the great helper of his mother and the role he always had with her. The strange behavior of Walter provides him with the justification to persist in this role. An intervention like this will kick Karl out of the family, and consequently will break the ongoing game, stopping Walter's psychotic behavior.

Paul: It's hard to know where to start with this. I see it quite differently. I see that you have a group of terrified people and they are terrified principally about what's gonna happen with mother and Walter. I had a fantasy at one point that Walter would run into the woods, and mother would run into the woods after him, and there would be three psychiatrists chasing both of them to take them to some institution.

I came to see the situation from a different point of view. And that is that people like this require information. This is a kind of information I am inclined to give them early in the first session. Such information would be related to what Karl said in terms of people being very preoccupied with their respective private thoughts: They are concerned about themselves, about what's going on in their heads. Therefore, what I'm inclined to do is to indicate that in instances where a family member, like here a father, has had a chronic disease for a year or about a year, that this will bear on the thinking of the other members as the disease progresses. They will either wish that the person were alive and totally well—in other words, that he miraculously recover from the illness, his cancer, or whatever disability he has—or they have frightening thoughts of wishing that the person were dead. That accounts for the form of anger that typically happens in such families. When people are in such a situation they usually experience a lot of anxiety. And the anger is very profound; it's related to being deceived, it's related to the numbness that they are experiencing, to the psychotic behavior that has been alluded to. I remember references made about it many years back by Elvin Semrod. He suggested that psychotic behavior generally represents a defense against one's incapacity to bear grief. And the grief can and does include anger. The anger, though, is generally regarded as taboo. It's a cultural taboo which demands a sanction if it is to be questioned. Here the therapist is the one who can indicate that anger tends to happen, not saying they have it, but saying that it does occur.

Another thing occurred to me about this: I see this as an instance of what does happen very often. One could call it an abortive, thwarted kind of mourning reaction for the patient who is incurable with cancer. What then to do with the family? In some hospitals in the United States there is a tendency to get the family together in an attempt to let everybody know what is happening. From Walter's point of view he was deceived, he was lied to. Yet that can generally be handled by indicating that in families where people are scared because of cancer or a coma or whatever that stretches out over time, their members don't know what to do. They feel very helpless, feel very scared, and they feel scared principally for the little children, the smallest ones. Usually little kids can understand that.

There are many other things that I would be inclined to do. To give an example: When Karl says he opens the door and Walter asked where is Daddy I would be inclined to ask: "What happened next?" What was the experience? Who was then called in, perhaps a minister or a priest or a mortician? In this way, the sequence of experiences becomes validated as real and important. Was there an open coffin? Did people say goodbye to the father? Did they touch the body? Anything that can be shared and expressed loses the sting of guilt. And the question is whether one is able to draw upon the empathic resources that are available. If one can do this, one can see in very short order a profound change in the inner being of the different members. It is extraordinary to see what can happen through legitimizing a person's experience, principally the anger. Certainly, that isn't the only thing they feel, but it's the feeling they struggle with the most.

Cecchin: It's interesting what you said because we have different opinions along with our different approaches. Within a systemic approach it would be more interesting to see the death of the father as powerful information given into the system. And while you started talking about how the family denied mourning as a unity, I pondered what happened to the system after death entered into it. What kind of organization did they build up? I got a little bit confused here. There are now big problems; for example, who is going to take the place of father, who is going to take the place of the son because also in a sense the son does not exist anymore. The mother gave up being a mother and now she wants to be the wife of the son. So there is a collapse of the whole system and that's the most important thing, not the mourning about the father. You say shared mourning is the normal kind of position. If the family is organized, then there is shared mourning and it will work naturally.

Paul: What you say is true in terms of the disorganization and attempted reorganization of the family system. But I do feel that human beings require what I think of as an affective input, the validation of certain affects as real, important, and normal. I don't see anything that is dissonant with what you are describing. It's just looking at the elephant from a different point of view.

There are other things that need to happen. Walter has to have the validation that he is real. He seems ready to fly off. His sense of his own unreality may stem from his disloyalty, principally to his father, who has in fact deceived him. There is a lot that is involved here. One of the things I do in this kind of proceeding is to videotape the family. I then let them see it, let them begin to externalize their experience as being both inside and outside. The main thing is to enable them to recapture some sense of organization as a family unit and as individuals in this family unit.

Wynne: People are using rather different terms to talk about this. As I hear it, the presenting issue has to do with some of the confusion which Dr. Selvini talked about. I would like to raise another question: What is going on with mother? She puzzles me at this point. I think another way of looking at it could be that she is presenting herself as a puzzle. This also relates to Dr. Cecchin's earlier point about the need to make sense out of this situation. And given this puzzling situation, this lack of sense, it is understandable they had not been able to solve the problem of what to do about the succession after father had died.

Further, the very fact that brother Karl contributed to the mystery by not sharing the fact of his father's impending death is another key issue here. At the same time, there have been some efforts to protect one another in a positive way or to conceal things in order to be able to maintain some coherence. So Walter is perhaps the one who has been the most mystified, the most "down." Secrets have been withheld from him the longest. His anger, his misbehavior, is perhaps understandable from this standpoint. But he is also identified as the one to, in a sense, rescue the family as a whole. He is instigating them, in effect, is getting them into this treatment situation. That we've often seen, of course: The presenting patient is on some level the savior of the family, if there is some prospect that therapy might indeed save them.

Selvini Palazzoli: I agree with Lyman. Tonight we will act in a sort of Shakespearian *Hamlet*. Shakespeare was a master in psychiatry. Concerning Ophelia he stated that there was something very wise in her craziness. Also Walter was very wise when he called his mother a witch. She is a witch, a very calm and pleasant one, but really a witch. She is maintaining an imbroglio. She started doing this long ago, when the husband was still alive. Madness has a very long history. But we have to look at the present situation. The death of the father brought with it the problem of succession. A problem for the boys, not for the daughters. Daughters were what we call "the subsystem of smoke-screens."

Willi: Who would like to focus on a different subject? Let's open the last round of contributions.

Boscolo: I would like to comment on this one point—where we talk about mystification. Walter is in a position of being mystified. I agree. I was impressed thinking about the fact that one daughter said that Walter is concerned about mother's future, that Walter and she herself are afraid that she, mother, could be ending up in a hospital. Walter and mother, both of them, did not deny this. My impression is that mother and Walter are in a different situation from the other three members of this family. All these three members present themselves as having their own family. In contrast, mother is a widow and the son has lost his father. So this young child is considering the possibility that in the future she will be sick because she lost this man. Now, I think Walter is being mystified because both mother and Walter would like to get together in the wake of the big loss which they both suffered. But the members communicate: It is because of Walter that mother is in trouble and that this compels them to stay together. So they blamed Walter.

They conveyed: We are getting together because Walter is bad. It is interesting to note that when they are all together or when somebody comes into the house after Walter misbehaved, then Walter is behaving well. So in behaving well when mother is together with a son or a daughter, Walter fulfills the injunction: We want to be together. At the same time, we saw that he has to be bad in order to make them come together. So he is in a paradoxical situation, that is, he is being mystified while he becomes the bad one. He has the job of putting them together and then he is blamed for that. But there is also a desire to be together. Therefore, if I think about an intervention, I would lean toward a counterparadox. I would think of a message to the family that addresses this need to be together and to not be together. So one thing I would do in the intervention is to connote positively Walter's decision of a few months ago to cause some trouble. Because by causing some trouble he brought the family here into therapy. And this he did very well. I would tell him: You wanted to solve the family's problem. Your father died and the family became very sad, your mother, your brother, and your sisters. So you felt the need to stay together, to mourn this man, and that's why once in a while you misbehave and as a result your mother connects with the others. Possibly we could describe a ritual. A ritual could for instance be combined with this task: Three times a week or once a week, according to the circumstances, the family members meet and think about their father. They would meet in a ritualized way. And at all the other times of the week they should not talk about father. In brief, I would put them together in certain moments of the week.

Willi: I would like the discussion to concentrate on a different point. It seems to me that we have different opinions here, yet there is also a consensus about the assumption that this is a family problem, without that ever being discussed. That is just taken as given and as a matter of course.

Now, we have here a congress for family therapy and in view of that a focus on the family seems justified. But I cannot imagine that all the people here are already convinced family therapists. Therefore, I want to put this question to the panelists: How can you prove that this is a family problem at all, or at least prove that family sessions and family therapy are superior to, let us say, individual therapy? Perhaps one can depict that a little more graphically: I could imagine a general practitioner saying something as follows: "For me, what all those therapists here fantasized is much too complicated. That sounds like what analysts said in earlier times. For me the matter is much more obvious. I have to start from what the patients present. In this case, Karl had contacted me to look for a better way to cope with Walter. Therefore, I have to concentrate on Walter. And there I can state that Walter has no father anymore; he is again looking for a father figure. Karl is the one who offers that to him at the earliest. It is not by accident that Walter is seated between Karl and the therapist. Well, maybe he is looking for me, the therapist, to be a father substitute. And this would make sense to me as a source of conflict for Karl. For Karl is now torn between his own family and the role of father he wants to fulfill for Walter." Well, this is just one possibility.

Also, I could imagine that an analyst would say the following: "Walter is now in puberty, he lives alone with his mother, he is completely at her mercy, he is much too close to her. As a consequence, there evolves an incestuous oedipal problem. Perhaps mother takes Walter to bed with her, as this happens rather often after a death: One's child is taken into the bed in order that one can feel again something warm and lively next to one's self. We see Walter as very resistant and filled with panic when confronted with such an incestuous offer. Understandably, he sees his mother as a witch and just as understandably he says 'You are not my mother at all.'"

Well, these are only two possible hypotheses or arguments that could have been made from the point of view of a general practitioner or of an individual therapist. And I would appreciate it if the panelists now try to convince this individual therapist, general practitioner, or analyst of the validity of a family perspective.

Boszormenyi-Nagy: I would like to just mention something about the process here because I feel that we are sort of speculating. Each of us is speculating according to our favorite way of looking at therapy, as of this time. And if the audience can still hear me I would like to draw the distinction between different types of therapy, namely therapy as basically trying to be more humane—which is a very pretentious word and I don't like it—by trying to be simply helpful in ways that would allow people to take the next step themselves, that is, by having the humility of holding their hand and finding out where they are struggling and trying to help them at that point, as, for instance, contrasted with the therapist's role as a self-appointed magician or someone who has to create a miraculous solution. I think that these are two different trends in the current scene and that people should at least be clear about it. In other words, there is one trend which says there is absolutely no need to be a magician because the straight trust and consideration of human beings is the greatest resource, and there is another notion that people may need the therapist in order to have a miraculous solution, expecting that in his mind or her mind there should be the solution for people's lives. This can take many forms but I think it is present enough, really. I could not continue any longer without making this clear.

Willi: Right now, could we perhaps come to the above point, because I think it is important to many of those who are not so familiar with this material. Therefore, once more my question: How and with what arguments could you prove that the family perspective is here to be favored as being superior to an individual therapy perspective?

Sperling: For me it would be important that the general practitioner get some clarity about what is shaping up as the next threat. Namely, Karl wants to leave his family in order to live in his mother's house. And I would hope that the family sessions bring out the reasons behind that so that he does not do it. To me that seems to be the most important point: Karl is about to leave his family in order to live with his mother and that would again result in dead persons, as it were.

Selvini Palazzoli: As a psychoanalyst in private practice, such as I was long ago, I had worked with Walter for years. Working as a family therapist, two sessions could be enough. Nobody will discuss what is better for the patient and for the family. But for the young people who are here in the audience, wanting to enter into private practice, I am very sorry to say: "Don't rely on family therapy in order to make your living. It is only as a salaried person in a public institution that you can afford the luxury to be so quick in curing people!"

Kaufmann: You ask what I would tell the general practitioner. At this point, there is the danger that we are defending family therapy and are making propaganda for it. But what the general practitioner wants is to get rid of the problem. Of course, it is also right, what Sperling said. Why family therapy? I wouldn't talk of family therapy at all but I would say: "Yes, it would be worthwhile to see the family together in order to find out which possibilities they have. But we can probably say right from the beginning that this, most likely, is not a case for family therapy." And providing this formulation I would then run some sessions. And I might also say: "It is possible that something will be happening and that something essential might change after several sessions, but I'm not really sure about it." But I wouldn't label it as family therapy. Otherwise, I would chase after the family and the whole definition of the setting would be wrong from the start.

Cecchin: I think the most convincing argument for the superiority of family therapy over individual therapy was given by Dr. Willi. The explanation you gave us as the one a family doctor or a psychoanalyst would give reveals a restricted view of the situation. When you have a boy who has a problem with his mother and you then focus only on the boy, you restrict your view. But even when you focus on the dyad—boy and mother—you restrict your view. You don't see all the consequences of the relationship between Walter and mother because there is also Karl and there are all the sisters and all the organization. So this would be a restricted view.

Another view, mentioned by Dr. Willi, is that the boy needs a father. He lost his father and now he needs a father. Therefore, he is given a therapist who becomes the father. Such a view, too, will prevent us from seeing all the consequences of such an arrangement. Walter will possibly feel much worse because Karl now has the mother all to himself and he, Walter, has a paid father. A father by payment. Understandably, he will feel even worse. So both this view and the medical point of view turn out to be restricted views because they reach from the individual to the dyad at the most. Instead, family therapy discovers the triad. And that means a total jump in logical levels. When we make the step from the dyad to the triad, we also make the step from relationship to organization. With that comes another level of thinking which gives us a much wider and more ecological view of what's happening.

Willi: We don't have much time left. We will hear a few more comments from panelists and then we would like to hear from Dr. Schmidt what really happened.

Wynne: I would agree, it would be desirable to do what Dr. Selvini and Dr. Kaufmann are suggesting, namely not to get into family therapy at this point and rather to do a consultation, maybe one other session of consultation before one reports to the family doctor, to the psychoanalyst, or to whomever. By then the situation will change so much that they, too, may change their minds about what they hypothesized and recommended at the beginning. But I think we do have a consensus here: We need to gain some experience and data with the family in such a way that the picture will change. Then it will be no longer a matter of arguing about that or this being better than that, but of just looking at what's going on here. That should be more or less self-evident at that point and there would be no more need to be involved in debates about which is better.

Boscolo: I would prefer to see the family. Also, I agree with the proposal not to define this as therapy but just as a meeting with the family. Further, I would not start therapy with the son because by starting such

an individual therapy with the son we would define him as a patient.
And by defining him as a patient in a family that is already looking for
a patient, the attempted solution—the therapy—would become the
problem. For this reason I think it is definitely better to see the family
and to avoid defining him as the patient.

Willi: Thank you. By now we have heard quite a few things. Nonetheless,
I would have liked to talk more about what might have happened from
now on. Also, I would have liked to hear from the panelists more of
what they think went on in the therapy from this point on. But we do
not have time enough for that because at the end of this meeting I
would also like the people in the audience to ask some questions or
offer some comments.

Well, Dr. Schmidt could you briefly report on what really happened
and could you give us a follow-up? Where is the family today?

Schmidt: First I want to say some words about the intervention. For us
the intervention is not only what we say at the end of the session. That
is the officially defined intervention, as it were, but that is just part of
the intervention. During the last years—and I talk now very much from
an Ericksonian point of view—we have tended more and more to introduce indirect information into the family via the questions that we pose
during the session.

During the preceding discussion the question came up whether these
questions are aimed only at eliciting sequences of behavior. To us this
looks different. We not only want to gather information during all the
interviews, we also want to feed information into the system. For
example, when we talked much of the time about who could comfort
whom, who could help whom, and so on, it was our strategy to focus
attention on this area. In this way we hoped to slowly induce a frame
of mind that disposed the members to think of each other in terms of
mutual help and comfort. We have the impression that the conscious
frame of reference of people is not flexible enough to take in such
information without resistance. So much about our way of putting
questions to the family. It is an indirect strategy of offering ideas to the
members.

After the interview we, too, had the impression that Karl was indeed
the main problem, that he was more of a problem than the others in
the family. Also, there was the problem of how to work with this family
that appeared not much motivated to us. In fact, they didn't want any
family therapy and this we had therefore to take into account.

What we told the family beyond that which could be gathered from
the video excerpts is something like this. We told them that we saw

in this family a lot of mutual support and solidarity with each other. We told them further we had the impression that the deaths of father and grandmother were still uppermost in their minds. As a result, there was a lot of pain and sadness in the family. We then said that there seemed to be a belief in the family that one could not cope openly with the sadness, that one could not talk about it, and that until now everybody had to be alone with his or her sadness. And that led us to make the point that now we were even more concerned about Karl. In a sense, we made Karl more of a problem. We conveyed that we were even more concerned about him than about mother, but made it also evident we were concerned about everybody in the family.

We continued by stating that Walter had taken on a very important role for the rest of the family, that he was doing a very important service for the family. First, he was bringing the family together so that the members could have more contact with each other and would not be alone with their painful feelings. Second, he diverted the attention away from those painful feelings. We said that a diverting of attention was obviously the family's main mechanism of coping with these painful feelings. Evidently, the family members thought that at this point they could not work through these matters in any other way. We also said that Walter obviously was trying the whole time to replace father. With that we also tried to approach the question of succession. But, so we continued, our impression was that he was overburdened. Nevertheless, we were of the opinion that he should continue with his behavior because at the moment this would be enormously important for the family. We also said it was our impression that in this family processes of mourning would need a long time so that it could perhaps be necessary to take a very slow and careful approach to such mourning and that, in our opinion, Walter was showing the needed care by diverting the members' attention to other topics, thereby ensuring that the necessary steps could be made slowly. As you can see, we tried to delineate Walter's behavior positively.

We continued by stating that Karl, in planning to move back to his mother's house, showed himself faithful to a tradition that in this family had been upheld for generations, namely a tradition that required everybody to sacrifice his own needs for those of others, so that one could say that in this family the other members' needs are much more important than one's own needs. Accordingly, we could very well imagine that Karl was now repeating something which in his father's case had already led to very heavy burdens. But as much as we had this impression, we couldn't say anything against it. We could imagine, so we added, that his decision to move back with mother would be very hard on his own family and that we could only acknowledge that and respect the fact that he was about to make such an enormous sacrifice.

We embedded still more information in our prescription. For example, we stated that one could imagine different ways in which to cope with the problems at hand. After having introduced such rather general information we expressed doubts as to whether this family would decide on coping more constructively with the problems. Then there was the question of how to proceed from here. We said that we could imagine that further sessions could be meaningful, but that on balance we would rather advise against a continuation of the sessions at this moment. We said it was our impression that this family had done much already. Certainly, further sessions might be useful, but it could well be that then more attention would be focused on these painful topics. Therefore, one could really wonder whether one should offer such sessions at all. We recommended that they should think about that at home very profoundly before they called to tell us whether they wanted another session.

In light of our present-day thinking we might have done something differently. Today we would say that we still do not know enough to decide at all. We do not yet know what to say and what to offer and that we therefore would like to do a second or, as we call it, even a third or a fourth initial interview. In the course of these interviews we then would try to offer more indirect ideas by inserting questions into the interview process.

During these "initial interviews" we try to change the map of the family in the manner I described earlier and only after we have done so we may say something that is definitive. With the help of this method we try to motivate a family to stay in contact with us. We had the impression that this family had little motivation to do so. Karl, too, expressed a lot of disappointment because he wanted Walter to be the center of attention during the session. Well, so much about our intervention.

For some time after the interview we didn't hear anything from the family. As I said earlier, we had not fixed a date with the family for a second interview. Eventually, the family decided not to come again. They did not want to have further sessions. We had expected that already and had tried to anticipate it in our intervention. We accepted their decision and told them that they thereby confirmed our view of the situation, namely that the family at the moment would rather prefer to cope with the mourning by diverting their attention to other matters. We said that we thought a decision like this one had to be respected and that we accepted it. At the same time, we advised them that Walter should continue to pay serious attention to his job of serving the family as he had done before. This we said about two or three weeks after the session. The family was not very enthusiastic about what we had to say. Then we didn't hear from the family for a long while. Half a year after this interview—it was the only interview with this family—we made a telephone contact with the family. I was the one to call them. We haven't seen the family since that time. Therefore, all the information I can give you derives from phone conversations.

The situation was then as follows. I called them and the daughter Anita answered. She was just paying another visit to mother and it sounded to me as if we had known each other for years. That is, she behaved toward me in a very familiar and friendly manner. She told me that their contact with us had been very important for them, and that they had decided it would not be useful for them to come for any more sessions. They felt then this was the right decision for them to make. I asked her how the situation with Walter had developed. She said she thought that that was a strange thing, which she couldn't explain fully. Approximately three weeks after the interview (and some days after the telephone call from the family in which we had repeated our reframing) Walter had begun to go to school again in a normal way. Sometimes he continued to act a little provocatively. For example, occasionally he would say "Mama, Mama, Mama" three times to his mother but he would do this less frequently than before. But about three months ago this strange behavior stopped altogether. Since that time he was going to school in a totally normal way, he was out of the house spending a lot of time with his friends, and there were no problems. As regards the topic of sadness, Anita said the members had preferred not to speak about it in the family. Instead, each had wanted to cope with that on his own. I could accept that. We then agreed that I would call the family again in longer intervals just to hear how things went on.

The last time I called them was about a month ago. This was also done with a view to this congress. I intended to ask the family once again whether it would be OK to show this tape. This time the mother herself answered the phone. She reported that everything was in best order. Since the last phone call Walter had not shown any problematic behavior. Also Karl was much better off. (I forgot to tell you earlier that after the initial interview Karl had changed his plans regarding his moving into the house of the mother—something about which he had al-

ready made up his mind. After the interview he had told the others that
he would have to think more of his own family and that older brothers
couldn't continue in the same way eternally; he ended up telling them
that he had decided to stay at home with his family.) Now mother
reported that he was much better. Her contact with him had loosened
up a little, whereas her contact with the sisters had become more intense. The sisters were visiting more frequently with mother. Walter
would not care so much anymore; after all, he spent so much time out
of the house with his friends. She continued to tell me that by now he
had finished school and was looking intensively for an apprenticeship.
That would be rather difficult nowadays but no more difficult than for
any other family. This much follow-up information we have at the moment, or more correctly as of one month ago.

Willi: Thank you very much. Now we have not much time left. Still, I
would like to hear one or two comments from our panelists. The question is: What was effective here? Does this follow-up confirm the
hypothesis of the Heidelberg team? Or are there other explanations for
this positive outcome?

Boszormenyi-Nagy: Again I would like to respond in a broader sense and
say that I want to caution against judging therapeutic goals and therapeutic effectiveness on the presence or absence of symptoms at any
given time. Even though society forces us to pay attention to symptoms
and that's part of our role to be helpful at that point. Evaluating what
has happened without understanding the human process involved just
by looking at the absence or presence of symptoms is not only mis-
leading but in a psychosis is a risky point of view. I want to make this
point because I will feel better leaving here having said that to just base
the therapy of psychosis on the absence of symptoms is in my judgment
a risky procedure which may lead to much more serious and more difficult kinds of problems.

Selvini Palazzoli: I would like to underline that not only did Walter's
symptom disappear, but Karl solved his problem with his family of
origin; he, too, was cured. The effect of a family therapy should be
evaluated not only through the success with the index patient, but also
through the change of the other family members. The follow-up was
very positive for the whole family (and, presumably, also for the Karl's
own young family).

Willi: OK, now please Dr. Kaufmann.

Kaufmann: One word only. If mother says now everything is in best
order I have my doubts about that. Because there seems to be no change
in this family law (or rule) which requires that one has to swallow

personal problems in favor of an altruistic stance. For me this family continues to be at risk whenever the members are confronted with new cases of loss or sadness. Of course, no system is going to change at once as soon as one allows the expression of sadness. But if these emotions don't come out, the system will not be able to organize itself in another way. And that will be exploited by this mother when the opportunity comes up. Thank you.

Willi: We have approximately another five minutes left in which questions and comments from the audience may be addressed to the panelists. May I ask the people on the floor.

First participant from the floor: I find it fascinating that you, as the moderator of this panel discussion, ask the panelists to respond to what a general practitioner or a psychoanalyst would need to hear in order to become convinced of the value of family therapy. To an outsider this is certainly a most fascinating question. But for the insider another question is more acute, at least it is for me, namely the question of how the differences between Mara Selvini and Ivan Boszormenyi-Nagy are to be dealt with. Because I have the impression that the course may become set here for the next decade. On the one side, we find those people who say "let's kick off an evolutionary process and then let it run it's course," and on the other side there are those who say "let's work through the problems at hand." I find it's a pity that you as chairman have rather smoothed away this conflict.

Willi: Thank you. Are there other comments or questions?

Second participant from the floor: Yes. I would like to comment on the remark made by mother that now everything was in best order. There was some expression of doubt regarding that. It was said that such a notion of order might reflect a certain bourgeois sentiment. But if this is so, I would like to know what kind of an order are these therapists striving for, given the fact that there exist so many different realities for families, for patients, and for therapists?

Willi: Thank you. Does anyone want to respond to this point?

Kaufmann: Yes, I think this is addressed to me. I admit that certain norms may be implied in my position. Nevertheless, I believe that we always must try to create those conditions that will enable a family also in the future to make optimal use of its resources. If we only care about the family's smooth functioning at any given moment, we will miss out on what it will need in the future. In brief, to me the family's prospects for future development are more important than its functioning in the present.

Schmidt: Let me say a few words on this point. Of course, we, too, are aware that not everything with this family was in best order. Also, we would have liked to do further work with this family, particularly from the point of view of prevention. But the fact is, one can work with a family only when it is present. And over the years we have been cured of our missionary zeal. Instead, we have learned to respect a family's decision even in cases where we cannot agree with it. On the other hand, there are indications that certain relational patterns have indeed been changed even though they were not explicitly worked through in the therapeutic session. Evidently, the members are experiencing their sadness and are coping with it, albeit doing this on their own. And that, too, could bode well for the future.

Willi: Thank you. Mrs. Paul, please.

Mrs. Paul: I would like to make a comment. You started off this talk by mentioning that, as a matter of course, half of the people on this panel should be women and half should be men. With that, you raised the issue of how women should be viewed and be represented. However, regarding the family session I noticed that there were two male therapists and that the mother was never once referred to as a wife. I'm not going to address the question whether individual therapy or family therapy is better. Whatever the therapy, I think it's very important to begin to see mothers as wives and mothers as daughters. The mother has already been betrayed by a husband because she was not told that he was dying. The oldest son was told, and perhaps that's the cultural pattern in the country. However, one betrayal leads to another. Perhaps she was betrayed by her own father and I am just saying that she may not be telling you the truth. Therefore, before you begin to treat women you must see them as really existing. You may call them the queens in the family, but whatever you call them, you have to be able to see them not only as witches but as human.

Willi: Thank you. Now a final comment or question?

Fourth participant from the floor: If you are interested in the opinion of a therapist who has worked with young people, let me tell you this: The segment from an initial interview which we just saw had a deterrent impact on me. In a situation like this one I felt it is not permissible to speculate openly on whether perhaps the mother or the son or both of them would be candidates for a referral to a psychiatric hospital. I was astonished to note how the interviewers in the session came to toss around questions in a manner which they demonstrated also in this very discussion, questions with which they deliberately wanted to direct the family members' attention to problem areas in which they hoped for better insights and constructive developments. I was surprised that they could bring such kinds of speculations into the session.

I would also like to address a second point: In a case such as this one I would not have seen any danger in declaring Walter to be the patient. Had I seen Walter alone, that is, apart from his family, I could have had a good exchange with him. Certainly, I would also have been in a position to get from him much more information than was possible in this family setting. For him to talk in the setting was extremely embarrassing. Understandably, this young lad looked on the videotape much more ill than he turned out to be in the further course of events.

Fifth participant from the floor: I have a question and a comment. The question is addressed to Dr. Schmidt. You told us that the daughters were back again with mother. Does this mean they moved back into mother's house or does it mean that the relationship between them and mother has improved? This is still not clear to me.

Schmidt: They have been visiting mother more frequently together with their children.

Fifth participant from the floor: My comment is this: Somebody said before that the conflict between the protagonists on this panel has been smoothed away. I would rather like to emphasize the things they have in common. After all, there are many different ways of helping people toward self-help, of tearing down barriers so that—individual as well as family—processes of self-renewal may get under way. And here I felt the systemic approach can work as well as a psychoanalytic approach. Therefore, I don't find it useful to get entrenched in polarized fighting positions.

Willi: Thank you. With that let us close the panel. I want to thank all of you who have participated and all of you who have listened actively. I hope that all of you have become sufficiently confused so as to feel that there are still many open questions and that there exist other therapeutic approaches besides one's own approach.

Closing Remarks on
the Panel Discussion

Gunther Schmidt and Fritz B. Simon

Looking back on the panel discussion, we feel that the way it material-
ized tallied very largely with the aims and expectations we hoped it would
fulfill. The idea was to offer the participants at the conference an opportunity both of seeing for themselves how we set about our work and of
being present at one of those rare encounters where leading proponents
of a variety of approaches to family therapy demonstrate, compare, and
contrast their fundamental positions on therapeutic procedure with reference to the same concrete case material. To our way of thinking, this
remains one of the best sources of comparison and stimulation for interested colleagues working in the same field.

We chose a first interview situation because such a situation leaves a
large number of therapeutic options open and the conduct of the interview and the choice of interventions are not so much a function of preceding interactions between family and therapist. We were also at pains to
select a situation involving factors which play a part in the theoretical
work of the participants in the panel discussion. And this was indeed the
case. The family shown was in a fairly acute state of crisis due to the deaths
of the father and the grandmother. We find ill-defined relationships,
aborted grief processes, and the attempts at stabilization and problem
solving along the lines of the "more of the same" principle, which, however, have the opposite effect to the one desired and lead to a further
escalation. A problem situation such as the one exemplified by this particular family can certainly be approached in a number of different ways,
using a variety of family therapy strategies. It is highly probable that due
to unfinished grief work the family is unable to exploit its resources for
constructive adaptation to the dramatic change in its situation. It would
obviously make sense to support the family in facing up squarely to the
psychological task of coming to terms with their grief. The generation

200

boundaries also appear ill-defined; greater clarity in this respect should be aimed for. "Legacies," in contributing to self-sacrificial behavior for the benefit of the others (particularly conspicuous in the elder brother, but noticeable in the other members of the family as well) are a factor also involved here; the debits and merits thus materializing could be taken up and worked through.

It seems to us that the discussion showed that there is no such thing as the "real" view of the family, nor can we expect to arrive at "the" appropriate therapeutic procedure, as any "reality" appears shaped by the therapist's concepts. The family we were dealing with here supports such view: It seems almost ideally suited to serve as projective test material—the family as a Rorschach blot for various family-therapy concepts—a new species of family Rorschach? There could certainly be endless discussion as to what perspectives and hypotheses, what therapeutic interventions would be most appropriate. But such a discussion is bound to remain unresolved. The procedures selected will always be largely dictated by the aims, criteria of functionality, and values (ethical, economic, etc.) which the therapists judge to be most important.

All the same, we found this particular discussion very valuable, enabling the participants and the audience to experience and compare various possible perspectives on the problem. For many colleagues, this can have a liberating, releasing effect, as it helps them to cast off the burden of family therapy dogmas. At the same time it involves the challenge of assuming more clear-cut personal responsibility for the decision to adhere to a given concept. The discussion could certainly have been tougher and more antagonistic but only if each participant had been more manifestly convinced that his concept was "better" than the others'. Is the lack of controversy in the exchange an expression of a constructivist collusion on the part of the participants?

Now for some remarks on our own approach. Some of the participants expressed a certain degree of surprise at the way we went about things; one member of the audience even went so far as to say that he had been shocked by it. He had, for example, the most serious misgivings about our readiness to entertain and enlarge upon the idea of hospitalization for the I.P. (index patient) and mother in the course of our hypothetical questioning. In his view, what he considered to be a fateful development could be exaggerated in this way, with dangerously severe strains resulting for the family from the questions. For this reason, we would like to say a word or two about the considerations that guided us in our approach.

Proceeding from a systemic view of things, we assume that symptoms (or other phenomena classified as requiring therapy) can be the expression of attempts at adaptation and problem solving by members of a system in situations involving changes or developments regarded as a threat to the survival of that system. If dangerous imbalances can be offset by the emergence of symptoms, then a new balance can be achieved. It is then frequently the case that the interactions of the members of the system are so attuned to each other that they contribute to a perpetuation of the symptoms as relatively stable, redundant interaction loops. These are determined by the rules obtaining in the system, including the rules of attribution (something is considered good, bad, healthy, sick, licit, illicit, dangerous, safe, etc.). We then see it to be the task of the therapist to induce changes at the level of behavior and/or of the attribution (the shared value system or system of rules upheld by the family). These changes should be such as to enable the family to activate resources instigating a more functional interaction process devoid of symptoms. We consider it to be frequently unnecessary, if not counterproductive, for intense emotional processes to be set off and worked through during the therapeutic sessions themselves. The aim of such sessions and the interventions by the therapists should be rather to bring about a change in the rules and behavior of the family in their everyday context (i.e., away from the sessions). In other words, the main part of the work should be done by the family outside the sessions.

Unlike, say, the systemic approach practiced originally in Milan, our view of the function of circular questioning is not primarily as a means of gleaning information for the therapists as a basis for their final intervention. While we do use circular questioning for that purpose too, our main application of it is as a vehicle to convey to the family a steady supply of new associative processes designed to change the family's epistemology, a flow of ideas provided by indirect, suggestive means. To this end we pose a large number of hypothetical questions which can anticipate certain developmental processes by functioning as a trigger for the enactment of certain eventualities on a purely mental hypothetical plane. If, for example, we spend considerable time going through the possibility of hospitalization of the I.P. and mother, using hypothetical questions to do so, this does not in our experience make the likelihood of that eventuality actually happening any greater—in fact quite the contrary. These questions almost invariably function as context markers, taking the "I-cannot-help-it" element out of such possible action and thus making it far less likely for family members to act on impulse in a way that would indeed lead to escalation and hospitalization. Hypothetical questions of this nature—as long as they systematically cover all the stages of an escalation spiral—very often assist patients in achieving more conscious awareness of the possible consequences of their interactions. Such awareness leads implicitly or explicitly to a greater willingness to assume responsibility for their behavior and activate resources for avoiding escalation while stimulating more constructive transactional processes. This is not to deny that such questions may put considerable strain on the patients. But it is not our therapeutic aim to make the families that come to us feel as comfortable as possible but rather to activate their intrinsic motivation in such a way as to institute change. In many cases, a certain amount of stress for the family during the session can have a very beneficial effect. In some cases, hypothetical questioning makes the family members' former behavior seem so amusingly absurd to them (and us) that the reaction is a humorous one, thus lightening the atmosphere. Another important aim of these hypothetical questions for us is the inducement of problem-solving associations and behaviors. In much the same way as Milton Erickson's hypnotherapy, we attempt to induce such associations and behaviors via questions, metaphors, connotations. For this reason, we have shifted the emphasis of our questions over the past few years for therapeutic purposes. Earlier, our main intention in posing circular questions was to gain an idea of which relational patterns and regulatory processes were contributing to the manifestation of the problem. Today, our interest concentrates mainly on the processes that will take place when that problem has been solved. In other words, our questions are oriented more toward the future. This does not of course prevent us from using this strategy in the classical systemic sense, to gather information on the ways the system has functioned so far, to use this information for positive connotation and for possible use in the final intervention.

Working with this particular family posed a number of problems for us. The most important factors that we felt should be taken into account were:

1. There seemed to be little motivation for the family to come to any further interviews as a family unit. The probability of their returning at all seemed very slight.
2. The family was adamant in defining their problem as an individual problem of the I.P. which affected them only indirectly. This definition seemed pretty firmly established to us.
3. They expected the therapists to concern themselves largely with the I.P., in fact to give him individual therapy.
4. The very obvious grief and despair at the loss of two close relatives was kept taboo in the first stages; any interactional connection with the "real" problem was denied.

5. The family's epistemology prompted them to essay a problem-solving strategy under the motto "more of the same." An instance of this was that the older son was on the verge of moving back in with his original family and temporarily leaving his wife and children. A further indication was the increasing concern to divert their attention from their own grief.
6. Extremely ill-defined relationships were to be found in the family and this made for cognitive confusion, not only in the I.P.

Taking these factors into account, we set out to bring about a distinct change in the family's view, in particular in their view of the various causes and motives they connected with their problem. And it looked very much as if we were only going to have this one opportunity. Many of the questions throughout the interview were designed to develop clearer definitions in the intrafamily relations. Our assumption was that a change in attributions and a better definition of relations might bring about changes in the behavior not only of the I.P. but of the other members of the family as well. Our intention was to use the information we had collected to redefine (reframe) the I.P.'s behavior as an attempt to help the family that should be respected as such. Also, we aimed to point up the connections between this positively connoted behavior and the bereavement processes and, in addition, offer the older son a kind of provocation that would prompt him to stay with his own family. We have telephoned the family at intervals over a period of almost two years to inquire how things have been shaping up. Those phone calls have confirmed that the aims we set ourselves have been fulfilled to a reasonably satisfactory extent.

Misgivings were also voiced during the discussion about our follow-up procedure and the report by mother or sister on developments since the interview. True, phone calls at intervals to inquire how things had gone after the family's encounter with us can hardly be viewed as satisfactory follow-up. It is certainly possible to object that the reports made by mother and sister were characterized by a "hello–goodbye" effect, in other words, that they could be expected to present a positive facade and cover up the genuine problems when asked how the situation had developed for the I.P. and family. One of the reasons for our decision to inquire by phone was that it seemed the most economical way of going about things. But there were other reasons that made us reluctant to invite the family to a follow-up session, let alone send someone out to visit them: The family did not appear strongly motivated; chances are that they simply would not have come. Their relationship with us after that one sole interview was not so close and profound as to prompt them to undertake a journey of some 30 miles to come and see us again. Quite apart from that, we doubt whether we would have gained any "genuine" information on this basis. We would probably have been treated to the same descriptions of the family, and then what? Probing and insisting further would have sealed a relationship between the family and us in which the therapists would have become something akin to detectives looking for evidence for something and subjecting the family to a "grilling." This could have the effect of a massive negative connotation on the family. And what would we have been looking for, checking out? How the relations "really" are, whether they are perhaps more "disturbed" than the family members describe them? Who is to define which is the "more real" description of the situation, what is "healthy," "sicker," or "more disturbed" in the family? The therapists, neutral observers, or the family members themselves? And at this point we become fully aware of a very fundamental problem. If we cast doubt on the family's own account and decided to "study" the family more closely (which would imply highly "linearized" observer–object relations), all we would find would be a picture of that family in terms of our own observation methods; that is, we would obtain nothing other than indications in accord with our own notions of relative values and functionality. We would also not say that the mother in this family should be called a witch. This also would be a simplified linear interpretation. She is as much, but also not more, contributing to the "family game" as the other members. Mother and daughter were clear about their definition of reality on the phone. And that means that in terms of *their* criteria the development is functional and "healthy," whatever we might happen to think about it. And for us that means that our mission is accomplished. We assume that the members of that family are competent to judge for themselves what is good for them.

Of course, we could always have asked the other members of the family what they thought, after we had heard the accounts of mother and daughter. But this would have suggested that we were cross-examining some members of the family to check up on the others. This could have triggered loyalty conflicts and made the therapists into agents of something like social surveillance. One danger of this, we feel, is that the family might then indeed be tempted to fall back on their old problem-solving strategies in order to fend off our probing questions. And this could hardly be said to be the desired effect.

Lunch Chit-Chat

We can safely pass over the discussion between our three friends in silence, as discussions about discussions are notoriously boring. Nor do we intend recording their final verdict on the conference as a whole. Suffice it to say that they all decided to attend the end-of-conference festivities in Heidelberg Castle. One of the items on the program was the family tragedy Instant Hamlet, *freely adapted from Shakespeare by Helm Stierlin. There was unanimous agreement that this was the high point of the whole conference. In fact a number of people were heard to ask whether it might not have been better to do without the rest of the proceedings and make do with the performance of the play on its own.*

Instant Hamlet

A family tragedy, in one act, adapted from William Shakespeare by Guilelmus Stierlinus
(First—and last—performance on Friday, 17 May 1985, in the Heidelberg Castle)

Dramatis personae:	Actors:
Claudius, King of Denmark	**Paul Watzlawick**
Hamlet, Son to the former and Nephew to the present King	**Helm Stierlin**
Polonius, Lord Chamberlain	**Ivan Boszormenyi-Nagy**
Gertrude, Queen of Denmark, and Mother of Hamlet	**Mara Selvini Palazzoli**
Ophelia, Daughter to Polonius	**Giuliana Prata**
Ghost of Hamlet's Father	**Lyman Wynne**
Laertes, Son to Polonius	**Norman Paul**
Horatio, Friend to Hamlet	**Carlos Sluzki**
Rosenkrantz Guildenstern Courtiers	**Luigi Boscolo** **Gianfranco Cecchin**
Fortinbras, Prince of Norway	**Theodore Lidz**
First Gentleman	**Jürg Willi**

Second Gentleman **Josef Duss-von Werdt**

Third Gentleman **Luc Kaufmann**

Fourth Gentleman **Max von Trommel**

Fifth Gentleman **Pekka Tienari**

A Lady **Rosemarie Welter-Enderlin**

Hamlet: The world is out of joint
O cursed spite
That ever I was born
To set it right.

Horatio: No reason to despair, dear Hamlet:
To set things right
We can now offer thee
Plenty of family therapy
For look around: you're in the midst
of thousands of family therapists!

Helm Stierlin, Mara Selvini Palazzoli, Lyman Wynne (in front), Giuliana Prata, Pekka Tienari, Norman Paul, Jürg Willi, Luc Kaufmann, Josef Dussvon Werdt, Paul Watzlawick, Carlos Sluzki

Hamlet: My dear Horatio, you're mistaken:
            Your inner map needs to be shaken
            There are more things in heaven and on earth
            Than are dreamt of in your episto-turf.

Ghost appears

            Look! There's a ghost
            Emerging from the void
            But lo, by Jesus, isn't that
            The ghost of Sigmund Freud?
            Leave me alone with him, I prithee.

Exit Horatio

Ghost: Yes, I am Sigmund's ghost
            Arising from the grave
            To tell a tale
            Of untold evil, wickedness, and wail.

Hamlet: Oh, I beseech thee, speak!

Ghost: I hoped that I in peace could rest
            Because the Queen, on my behest

Giuliana Prata (Ophelia)

Norman Paul (Laertes), Helm Stierlin (Hamlet)

Would never, never be amiss
In being a proper analyst
But then your uncle came, that lout
Corrupted by the Palo Alto crowd
And with systemic trickery and cunning
(How dreadful, yet also how stunning!)
He caused her downfall.
Ay, that incestuous, that adulterate beast
With witchcraft of his wit he had a feast!
O wicked wit and gifts that have the power
To turn around this queenly flower
And arrogate her to his shameful lust
O what a mess is this, o what a bust.

One hears a cock's crew

I must be gone—the cock is crewing.
O Hamlet, in what mess I'm stewing!!

Hamlet: Poor pitiable ghost!
I promise thee, I'll do my best
To put forever you to rest.

Mara Selvini Palazzoli (Queen Gertrude),
Paul Watzlawick (King Claudius)   *Ivan Boszormenyi-Nagy (Polonius)*

Enter Claudius, the King, and Gertrude,
the Queen

But lo, behold!
There comes that wicked, that incestuous pair!
I hide myself, b'cause they must not find me here.

He hides behind trees

Gertrude: Who is so firm that cannot be seduced!
Not me, your Gertrude, for I feel bemused
By all your charme and erudition
O let me sink into oblivion
And take on the one-down position
Before you, my dear king and savior
My heart was never pounding heavier!

Claudius: O never, prithee, on your knee
I hate complementarity
You are my goddess, are my queen
Such as the world has never seen

Kisses her

Theodore Lidz (Fortinbras), Carlos Sluzki (Horatio)

However, if we jointly go to bed
We will, for sure, drive our poor Hamlet mad.

Hamlet rushes forward from behind the tree

Hamlet: Indeed, you will!
Already I feel deeply shaken
By raving madness o'ertaken,
O horrible, o horrible, most horrible!

Claudius: No doubt: he's mad, that is not nice
To cure him now we need professional advice.
For that, let's turn to our dear Polonius
Who always is so graciously harmonious.
O luckily I see him coming.

Enter Polonius

Polonius, we need your help:
Dear Hamlet raves about our badness
But our concern is *Hamlet's* madness
What can we do?

*Mara Selvini Palazzoli (Queen Gertrude),
Gianfranco Cecchin (Guildenstern), Luigi
Boscolo (Rosencrantz)*

Lyman Wynne (Ghost)

Polonius:	You must, at first, make straight amend For merit and entitlement Then you must take a proper plea For invisible loyalty And then apply, I implore thee Just pure contextual therapy!
Claudius:	I am afraid, that will not be enough I know our Hamlet: he is tough We need some stronger medicine To really do that upstart in Oh, Gertrude, you, who are so clever Tell us, what should be our endeavour?
Gertrude:	As paradox with paradox one counters So madness one with madness launders Let Hamlet fall so utterly in love That love's own madness will be quite enough For him, so that then we, in splendid unity Are henceforth spared his importunity. Let fair Ophelia, this ravishing dame Set our dear Hamlet's heart aflame!

Enter Ophelia

O lucky us—there she comes!
We all will hide behind this acorn tree
So that, ourselv's unseen, we can, what is to
happen, see.

*Gertrude, Claudius, and Polonius hide behind
the tree while Hamlet and Ophelia meet each other*

Ophelia:	O my poor heart is beating faster Look, there is Hamlet! I wish he were my prince and master And take me straight into his princely bed But that's impossible, for he is *mad* Not even love's most tender ministration Might mitigate such perturbation. But come what may—I'll try to win him over

She approaches Hamlet seductively

Hamlet: Get thee to a nunnery, and fast!
                 Such trickery, I am aghast
                 There is no decency, no wit
                 No definition of relationship.
                 I shall not see you anymore
                 You are a pest, you are a bore
                 Off to a nunnery!
                 And never speak of love or bed!

Ophelia: I knew it: he is ghastly mad!

Hamlet: Off to a nunnery, out of my sight

Ophelia: O terrible, terrible is my plight!
                 There is no sense in living anymore
                 It's better to be dead than be a bore.
                 Therefore, I rush to end my useless life
                 Not fit to be a mistress nor a wife

Ophelia rushes off to drown herself

Polonius: Help, help—let's catch
(from behind   That Hamlet dead or alive
the tree)

                 *Hamlet turns suddenly around and stabs
                 Polonius with his rapier*

Hamlet: Aye, never alive, it is too late
                 Now see: that's a revolving slate!

Hamlet rushes after Ophelia until he is out of sight

Polonius: O how could he so totally
(dying)   Misunderstand our theory.
                 (That is so boringly lineal,
                 could you at least make it circular.)
                 Because his judgment was erroneous
                 There must now die poor old Polonius.
                 Look, I am dead and gone!

Gertrude: He is, for sure, so starkly dead
                   As our Hamlet's raving mad!

Claudius: That is enough, indeed:
                   We must now speedily proceed
                   To make a plan whereby one stops
                   For good this madman's deadly flops
                   There is a lesson he must learn
                   From Rosenkrantz and Guildenstern.
                   How nice, I see them coming!

                   Enter Rosenkrantz and Guildenstern

                   Good friends, we will be truly blessed
                   If you fulfill us one request.

Rosenkrantz
and   To do so, gracious king and queen
Guildenstern: We are both ready, fit and keen

Claudius: Well, then listen:
                   Poor Hamlet's gone out of his mind
                   Therefore I ask you, be so kind
                   And get him to that blasted town
                   Where he with other fools may clown
                   Or in the Neckar river drown
                   Get him to Heidelberg!

Rosenkrantz: Old Heidelberg, my noblest master
                   That dreadful name does spell disaster
                   For sane and insane men galore

Guildenstern: A fact we honestly deplore

Rosenkrantz: Yet we shall carry out this chore
                   And execute your delegation
                   As does befit our humble station
                   We're off to Heidelberg.

                   Exeunt Rosenkrantz and Guildenstern
                   Enter Laertes

Laertes: I am Laertes and irate
                    About my family's dreadful fate:
                    Polonius, my father, slain
                    Ophelia, too, went down the drain
                    All operant mourning is in vain!
                    She was a sister dear to me
                    O horrible inequity!
                    Now she is gone and I'm alone

                          Turns to Claudius

                    O Thou, who sits on Denmark's throne
                    Tell me, O Sir, who is the one
                    Who all these monstrous deeds has done?

Claudius: It is a man whose conduct we bemoan
                    A great and noble mind, but now so o'erthrown
                    That he's a parody of his once princely features
                    A danger to all living creatures
                    We need all help we can obtain
                    To get this foe of mankind slain
                    Alas, it is none other than our Hamlet!

Laertes: To take care of him, count on me, my Lord.

Claudius: I know, Laertes, that we must
                    Endow you with our greatest trust.
                    And now, to expedite your task
                    Accept this rapier and this flask

                          He hands Laertes a rapier and a bottle

                    The rapier with its venom-coat
                    Will let your foe to heaven float.
                    The flask contains a pois'nous potion
                    That quickly sets the blood in motion
                    Of whosoever drinketh it
                    Use both, I prithee, as you see fit.

Laertes: I shall do so and properly employ
                    These hefty tools so that we all enjoy

A splendid opportunity
To cope with crisis in a family
But lo! There's Hamlet coming.
Let me handle him
While you, I prithee, be just seated
Until the monster is defeated.

Claudius and Gertrude sit down on a table on
which Laertes places the bottle, then he turns
provocatively to Hamlet

Hey Hamlet, why so fast, I prithee
Your mood, dear prince, seems dark and miffy
May I, with humbleness and wit,
Lighten it up a little bit?

Hamlet: Indeed, you idiot, you may:
                 Just get yourself out of my way!

Laertes: Never! I dare you to a fight
                 That will set the record right
                 And therefore I, with all my might
                 Send you to hell, Hamlet: good night!

Both fight with rapiers

Take this, and this, and this!

Hamlet: Oh gee, I feel, I've just been hit
                 By this incredible misfit.

Laertes: Yea, Hamlet, curse me, 'tis in vain,
                 That stab's been poisoned: you are slain!

Hamlet: But ere I never more shall be
                 I'll take you fiendish hound with me

He grabs Laertes' rapier, stabs him with it

Ha, take this!

Laertes:	Dear Jesus—to our souls be kind Now that we are in death entwined.

Claudius:	We watch the sordid termination Of a symmetric escalation!

Hamlet:	Ha scoundrel, with your trivial wisdom You, too, are bound up with this system And therefore, without further fuss We take you down to hell with us.

With a final effort he grabs the poisoned rapier
and stabs Claudius with it

Claudius: *(dying)*	I die, but I am forced to mention: That was a stupid intervention!

Gertrude:	Indeed, I also must confess: This is an awful bungled mess Ere into this morass I sink I need to have a little drink

She drinks from the bottle on the table

Claudius:	Oh wretched woman, that's the end: Your days on earth are also spent That drink, that was no anodyne Instead, thou hast drunk poison'd wine And thus, without further ado With us from this damn'd world you'll go.

Gertrude:	Oh God, I feel it: it is so!

She also dies with the others
Enter Fortinbras and Horatio

Fortinbras:	A sordid ending 'tis indeed To show us whereto it may lead When members of a family Fail to resort to therapy.

Horatio:	Therefore, avoiding all delay We'll go to demonstrate what may (Such massive problems notwithstanding) Unfold as a much happier ending:
First Gentleman:	Hamlet, our o'ertaxed delegate Will realize, ere it is too late What once a wise man thus expressed: Vice may be nice, but incest's best.
A Lady:	And therefore without conscience's sting He will embrace the queen and king And gladly watch their frolicking.

Hamlet embraces king and queen, and then watches how they frolick

Second Gentleman:	While he, with all delib'rate speed Ophelia to his bed can lead

Hamlet picks up Ophelia and leads her around

Third Gentleman:	And thereby fill with happiness Polonius and Laertes

Polonius and Laertes step forward and happily embrace Hamlet and Ophelia

Fourth Gentleman:	While Rosenkrantz and Guildenstern Old Heidelberg to love will learn

Rosenkrantz and Guildenstern appear with a bottle of wine and a poster of Heidelberg

Fifth Gentleman:	And Sigmund's ghost, may he be blessed Will find his well-deserved rest.

Ghost appears and stretches comfortably on a chaise

Chorus:	So come that you now all may see

Our cast in splendid unity
Forgetting all that butchery
And constructing in harmony
Our FAMILIAR reality!

All players get together, the diverse subgroups
embrace each other and present themselves finally
as one happy group to the public.

Index

221